AYURVEDA

AYURVEDA

Ancient Wisdom for Modern Wellbeing

Geeta Vara

First published in Great Britain in 2018 by Orion Spring
an imprint of The Orion Publishing Group Ltd
Carmelite House, 50 Victoria Embankment
London EC4Y 0DZ
An Hachette UK Company

3 5 7 9 10 8 6 4 2

A CIP catalogue record for this book is
available from the British Library.

ISBN: 978 1 4091 7793 7
Ebook ISBN: 978 1 4091 7794 4

Printed and bound in Great Britain by Clays Ltd, Elcograf S.p.A.

www.orionbooks.co.uk

Every effort has been made to ensure that the information in the book is
accurate. The information in this book may not be applicable in each individual
case so it is advised that professional medical advice is obtained for specific
health matters and before changing any medication or dosage. Neither the
publisher nor author accepts any legal responsibility for any personal injury or
other damage or loss arising from the use of the information in this book. In
addition if you are concerned about your diet or exercise regime and wish to
change them, you should consult a health practitioner first.

For the four most illuminating energies in my life,
Shaan, Amaia, Nia & Yash

Contents

Section 1:

The Science of the Body and Mind

Introduction

Ayurveda is the oldest known medical science, and takes a total holistic approach to life and wellbeing, embracing the mind, body, emotions and soul as well as the effects of the environment, seasons, moon and sun cycles. Ayurveda is often coined as the science of life and I believe it truly is a way of living, governed by the laws of nature. This ancient wisdom is more pertinent today than it has ever been, as we continue to move further away from our natural biorhythms. Embracing the natural flow of life and getting in touch with our 'self' is the best gift we can give to ourselves in a world that has become technologically and synthetically dependent.

I am a passionate practitioner and, in this book, I will give you an introduction to the principles of this ancient system and a practical guide to applying its simple techniques in your day-to-day life, to keep your mind, body and soul healthy and vibrant. You will discover an Ayurvedic diet and lifestyle that is appropriate to your body type. As a preventative approach to healthcare, the daily rituals and guidelines of Ayurveda will help you to nurture your wellbeing the way nature intended.

I strongly believe that the discussion around health needs to evolve from the focus on illness, and start embracing wellness. A paradigm shift of prevention over cure. The simple, daily applicable wisdom of Ayurveda outlined in this book can help lead you out of the doctor's surgery, and on a journey towards self-healing. I want to help empower you with this holistic approach to wellness and remove the helplessness that many people feel when they go to the doctor.

Ayurveda teaches us to reconnect with the flow of life and be in synchronicity with our natural circadian rhythms: the life clock, the day clock, the seasonal clock and even the moon clock. Nature is our best teacher – and you only have to observe the ebb and flow of the natural plant and animal kingdoms to understand. My desire is to encourage people to get intimately acquainted with themselves, and notice their 'dis-eases' as an indicator of imbalances that can potentially manifest into full-blown health issues. It's time to move away from a 'pill for every ill' mentality, and towards a holistic and preventative health approach.

Since the start of my practice in 2008, my purpose has been to share the wealth of this profound ancient Ayurvedic wisdom in an uncomplicated and easy-to-apply way without compromising its authenticity. I am often asked how I got involved in Ayurveda, and I guess I was involved even before I realised it! As a born and raised British Indian with an African twist (both my parents were African-born), many of my lifestyle routines and dietary habits were naturally Ayurvedic, taught to me as a child by my grandparents. I quickly became curious about my family's day-to-day rituals and food habits, since they differed from my peers'.

My upbringing was a marriage between Western and Indian cultures. At times, this was confusing and even led me to feel a loss of identity. I never had any major health concerns growing up, but I lived in a world where my lifestyle at home contrasted strongly with that of my Western schoolmates. As time went on, I realised that the cultural challenges of my childhood had become my biggest blessing by helping me to appreciate the delicate nature of an integrated lifestyle. This has enabled me to translate the wisdom of the *Vedic Samhitas*, the ancient scriptures that were written to enrich every aspect of our lives. My experiences enable me to help clients apply the principles of Ayurveda to their lives, regardless of their location, age, gender or culture.

Although my first degree was in business, I had a strong pull towards natural healthcare, which was already fast becoming a part of my personal development and spiritual growth. I was more and more curious as to why people still 'felt' unwell, despite their diets being seemingly healthy, and why there was a dearth of understanding around the impact of our emotions and mind on our physical health. Out of this curiosity and the desire to follow a more fulfilling life purpose, I was intuitively guided towards the science of Ayurveda. This profound system of health and wellbeing helps you to analyse your body's particular constitution. When you are aligned with your constitution (prakruti), your true natural state, even the simplest lifestyle changes can reap some amazing health benefits.

I believe in living an expansive, peaceful and fulfilling life. A life where we truly connect with people and nature at large. A life where we measure happiness by our state of being, and not by a collection of achievements or material possessions. Through the guidance in this book, I invite you on a journey of health promotion and disease prevention. I am excited to be sharing very profound but practical self-healing wisdom, tools and techniques to empower you to take health and wellbeing back into your own hands.

Note on the text: You will find a glossary at the back, with explanations of all the important Ayurvedic terms and concepts that I refer to in this book. Where a word appears in bold in the text at the first instance, you will find it in the glossary.

CHAPTER I

Our Current State of Health

'It is health that is the real wealth and not pieces of gold and silver'

Mahatma Gandhi

What is health?

'sama dosha, sama agnischa, sama dhatu, mala kriya
prasanna atma indriya manaha, swastha iti abhidheeyate'

Sushruta Samhita

The above is a **Sanskrit** verse taken from the ancient **Vedic** health scripture, the *Sushruta Samhita*, one of the earliest writings of **Ayurveda**. This quote describes what constitutes a healthy person: according to Ayurveda, a person is healthy when he/she has balanced bioenergetic forces, strong digestive fire, nourished body tissues, well-functioning body processes, a calm mind, balanced emotions and clear senses. Ayurveda addresses the underlying imbalance in the mechanisms of the body that gives rise to a disease and, as you read this book, the profound meaning of this verse will become clearer. It really is a shift in our current thinking, yet the knowledge spans back more than 5,000 years. This system looks beyond 'what' the disease is and focuses on the question of 'why' there is a disease and what is driving it. The short verse above encompasses every possible mechanism of your body, mind and soul that needs to be taken care of for complete wellbeing and disease prevention.

If you consider a more recent definition of health, by the World Health Organization (WHO) in 1948, the philosophy is similar:

> 'Health is a state of complete physical, mental and social wellbeing and not merely the absence of disease or infirmity'

It's clear that being 'healthy' is far more than the absence of disease. Ayurveda aims to connect the dots between all the possible causes of disharmony in our biological ecosystem. It never dismisses anything, regardless of how unrelated it may seem to your ails. A disharmony in any part of your life can create an imbalance in your microbiome or, in other words, the environment of your body.

Optimal health is a state of balance according to Ayurveda, and you don't need to be a rocket scientist to figure it out. You just need to listen to your intuition and follow nature's lead. As a multidimensional approach, you can heal your own life with food, exercise, sleep, rest, a suitable routine, herbs, breathing, meditation, prayer and connection to your higher self.

A healthcare deficit in the West

In the UK, we are fortunate enough to have a system of healthcare like the NHS, making treatment accessible to all.

However, what we are missing is the deeper comprehension of who we are in relation to everything and everyone around us. I don't mean your religion, age or the job that you do; I mean in terms of the structural and energetic composition that makes you a unique individual. Is your external environment balancing or unbalancing for your internal environment?

This is where Ayurveda flourishes, by understanding the

systems and networks that connect your mind and body rather than purely examining the symptoms.

A tale of two worlds – East and West

Let me ask you a question. When you think of Eastern medicine, does it conjure up images of yogis meditating under a tree, mystical medicines brewing in a pot, or people walking in nature completely blissed out? Or how about an array of body treatments with unpronounceable names, all of which seem a little primitive and low-tech? Well, it is no surprise that Eastern philosophies and medical systems remain somewhat of a mystery to the modern man. In this book, I hope to bring you closer to understanding the science and the connection of your body and mind, not just by reading about it, but by experiencing the health benefits first-hand through the recommendations I introduce.

In the West, we separate the entities of mind and soul from the body. We see our GP for issues pertaining to the body, a psychologist for issues of the mind, and our religious leaders for issues connected to faith and spirit. As we go through the medical system, we further compartmentalise ourselves by seeing different doctors for various body parts – neurologist, cardiologist, gastroenterologist, and so on – and we can often end up with several different prescriptions without a full understanding of how each drug interacts with another. For me, there is a complete lack of connectivity in this model. Our bodies are treated as no more than a mechanical organism, much like a car or computer.

Western medicine takes an evidence-based approach. New state-of-the-art technology, clinical methods, laboratory research and innovative medicines are viewed as the biggest breakthrough. You believe it when you see it. In contrast, Eastern medicine relies on the profound knowledge that has taken centuries to perfect. Practitioners not only have a proven track record of scientific efficacy but are also immersed in a faith-based approach. More of an 'I will see it because I believe it' attitude. One medical system is neither superior nor inferior to the other, as they all have their unique offerings, including allopathic medicines (the system of our current medical practice) – especially in emergency situations – and surgical advancements.

It is worth bearing in mind that when modern medicine researches or tests a herb, diet or any Ayurvedic modality against a hypothesis in isolation within the framework of a lab, this approach is a reductionist one. It does not consider the holistic approach that is applied in a clinical set-up with each patient and their distinct set of presenting issues, so the results are skewed and inconclusive. Our inquiring intellect needs some proof, but let's also acknowledge the fact that some things may be felt by us in our physical or energetic body and yet may not necessarily be seen or have the capacity to be scientifically proven.

There is increasing concern around the resistance to antibiotics. The misuse and overuse of antibiotics has increased our dependency and diminished the power of our body's natural defences to fight infections, not to mention the potential side effects of taking them, such as nausea, diarrhoea and fungal infections of the digestive system, mouth and genitals to name a few. Moreover, there is an increased risk that useful body bacteria are also killed off in the process, weakening our system at the core. I find that the more people understand these risks, the more they are drawn to natural medicines like Ayurveda, which strengthen the body's natural defences, without harmful side effects.

Most Eastern philosophies will promote the view that the mind, body and spirit are all part of our ecosystem and completely intertwined with one another. In traditional Eastern practices such as Ayurveda, your practitioner will see the whole you and not a compartmentalised section of you. Maybe the root of your physical health issue stems from an emotional trauma or from mental stresses.

'What really called my attention to Ayurveda is the holistic way it looks at the individual – not only the physical but also the psychological, emotional and spiritual.'

Aline

A shift in the health paradigm

Ayurveda is the polar opposite of the 'one size fits all' approach to treating people who present similar conditions. As clichéd as the word 'holistic' sounds, Ayurveda really does take a 'whole-istic' view, placing the person at the centre of treatment and not the disease.

An Ayurvedic practitioner will really take the time to listen for the spoken and unspoken signals of the patient. Attention is given to every element of your life, to gather a detailed understanding of your history or, as I prefer to say, 'your story'. Every aspect of your body, your mind and your emotions, the impact of the seasons, your age, your relationships and your environment all play a role in your overall health.

Using traditional diagnostic techniques such as checking the pulse and tongue, we can start to discover the level of toxins in your body and where your imbalances might lie. From here, a practitioner can prescribe a suitable diet, herbs, treatments, detox and rejuvenation programmes, **yoga**, breathing and meditation to support optimal long-term health.

In my practice, I like to pay close attention to the 'language' my clients use in a consultation; this can give me a clear indication of their attitude to their health, life and outlook on healing. I have often heard in clinic the phrases 'He is such a pain in the neck' and 'He is a pain up the backside' from patients presenting physical pain in the same areas of the spine. I hear, 'I have no choice, I just have to get on with it' or 'I have this condition, so I just have to live with it' – all in all, very disempowering language. I encourage you to notice the language that you use to talk about your health and also yourself as a whole. Are you using language that disempowers you or is self-pitiful? How can you change this?

Ayurveda aims to treat the root cause not just the presenting symptoms. This discourages diseases from reappearing. It's kind of like weeding the garden. If you take the weeds out from the root they are not likely to come back anytime soon, if at all. As such, if your mind is stuck in negativity so too will your body be.

Be your own doctor

Do you know the meaning of 'doctor'? The word actually stems from the Latin verb 'to teach', but the current understanding is that of a person qualified to treat people who are ill. The modern-day doctor is so inundated with patients at his practice that he is often limited to the prescription of drugs to give symptomatic medical relief. From time to time this is necessary as it brings fast pain relief, but this is not a long-term solution.

Why spend time in the surgery trying to fix an issue when you can create health and happiness by teaching yourself the tools and techniques that can keep you out of that surgery? By spending money and time eating and exercising in the best way for your body type, you can nurture your 'self' in a holistic way.

You have a choice in every moment to make it healthful. Be present, in each moment. You have the power to choose a food or an activity that is balancing or unbalancing. The science of Ayurveda enables you to maintain balance that is unique to you by getting to know yourself intimately in relation to everything around you. I always encourage my clients to take one small step at a time in order to form new life-promoting habits.

Make changes at a pace that suits you and then adopt more changes when you feel ready. Once you start to feel the benefits, you will naturally be inclined to incorporate more changes into your life. The point I am trying to make here is that every moment is a choice, your choice. Are you choosing well? What to eat, when to sleep, whether to exercise or not, who to spend time with, when to shut down your computer. No one is in charge of your life except you!

The idea is for you to be authentic and realistic about what will elevate your health. I urge you not to conform to any ideology or fall into any media traps of 'perfection'. This mindset will lead to constant dissatisfaction and disappointment. What will become apparent is that your life and health is always in a constant flux, and getting to know your whole self more intimately is the key to true preventative health.

I always like to refer to the analogy of water being stronger than a rock. Though rocks appear to be hard and indestructible, they are also innately rigid. In contrast, water is so soft yet through its flexible, adaptive and consistent nature, it has the strength to erode and carve rocks. Change happens over a long period of time, and if you remain flexible to change and flow like water, over time you too can make a significant impact on your life with small changes, drop by drop. Any obstacles, blockages or unhealthy habits can be overcome. Consistency in your approach to healthful changes will ensure that you get the results that you desire. It can be as simple as having your hot lemon water every morning. Start where you feel comfortable, but be consistent. 'Sometimes' won't help you drop the excess weight, clear that skin rash or sleep better. Since the only thing we have control over is ourselves, it's time to take responsibility.

The principles of Ayurveda help you to identify the changes and practices you can adopt so that you can be aligned to a life of wellness. This is a personalised system of medicine and a system that grants you freedom from illness. It is a transition from a life of mediocrity to a life of vitality. It is not about just getting through the day but living fully with energy and enthusiasm. If your energy reserves are low, then how can you be of service to your family, friends and community?

Common health issues

As I reflect at the end of each day in clinic, I feel truly blessed to follow my path of passion and turn it into work that doesn't feel like work. Ayurveda has been such a transformative part of my life and it is the greatest gift that I could have asked for. Guiding people on their journey to wellness is more rewarding than I imagined was possible and I truly believe that when my clients come with a strong intention to heal, miracles can happen; my role is simply to facilitate their journey.

I see a broad spectrum of health ailments in clinic, from IBS, leaky gut, indigestion, insomnia, asthma, chronic fatigue, sinusitis, skin irritations, migraines, peptic ulcers, sciatica, obesity, diabetes, anxiety, depression, high blood pressure and cholesterol, to name a few. One thing that is for sure, many of the presenting physical ailments stem from either an emotional or mental stress. Some people are drawn to Ayurveda to address specific health issues and others purely to learn about their mind/body type and to be more aligned with their true self. Regardless of the ailments, the focal point is always on correcting and balancing your gut health and aligning to your natural mind/body type.

Client story

'I have struggled to maintain a healthy weight since childhood, and have tried quite a few different diets and fads, always trying to adhere to the conventional wisdom of what a "healthy diet" looked like.

I have made several changes to my daily routine, including starting the day with warm lemon water, keeping breakfast cooked and light, avoiding an excess of raw foods and switching my main meal of the day to lunch. These changes have helped to bring me closer to a natural alignment, both in my internal and external world. These new ideas went against what I had been taught at first about food consumption, but I went with it and started to get positive results, which made me look at other patterns and habitual behaviours in my life that may not be serving me.

With the support of Geeta, I have experienced weight loss, better sleep, increased energy levels and better concentration.'

Dugald

I hope that this book inspires you to live a life aligned to your Ayurvedic mind/body type so that you can become a healthier and happier version of yourself. Whether you make just a few small adjustments or embrace the fuller Ayurvedic way of life, the practical and simple-to-follow guidance in this book will ensure that you feel positive shifts in your wellbeing. Everybody responds differently, so I ask that you apply patience and perseverance as you make new, healthful changes. Some people feel the benefits from small changes within days, while the benefits of deeper changes to your diet and lifestyle can be felt within weeks. Breathing exercises will leave you floating on clouds within minutes. While some changes will fit like a glove, others may be suited just for a season or until you intuitively feel aligned – after all, our health is not static. Remember that, like the entire universe, our body is evolving and changing at its own pace, so give it the support it needs and have faith. Think of your body as a sunflower: you plant a seed, you take care of it properly, water it, give it food and exposure to sunlight and, for sure, the flower will blossom at the right time. You can't rush the process and neither will you keep digging the soil to see how the seedling is getting on; you just have patience and wait for it to bloom. It is the same with Ayurveda; there is no quick fix to long-term wellness, but with small lifestyle changes, you will experience many benefits.

You can implement the advice in this book straight away. The aim here is to incorporate the advice as lifestyle changes, as this is when you will truly start to reap the benefits of preventative healthcare. More importantly, the changes you implement should feel positive, natural and meaningful, and ultimately leave you feeling good. If you have good health, all aspects of your life can flourish.

CHAPTER 2

Ayurveda – Personalised Healthcare

'Every human being is the author of his own health or
disease'

Siddhartha Gautama (Buddha)

History in a nutshell

Ayurveda is the oldest known medical system, dating back 5,000
years, and it aims to treat the root cause of an illness. Known as
the knowledge (*veda*) of life (*ayus*), Ayurveda is a traditional
philosophy born outside of medical labs, long ago. Sages and
rishis, or the 'seers of truth', downloaded this wisdom of life,
known to them as Ayurveda, through deep meditation. In Vedic
mythology, Lord Dhanvantari was the first incarnation to impart
the wisdom to mankind. It is through these insights that the basis
of Ayurveda was formed.

These rishis passed the teachings on to their students by the
oral tradition, until sages such as **Sushruta** and **Charaka**
transcribed this knowledge into the earliest authoritative written
texts, around 1000 BC. These texts were called *Sushruta Samhita*
and *Charaka Samhita*. It is from these and other similar scriptures
such as Vagbhata's **Ashtanga Hridayam** that practitioners like
myself learn this ancient wisdom even today. This universal
knowledge is now accessible to people across the globe. Ayurveda
is one of the few indigenous sciences that still thrives in our
modern world, despite the fact that it was outlawed in India at the

time of colonisation. Today, Ayurveda flourishes all over India and
is being seen once again as a credible approach to wellness in the
West.

The philosophy of Ayurveda

At the heart of Ayurveda is the **Samkhya** philosophy of creation
and the evolution of life, explained by the great sage Kapila.
Purusha is the formless and pure consciousness pervading all
concepts of time and space. It is considered to be the male energy
and exists as a passive awareness. Purusha is reflected as creation
in the form of **prakruti**, the creative force responsible for all
manifestation, physical and energetic. Prakruti is a physical
counterpart that is considered to be the female energy. It is
believed that all evolution of nature is governed by the interaction
of these two forces. This stimulated a chain of evolutions, starting
with the rise of the universal intellect (**buddhi**), then ego or the 'I'
(**ahamkara**), before the ego split to create the three **gunas** (**sattva**,
rajas and **tamas**). Sattva gave rise to all the senses and the organs
of perception, as well as the mind (**manas**). Tamas gave rise to the
five elements (ether, air, fire, water and earth). Rajas is the force
that interacts between sattva and tamas.

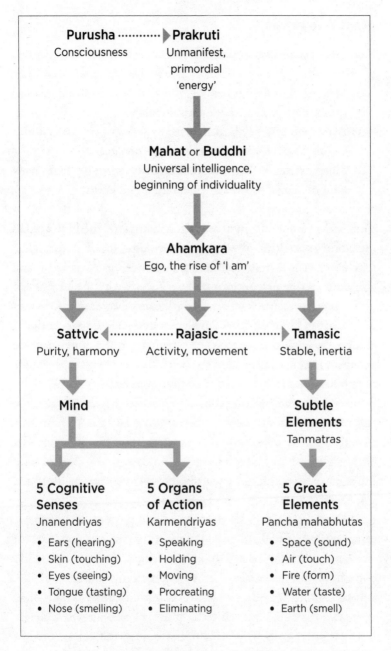

Samkhya Philosophy of Creation

What is Ayurveda?

Your body is the most sophisticated engine you will ever operate in your life. It has an intelligence far beyond our own comprehension. It desires healing; it wants to be well and gives us a multitude of signals if there is an imbalance.

Ayurveda has two key health goals:

1. Curative – to reverse diseases where possible.
2. Preventative – to promote longevity through diet, daily lifestyle, yoga, breathing, meditation and herbs.

The wider scope of Ayurveda is a complete medical system including specialism in surgery, toxicology, internal medicine, psychiatry, ENT, rejuvenation, paediatrics, gynaecology and aphrodisiacs (life promotion).

Though the science was born on the Indian subcontinent, Ayurveda is not exclusive to India or Indian people. The knowledge is universal and can be applied to anyone, anywhere, since it is a personalised system of health. It is a timeless teaching that is so old yet so applicable to our lives now, and will continue to be for millennia to come.

In order to be healthy, your body needs to perform its vital functions optimally; it needs to digest foods and absorb nutrients, eliminate toxins, process information, maintain free-flowing body channels etc. If you take care of the fundamental processes with the right diet and lifestyle, your body will take care of itself and stay healthy.

Without managing the root cause, the problem may subside temporarily but will either lie dormant, persist at some level, or reoccur. Ayurveda uses diet and nutrition, lifestyle guidance, natural medicines, body therapies, breathing and meditation, detoxification and rejuvenation processes and spiritual counselling to treat a patient. Through these practices and lifestyle choices, we can dance to the ebb and flow of nature and connect to the reality that everything is dynamic energy.

We all make excuses

How do you create a new habit pattern and how do you stay committed and focused on making a healthful transformation? I sometimes see clients who have a desire for better health but have a string of excuses as to why they 'can't' make changes. Of course, these are always very valid and genuine reasons. However, if you want to see a result from your underlying desire for wellbeing, your strong intention is not enough – it needs to be met by action. This is only half the equation, though. If you don't value your intention, have a belief in your power to heal or hold your health as a priority in your life, there will always be room for excuses. This applies to everything that we do or want to achieve, and not just health. We are not striving for perfection, but authenticity.

These are some of the excuses I hear:

- I don't have time / I'm too busy
- I will deal with it when something goes wrong
- It can be costly to eat well
- I can't cook
- I can't take on the additional stress
- I work long hours
- I started the day badly, so no point in trying to be healthy now
- I will start tomorrow – but tomorrow never comes!
- I don't have the willpower
- I can't survive without my coffee or afternoon sweet treat
- It's already in the fridge so I can't resist
- It's hard to stick to a healthy plan when I have such an active social life
- I'm always too tired
- My children take up all my time
- Something always comes up
- I just don't enjoy exercise
- I need more food when I feel sad / stressed
- Life is too short, so I just enjoy my indulgences

How many of these have you said to yourself? Firstly, it's time to drop any guilt about previous shortcomings. The past is not something you can change, but every morning you wake up you are reborn. So, don't let the 'you' from yesterday get in your way today. Here are my key steps to changing your health habits, which can help you apply the guidance that follows in this book in an achievable way.

Time

When we use time as an excuse, what we are really saying is, 'I am choosing not to make this a priority in my life right now.' Everything you do is ultimately a choice, even if it seems you are sometimes bound by work, family, finances or health stresses. When you put yourself and your health first, I find that you are able to stretch time and energy for everything else in your life. Can you carve some time for yourself by getting up fifteen minutes earlier?

Action

You will instantly start to feel a shift when you start to make healthful changes one step at a time. What is important is that you take that first step. To see the lasting results that you so desire, action is required.

Consistency

Commitment to persistent patterns of positive change is key to any lasting lifestyle change. In my experience, it can take thirty to forty days to turn a change into a new habitual pattern. Prioritise your intentions and avoid falling into the trap of negative influencers. Those friends who egg you on for dessert or another glass of wine, even though you don't really want it. This is also about not falling into the media traps of what is portrayed as perfect or the latest fad/trend.

Flexibility

Flexibility makes you stronger. If you slip every now and then, don't be hard on yourself and don't carry guilt, as these are harmful emotions. Flexibility in mind and body will give you the vibrancy that you crave. Remember, be like water!

Faith

Have faith in yourself. You must believe in yourself. What are your core values? Connecting with your mind or body is connecting to the divine. Do you believe in your ability to be well?

Twelve tips to stay on top of your Ayurveda A-game

1. Let go of negative self-talk. It's time to feel good about yourself. Who are your role models for how you aspire to grow?
2. Surround yourself with supportive and like-minded people, but only seek approval from yourself.
3. Start to master your weaknesses and the factors that trigger behaviours, such as overeating or excessive exercise. Are you forming unhealthy patterns? Find alternatives and work on those with loving kindness.
4. Change takes time! Remember, Rome wasn't built in a day. Make bite-sized changes that feel comfortable to you. Keep adding to them slowly. Over a year, your overall lifestyle will have transformed.
5. Follow a routine that works for you, especially when it comes to sleep, exercise and diet – your three pillars of health. This will be based on your mind/body type. See chapter 4.

6. Change your language from 'I can't' to 'I can'. Don't just pay it lip service. Really believe in yourself.
7. Sit less, move more. Take the stairs, shop in store rather than online, go for family walks.
8. Slow down and take the lessons from nature. Does the sun ever decide to not show up? Create your routine and stick to it.
9. Make yourself your number one priority in your life. It is time to take responsibility for your health. If you don't, no one else will. You will have more energy to serve others in the long run.
10. Write a gratitude journal. It will help you to stay present, appreciate the smaller things and give you the space to recognise your milestones.
11. Don't be too rigid and take life too seriously. Laughter really is the best medicine.
12. Seek help from a professional to give you support and guidance for your journey to wellness.

My equation for better health

Time + Action + Consistency + Flexibility + Faith
= Health and Harmony

Geeta Vara

CHAPTER 3

The Making of Your Mind/Body Type

'Everyone has a doctor in him or her; we just have to help it in its work. The natural healing force within each one of us is the greatest force in getting well'

Hippocrates

The five great elements – the pancha mahabhutas

The foundations of Ayurveda are rooted in the principle that the entire universe is composed of five great elements, as explained in the Samkhya philosophy. Our body is composed of the same five elements. We are a microcosm of the macrocosm. We are one individual cell in the organism of the universe, just like we have trillions of cells in our entire body. These five elements are known as the **pancha mahabhutas**:

- **Akash** – ether/space
- **Vayu** – air
- **Agni** – fire
- **Jala** – water
- **Prithvi** – earth

Akash, or space, is the subtlest element in which everything exists and happens. As akash started to vibrate, it created air; the friction of air gave rise to heat, and the moisture from this heat created water; the water solidified and turned to earth, the fifth and final, densest element. All organic and inorganic matter are varying combinations of these five elements. Our energy is in constant interaction with everything that surrounds us, and everything is constantly changing and evolving. All matter has an individual existence, yet nothing can exist independently. Our internal body energy reflects the great cosmic energies of the external. Our entire existence and survival is based on our relationship with these elements and if you are in harmony, you will flourish in optimal wellbeing.

These elements, of course, correspond to 'real' and tangible expressions of the elements space, air, fire, water and earth, but also the subtle and abstract expression, so try not to always interpret them in a literal sense, as they can often be invisible. To grasp some of these concepts fully, we need to disengage from our logical left brain and rely on the creative, qualitative right brain to understand. The qualities of these elements can be experienced in our daily physical, mental and emotional being and can be identified by their inherent qualities, such as the coolness and dryness of air, heat or light from fire, or the moisture of water or groundedness and stability of the earth.

These elemental qualities can be seen in everything: your body, your food, your activities, the environment and the seasons. If there are cracks in your relationship with these elements, you will experience disturbances in your body, which can give rise to various health issues.

The five elements in the body

1. Ether – Space is omnipresent and allows all the elements to exist and interact. In the body, space is translated as open cavities, such as in the heart, abdomen, bladder, mouth and nostrils, as well as intracellular and synaptic space. Ether is a contributing element to the **vata dosha.**

2. Air – Wind is the dynamic and mobile element that governs all the movement, change and actions in the body. For example, muscular functions, breathing, blood circulation. This is the main element that gives rise to vata dosha.

3. Fire – Fire is present in everything that requires digestion and transformation. Body temperature, intelligence, digestive enzymes, metabolism and acids are examples of the element of fire. This gives rise to the **pitta** dosha.

4. Water – Water represents all liquidity that flows throughout the body. Body fluids such as plasma, blood, saliva, mucus and intracellular fluids form the largest represented element in the human body. Water is a contributing element to the pitta and **kapha** doshas.

5. Earth – Earth shows up as all visible solid matter that we call the body. The earth gives your body structure and form, such as bones, teeth, tendons, muscle, skin, hair, organs, and so on. Earth is the key element for the kapha dosha.

Understanding these five elements helps us to interpret our outer universe but also our inner world too. The combination of these elements with each other determines our unique mind/body type, habits, personality and our predisposition to health issues.

You can interpret the elements of the environment at a subtle level through your five senses in the following way:

Element	Subtle element	Sensory perception by
Space	Sound	Ears
Air	Touch	Skin
Fire	Sight	Eyes
Water	Taste	Tongue
Earth	Smell	Nose

The concept of existence fills me with wonder and awe. We come into existence, consume the plants, herbs, minerals and water of this planet, and eventually our body returns to the same land. This confirms to me that we are just different compositions of the same elements, and how cyclical our existence really is.

Doshas demystified

One of the most practical cornerstones of Ayurveda is the idea that our physical characteristics and personality are born from the doshas. The three doshas, vata, pitta and kapha, are derived from varying combinations of the five elements in a condensed form that are present and functional in the body.

Every person can identify with one of Ayurveda's three broad dosha types. Although everybody is made up of the same five elements, the differing combinations of these elements give rise to your mind/body type, which is as unique as your fingerprint – it is your exclusive blueprint of existence. This unique physical and mental constitution is known as your **prakruti**. You may have explored a similar theory in modern science that identifies a healthy person to be one of three physical body types: ectomorph, endomorph or mesomorph; however, this concept does not elaborate past the physical body.

This information of physical body types remains as only information in modern science but in Ayurveda, understanding our mind/body type – physical and beyond – empowers us to tap into a wealth of wisdom about how our body works and what we can do to stay in a healthy balance. For example, an ectomorph body will never be able to have the musculature of mesomorph and an endomorph will never be a size-zero catwalk model, despite the endless dieting. Ayurveda teaches us to honour and work with our unique body type to stay well and healthy.

The doshas are the bio-energetic forces in your body that sustain life. Without any one of them, life would not exist. Not only do doshas form your prakruti, they also have a functional role and regulate everything that happens in your body. Each and every cell in our body contains all three doshas, along with their specific actions:

- Vata is the principle that governs movement and regulation
- Pitta is the principle that governs heat and transformation
- Kapha is the principle that governs structure and growth

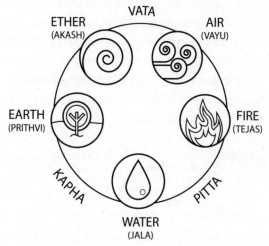

The Five Elements and the Tri-doshas

The three doshas are responsible for all physiological and psychological processes; they are the dynamic forces that determine growth, transformation and decay. They are constantly in flux, as they respond to your actions, thoughts and emotions, to the time of day, the season, the foods that you consume – all of which influence the function of your mind and body. This means you could associate a dosha and its characteristics to everything.

The presence of vata can be correlated to modern medicine as activity of the nervous or muscular system. Pitta correlates to all the chemical processes that take place in the body, such as hormone release and digestion. Kapha can be correlated to the physical mass of the body and skeletal system. Doshas are not the substances themselves but the forces that manifests them into existence.

When the doshas are in close balance (a state of equilibrium) to your natural state (prakruti), you will experience good health, vitality, agility, strength, flexibility and emotional wellbeing. You will be the best version of yourself and your doshas will showcase healthy physical, mental and emotional signs.

The literal translation of dosha is 'fault', or that which is prone to getting spoilt. When you go against your intrinsic nature and follow diet and lifestyle patterns not aligned to your prakruti, you will trigger your doshas to become imbalanced or 'faulty'. We call this *prajnaparadha* (crimes against our better judgement). How many times have you known that taking an action or consuming a food would not be healthful, but decided to override your intuition, only to suffer afterwards?

Characteristics of tri-doshas

Vata	Pitta	Kapha
Light	Hot	Heavy
Cold	Penetrating (sharp)	Slow/static
Rough	Liquid	Oily
Dry	Oily	Smooth
Mobile	Light	Cold
Subtle	Malodorous	Stable
	Fluid	Soft

The role of vata in your body

Formed of ether and air elements, the vata dosha is what keeps your body moving and your mind motivated. It's by far the most dominant dosha of the three, as it supports life and initiates all activities; it simply loves to be involved wherever it can. It is the supporting force behind the pitta and kapha doshas, which require the movement of vata in order for them to function. Vata has distinct characteristics: it's cold, light, dry, rough, mobile and subtle.

The 'dry' characteristic of vata is easily identified in dry skin, hair, nails, bones or bowels. 'Roughness' is found in the texture of nails, skin, hair, lips and a hoarse voice, while 'lightness' is seen in light body weight or light sleep. 'Cold' qualities are displayed with resistance to cold climates. The 'subtle' quality is exhibited as creativity and expression. The 'mobile' quality lends itself to multitasking and fast movement.

Some of the key jobs for vata in the body include the blinking of your eyes, inhalations of breath, pulsation of your heart, nerve impulses, moving your food through the digestive system to elimination, and circulating your blood all around your body.

Mentally and emotionally, vata gets to work by assisting your thought processes and mental adaptability, encouraging your spiritual aspirations, supporting your imagination and visualisation, and balancing fears and anxieties.

The role and function of vata is broken down into five sub-doshas: *udana, prana, vyana, samana* and *apana*, which oversee different parts of your body. Understanding which sub-dosha is involved in a health issue enables a practitioner to tailor your treatment. In this book, I refer to the overall role of the doshas.

The role of pitta in your body

Pitta dosha is formed of the fire and water elements. What happens when these elements coincide? They generate heat and create a boiling effect, and this is what keeps your body warm and in a constant state of transformation. Its qualities are hot, penetrating, oily, light, liquid, malodorous and fluid.

The 'hot' quality is expressed in the body as heat in body and emotion, and strength of metabolism. The 'penetrating' effect is displayed as the intellect and the drive to get things done. The 'liquidity' of pitta is seen as gastric juices or sweat. The 'oily', unctuous quality is seen in the softness of the skin. You are easily able to spot the 'malodorous' quality as bad odour in the body or mouth.

Pitta also has five sub-doshas in the body: *alochaka*, *sadhaka*, *ranjaka*, *pachaka* and *bhrajaka*. Between these five fiery sub-doshas, they manage all the various digestive activities in the body, whether it is from food or from stimuli through the sensory organs. It is the force of pitta that gives warmth to your body and stimulates your sense of hunger and thirst. This dosha gives colour and lustre to your skin, hair and eyes.

Emotionally and mentally, pitta takes care of your ability to judge and discriminate; it takes care of your mental perception and processes, your willpower, control and enthusiasm. But also the joy, laughter and courage that reside within you.

The role of kapha in your body

The soft, cold, oily, heavy, stable, static, slow and smooth qualities of kapha are made from the water and earth elements. Without kapha, your body would have no structure, moisture, growth or protection. All body tissues, bones, muscles and body fluids need kapha dosha to give them form.

Some of these kapha qualities stand out a mile. 'Heaviness', for example, is seen easily as big bones, muscle mass or excess weight. The 'static' quality can be identified as a slowness or sluggishness. 'Oiliness' will display itself as lubrication in the joints, skin and hair. The 'smooth' quality can be seen as supple movement of joints and body and a gentle personality. The 'cold' quality is experienced in the coolness of the skin. The 'soft' quality might be seen in the eyes, skin or a kind heart. The 'stable' quality will be seen in loyalty and a calm mind. The 'slowness' is displayed in slow eating or having a slow gait.

Kapha has five sub-doshas: *avalambaka*, *kledaka*, *bodhaka*, *sleshaka* and *tarpaka*. These govern various parts of the body. Kapha gives your body strength and stability, protection, and lubrication to mucous membranes and joints. Kapha ensures that you have a balance of fluidity in the body and gives you your sense of taste.

Kapha supports a strong memory, patience, calmness, compassion, forgiveness, loyalty, a sense of belonging, devotion and love. Kapha is emotionally very nurturing.

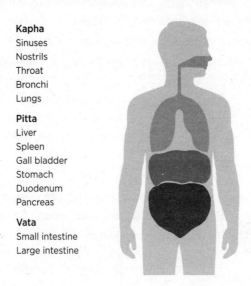

Kapha
Sinuses
Nostrils
Throat
Bronchi
Lungs

Pitta
Liver
Spleen
Gall bladder
Stomach
Duodenum
Pancreas

Vata
Small intestine
Large intestine

Body Parts and Organs influenced by the Three Doshas

The subtle energies

Prana, **tejas** and **ojas** are the three corresponding subtle energy forms of the three doshas which have an influence on our overall wellbeing when our body is balanced or near-balanced. This trilogy of subtle energies contributes to our vitality. It is that person who is strong, who glows and is full of beans and you wonder what is their secret?

Prana

Prana is your life force energy, that which gives you life. It is the subtle energy of vata and can be correlated with a similar concept in other Eastern cultures – *qi* in Chinese or *ki* in Japanese. Have you ever practised qigong by rubbing your hands together and then holding them opposite each other as if you were holding a football? As you gently feel and massage this invisible ball you will feel a force of energy. This is prana between your hands. Prana exists everywhere, and this is a physical way to understand it. By choosing foods that are vibrant and full of life, exercising your breathing and body, and taking appropriate rest, you will support the prana within you.

Tejas

Tejas is the subtle energy of pitta that illuminates the radiance within you. It is the force behind that which gives you the lustre in your eyes and skin. Tejas is the energy that allows communication between the mind, body and soul, allowing the translation of physical activity to the mind faculty and vice versa. The aim is to keep tejas optimal in the same way as prana.

Ojas

Ojas is the subtle energy of kapha and displays itself as the vigour and strength within you. It is the essence of all tissues formed from the digestion and assimilation of your foods, thoughts and impressions. Pure and vibrant food, supported by a strong digestion, will ensure that your ojas remains strong, keeping your body and organs healthy. Ojas is like the glue that holds everything together and is created while you sleep at night, so a good night's sleep is essential for good health. Physical and mental weakness or immune deficiency is a sign that ojas has become compromised.

CHAPTER 4

Discover Your Unique Mind/Body Type

In this chapter, you will discover your unique mind/body type – the cornerstone of holistic healing with Ayurveda. You will identify with a variety of characteristics from three broad mind/ body types, and this will give you an insight into your health vulnerabilities and help you recognise the signs and symptoms in the early stages, so you can manage your health. Once you become acquainted with your prakruti, you will open the doors to a wealth of natural, easy-to-apply tools and techniques that will help you maintain a balance that is more aligned to your natural state.

Your prakruti

Your prakruti – also known as your constitution, dosha type or mind/body type – is your natural state of balance and is unique to you. It is established from a combination of your parents' prakruti, their mental and emotional state at the time of your conception and your mother's diet and lifestyle through pregnancy. This is your personalised key to health and harmony. Your prakruti determines personal traits such as your body frame, temperament, digestive capability, sleep patterns, personality and approach to life, physical stamina and other body habits. It also helps you to identify your predisposition to certain health ailments, which I discuss later in this chapter.

Your prakruti, like your DNA, does not change. However, the various influencing factors of environment, season, age, diet and lifestyle can cause you to enter an imbalanced state called **vikruti**. Vikruti is the term used for your *current* state of balance, when doshas have deviated from the natural state that is your prakruti. Vikruti is in constant flux and ever-changing as you are influenced by internal and external factors. The tendency is to become imbalanced in our natural dominant dosha. For example, a person with a vata-dominant prakruti is likely to see an imbalance in this dosha first. Bringing vikruti back to a normal state is the key aim of Ayurvedic treatment.

If you are of a single-dosha constitution, you are likely to have very distinct characteristics. Most individuals, however, are usually a dual-dosha prakruti, presenting characteristics of one or two doshas more strongly. For example, if you are a vata/pitta type, then you will have a dominance of vata characteristics followed by pitta. If you are a pitta/vata type, then you will display strong pitta characteristics followed by vata characteristics, and so on. The rare occasion that all three doshas present themselves in near-equal amounts is referred to as **tri-doshic**. Do bear in mind that every person has *all three* doshas – here, we are simply referring to the dominant display of the doshas in your prakruti. Therefore, going forward, 'vata type', 'pitta type' and 'kapha type' refers to the dominant presenting dosha in the individual, indicating the elements that are in higher proportion in your body.

You may associate yourself with multiple characteristics of vata, pitta and kapha, and that is OK; we are complex beings, after all. We cannot be rigid in our approach and your type does not limit you or diminish your individuality. Two individuals who take a dosha test may get the same result, but this does not mean that they will hold identical characteristics; on the contrary, dosha traits manifest differently in different people. One person might display vata in their eyes, skin or temperament, and another person may display vata in their body frame and speech. A similar result means that the forces present in our body are at a similar ratio, yet they might show up differently in characteristics. This is the individuality that makes Ayurveda a personalised system of medicine. It also means that people will react differently when exposed to the same food, environment, exercise or stress.

One prakruti is neither superior nor inferior to another, but one thing is for sure: you have to learn to love yourself as you are and work to your strengths. A kapha body type will never be a size-zero, and a vata type of person may not have the natural stamina of a kapha person; pitta types might never have the flexible attitude that vata types possess, and kapha types may not have the fire, focus and determination that pitta types do. Your goal is to maintain your balance according to your unique mind/body type.

Identify your prakruti – take the test

To help you determine what your natural dosha type is and where your imbalance lies, an Ayurvedic practitioner would take a detailed case history and use various traditional diagnostic tools and close examination of body habits, hair, nails, skin, digestion and temperament. But you can self-identify with one of ten body types by answering the prakruti/vikruti questionnaire that follows.

You should answer the questionnaire twice. When filling out column one, think back to how you have always been, your natural tendencies since you were younger and how you are most of the time when you are feeling good, and answer each question accordingly. If you fall into more than one category, then tick all the ones that apply. The result will indicate your prakruti.

Then, when you fill out column two, tick the answers that represent your current state – and be honest here. Again, tick all the answers that apply for each question. This will highlight your vikruti, your imbalance. You can then compare this to your first score and see how far out of balance you are.

	VATA	1 Prakruti	2 Vikruti	PITTA
Age	55+	❏	❏	17–55
Body frame	Thin, prominent bones	❏	❏	Moderate build
Height	Taller or shorter than average	❏	❏	Medium
Hair	Dry, curly, thin, brittle	❏	❏	Soft, greys, balding, red/blonde, straight
Teeth	Big, uneven, receding gums, gappy	❏	❏	Moderate size, soft gums
Head & Face	Thin or small face, irregular features	❏	❏	Moderate, contoured face
Nails	Brittle, thin, cracking, white spots, breaks	❏	❏	Pink, soft, medium, long, flexible
Nose	Small or long, crooked	❏	❏	Straight, pointed, medium
Eyes	Small, sunken, black/brown, dry	❏	❏	Reddish, sharp, penetrating, light sensitive
Skin	Dry, rough, cool, thin, cold extremities	❏	❏	Soft, warm, oily, rosy, freckles, irritable
Muscles	Underdeveloped, thin muscles	❏	❏	Average muscle structure
Weight	Low, underweight	❏	❏	Moderate
Appetite	Variable/grazer	❏	❏	Strong, regular
Hips	Narrow	❏	❏	Medium
Lips	Thin, dry, cracked	❏	❏	Medium, soft, moist
Bowel habits	Dry, hard, constipated	❏	❏	Regular, soft, loose, burning
Hands & Feet	Small, thin, dry, cold, prone to cracking	❏	❏	Warm, pink, moist, healthy
Thirst	Variable thirst, prefers warm	❏	❏	Strong thirst, prefers cool
Physical activity	Very active	❏	❏	Moderate
Temperature	Dislikes cold windy weather	❏	❏	Dislikes excess heat/ strong sun

1 Prakruti	2 Vikruti	KAPHA	1 Prakruti	2 Vikruti
❏	❏	0–16	❏	❏
❏	❏	Broad, solid, curvy, stocky	❏	❏
❏	❏	Medium to tall	❏	❏
❏	❏	Silky, smooth, thick, wavy	❏	❏
❏	❏	Strong, white, strong gums	❏	❏
❏	❏	Large, round, pale	❏	❏
❏	❏	Wide, white, strong/thick	❏	❏
❏	❏	Large, wide, rounded	❏	❏
❏	❏	Large, thick lashes, blue, white, calm, gentle	❏	❏
❏	❏	Thick, soft, oily, cool, pale	❏	❏
❏	❏	Solid, large, well-developed	❏	❏
❏	❏	Heavy, overweight	❏	❏
❏	❏	Slow, constant	❏	❏
❏	❏	Wide	❏	❏
❏	❏	Large and smooth	❏	❏
❏	❏	Formed, heavy, slow, sluggish	❏	❏
❏	❏	Large, thick, cool, damp	❏	❏
❏	❏	Low thirst	❏	❏
❏	❏	Lethargic	❏	❏
❏	❏	Comfortable in warm weather, dislikes cold and damp	❏	❏

	VATA	1 Prakruti	2 Vikruti	PITTA
Walking style	Fast paced	❏	❏	Steady and purposeful
Energy level	Very active, spurts of energy, tires easily	❏	❏	Active, determined, pushes hard
Sleep	Light, disturbed, insomnia	❏	❏	Moderate/good, short
Speech	Enthusiastic, talk-ative, talk with speed, interrupts, animated	❏	❏	Sharp, direct, clear, concise, logical
Profession	Artist, creative, actor, singer, philosophical	❏	❏	Professional leader, analytical, politics, teacher
Dreams	Fearful, flying, running, jumping, anxious, active	❏	❏	Fighting, anger, fiery, colourful, passionate
Mind	Restless, active, adaptable, creative, quick, indecisive	❏	❏	Critical, intelligent, decisive, logical, sharp, organised, ambitious
Beliefs	Changeable, erratic	❏	❏	Focused, fanatic
Creativity	Inventive, abundance of ideas	❏	❏	Technically creative
Work ethic	Active and busy	❏	❏	Organised and focused
Temperament	Nervous, fearful	❏	❏	Irritable, impatient
Memory	Grasps and forgets quickly, poor long-term memory	❏	❏	Clear/sharp
Emotions	Enthusiastic, intuitive, lively	❏	❏	Warm, perceptive
Emotions when stressed	Anxiety, fearful, anxious, worry	❏	❏	Jealous, irritated, aggressive, angry
Learning ability	Quick to learn, quick to forget. Loses focus multitasking. Learns by listening	❏	❏	Learns at moderate speed, absorbs information well, visual learner
Body strength	Low, poor endurance	❏	❏	Moderate endurance

1 Prakruti	2 Vikruti	KAPHA	1 Prakruti	2 Vikruti
❏	❏	Slow and relaxed	❏	❏
❏	❏	Strong endurance, slow to get motivated	❏	❏
❏	❏	Deep, prolonged	❏	❏
❏	❏	Slow and purposeful, clear, soothing voice	❏	❏
❏	❏	Carer, healthcare worker, chef, self-employed	❏	❏
❏	❏	Gentle, romantic, water-based	❏	❏
❏	❏	Calm, relaxed, slow, compassionate, patient, methodical	❏	❏
❏	❏	Loyal, constant, conservative	❏	❏
❏	❏	Business oriented, methodical	❏	❏
❏	❏	Slow and methodical	❏	❏
❏	❏	Easy-going, calm	❏	❏
❏	❏	Slow to learn, retains info, good recall	❏	❏
❏	❏	Calm, loyal, love, dependable, stable	❏	❏
❏	❏	Attached, withdrawn, depressed, greedy, self-pity	❏	❏
❏	❏	Learns slowly but does not forget information	❏	❏
❏	❏	Strong endurance	❏	❏

	VATA	1 Prakruti	2 Vikruti	PITTA
Sweat	Light perspiration, no smell	❏	❏	Profuse perspiration, sometimes with strong odour
Movement	Active	❏	❏	Moderate
Eating habits	Erratic hunger, irregular meals, indulges or skips meals	❏	❏	Regular meals, strong hunger. Never misses a meal
Immunity	Variable, poor or weak	❏	❏	Medium, prone to infection
Sensitive to	Noise	❏	❏	Bright light
Sex drive	Changeable, low stamina, can be intense	❏	❏	Moderate, passionate, dominating
Spending habits	Spends easily, impulsive, low savings	❏	❏	Considerate spender and saver, splurges on luxuries
Social	Sometimes shy in new situations, otherwise friendly and chatty	❏	❏	Outgoing, assertive, likes attention
Digestion	Irregular, gas formation	❏	❏	Quick, good, hungry quickly
Disease tendency	Joint and body aches/pains, easily stressed, nervous disorders, bone issues	❏	❏	Prone to inflammation, hyperacidity, skin rashes, fever
Hobbies	Art, music, esoteric subjects, dancing, travelling	❏	❏	Competitive sports, political debates, luxury holidays, self-care/looking good
Menstruation (women only)	Irregular, clots, intense cramps, scanty flow, PMS, dark colour	❏	❏	Regular, heavy, long bleeding, red, intense PMS, cramps, irritable
Total		❏	❏	

1 Prakruti	2 Vikruti	KAPHA	1 Prakruti	2 Vikruti
❏	❏	Moderate, consistent, pleasant odour	❏	❏
❏	❏	Slow	❏	❏
❏	❏	Steady hunger, craves food, can go for long periods without food	❏	❏
❏	❏	Strong	❏	❏
❏	❏	Smells	❏	❏
❏	❏	Slow, constant, loyal, devoted	❏	❏
❏	❏	Thrifty, accumulates cash, spends carefully, but likes to spend on food	❏	❏
❏	❏	Quietly sociable and makes loyal friends	❏	❏
❏	❏	Slow, creates mucus	❏	❏
❏	❏	Conditions of the respiratory system, obesity, high cholesterol	❏	❏
❏	❏	Relaxing at home, watching TV, nature walks, eating out, baking/cooking	❏	❏
❏	❏	Regular, easy, water retention, mild PMS, dull cramps	❏	❏
❏	❏		❏	❏

Total column one for vata, pitta and kapha. If, for example, your score for vata was 30, for pitta, 23, and kapha, 14, then your dosha type is vata/pitta. If you scored, say, 24 for kapha, 18 for pitta and 9 for vata, then you are a kapha/pitta. If your score for vata was 34, 8 for pitta, and 10 for kapha, then your constitution is likely to be vata-dominant. If you scored 20 for vata, 18 for pitta and 18 for kapha, you're likely to be tri-doshic. In the same way, total column two to establish your current state.

Now that you have identified which one of the ten dosha types you are, you can follow the guidance in this book that is right for you. If your current state indicates a significant increase in one dosha then follow the advice for this dosha in the first instance. Ayurveda does not have a single answer for one ailment, but rather looks at all the influencing factors in choosing the best route to healing. This tailored approach is what makes Ayurveda unique. By recognising when your individual doshas are unbalanced, it can help you prevent diseases from manifesting by using a multifaceted approach to healing.

Here is an overview of the ten different dosha body types.

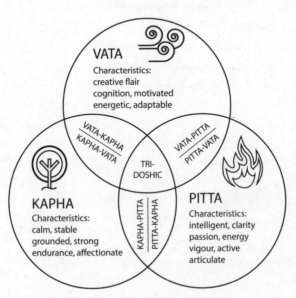

Your Prakruti (mind/body type)

Vata

Vata types usually have a lighter bone structure, less fat and a thinner build, with cool or darker skin and skin that tends to be on the drier side. Their joints and veins are often visible. The vata body type can be compared to an ectomorph.

Due to the natural mobility of vata, these types tend to be quick-thinking and fast-moving. They will have short bursts of high energy and get lots done, but then tire easily and need to take a rest; they need to fuel the body often, so that they can get going again. Due to the cold characteristics, vata types are sensitive to cold foods and weather.

Emotionally, they tend to be blessed with sensitivity, but also prone to worry. The vata mind is creative and imaginative, and they are able to think outside of the box; they are excited easily and can be spontaneous by nature, and so are happy to go with the flow.

Vata's changeability means that vata types have varied sleeping and eating patterns, and engage in an array of activities. They tend to pick up information quickly but can forget just as easily. A balanced vata person will be vibrant, energetic, creative, vivacious and excitable. When vata types are in balance they are truly dynamic, accomplishing lots of tasks. They do have a tendency to fidget – playing with their hair or a pen, pacing up and down. If they become imbalanced, they tend to suffer from dry bowels and skin, and can be prone to cold hands and feet.

Here are some more typical vata characteristics.

Physical vata characteristics
- Naturally slim frame, often with protruding joints
- Tall or short in height
- Small eyes, usually dark in colour
- Underweight, or finds it difficult to increase weight
- Skin can be on the dry side and often thin, with visible veins

- Hair can be thin, dry and brittle
- Quick and agile with short bursts of energy and enthusiasm; can then often feel exhausted
- Susceptible to cold hands and feet
- Variable appetite and inconsistent meal patterns; can often skip meals or equally be indulgent
- Light sleep with flighty dreams
- Walks and talks quickly
- Variable sex drive
- In women, menstrual cycles tend to be irregular and are often accompanied by pain
- Prefers warm, tropical climates
- Poor or weak digestive fire; can digest food well one day and poorly the next

Mental/emotional vata characteristics
- Creative and artistic
- Adaptable and flexible to most situations
- Enthusiastic and spontaneous – loves action, adventure and change
- Emotionally sensitive
- Quick to grasp new information but can easily forget it too
- Impulsive spending
- Compassionate
- Charismatic, with strong or animated communication skills
- Intuitive and spiritually inclined
- Great sense of imagination and perception
- Life and soul of the party
- Loves to travel

Pitta

With a medium build, similar to a mesomorph, pitta types tend to have a well-proportioned shape and features, as well as sustained energy levels. Their bodies are prone to getting hot easily.

Pitta types have a keen intellect and a determined and focused mind, and tend to make good leaders and public speakers. They are outgoing, affectionate and they love challenges. They are passionate and driven in life, and are super-alert. They have good attention to detail and possess a sharp memory, meaning they can complete multiple projects at the same time. They are organised, efficient and decisive, and great critical thinkers.

The fire present in pitta means that pitta types have a tendency to display colour in their body, evident as freckles or as red hair. They also tend to go grey or bald at an early age. When they exercise, they get red and tend to sweat easily. They can become irritable, judgemental, impatient and angry when this dosha is out of balance.

Physical pitta characteristics
- Medium and well-proportioned build
- Average and stable weight
- Fine hair, often lighter or red in colour; premature greying or hair loss is common
- Delicate skin, prone to freckles and moles
- Medium-sized, bright and penetrating eyes
- Thin and pointed nose
- Sleep is light–moderate but undisturbed, eight hours usually will suffice
- Excellent appetite, strong hunger, good digestion and easy elimination
- In women, menstruation is regular and can be heavy and long-lasting
- Perspires easily and heavily
- Feels uncomfortable in hot climates

Mental/emotional pitta characteristics

- Driven by routine, order and cleanliness
- Gets irritable if a meal is missed – what is humorously referred to as getting 'hangry'
- Witty and outspoken
- Joyful and contented
- Determined and persevering – natural-born leaders
- Focused, perceptive, intellectual and goal-oriented, with a sharp memory
- Articulate and concise, with strong communication skills – they make excellent public speakers since they can easily project their voice
- Able to perform under pressure
- Perfectionist and impatient nature
- Thrifty with finances, but enjoys an occasional splurge
- Strong sex drive and easily aroused
- Likes competitive sports
- Adventurous and brave

Kapha

Similar to the Western body type of an endomorph, in the physical body, kapha types tend to have a solid frame and strong bones, smooth skin, large eyes and thick, wavy hair. They have physically strong bodies, with supple but firm muscles. Due to the earth and water elements, kapha types tend be slow in their movement; they are long, heavy sleepers and are uneasy in cool and damp environments.

Kapha types are slow in their learning. They need time to soak up information, but once knowledge has been absorbed, it becomes ingrained in their mind and they generally have a sound memory.

Kapha types have a calm, tolerant and relaxed temperament. They tend be loyal, compassionate, patient and forgiving. They are steady in their emotions and are rarely angered. These are the characteristics of a kapha type that are positive and balanced. If a kapha person becomes imbalanced, they can easily put on weight, sleep excessively and become lazy.

Physical kapha characteristics

- Broad frame, curvy, with heavy bones
- Thick, oily and curly hair
- Large, lustrous eyes
- Large, strong and white nails and teeth
- Oily and smooth skin
- Moderate appetite and hunger, with possibly a slow digestion
- Slow and graceful movement
- Physically strong, with good stamina and stability
- Calm and relaxed voice
- Sleeps long and deeply, often with pleasant dreams
- Prefers dry and warm climates
- Steady desire and drive for sex
- Capable of vigorous and prolonged physical exercise – they make great long-distance runners, although they might prefer to avoid physical activity
- Well-formed and regular stools
- Likely to be fertile; 'child-bearing hips' common in women

Mental/emotional kapha characteristics

- Calm and collected disposition
- Rarely complains
- Thrifty and savvy with money
- Warm and compassionate
- Tolerant of others and forgiving in nature
- Patient, with great listening skills
- Often a creature of habit
- Intelligent but can take a while to grasp new concepts

Dual-dosha types

If you identified with characteristics from more than one of the types above, you will be a dual-dosha type. In this case, one dosha might become dominant under certain circumstances, while the other dosha might become dominant under different circumstances. For example, if you are a pitta/vata or a pitta/kapha type, pitta will be dominant over the summer and vata or kapha dosha will become stronger over the autumn/winter. My advice is to follow the diet that balances your strongest dosha imbalance, taking into account the seasonal effects.

Vata/pitta or pitta/vata

A dual-dosha type where either vata is dominant over pitta, or pitta is dominant over vata. For example, if you are a vata/pitta type, you may still have the slender build of a typical vata but have a greater resistance to environmental influences. You may also be more emotionally stable and generally have better digestion, due to pitta influence. Alternatively, a pitta/vata person may have a sharp mind and digestion, but the vata dosha may influence a creative flair or erratic eating patterns or elimination. In someone with these dual-dosha combinations, there will be an overlap in qualities, such as lightness, but there will also be qualities opposite in nature, such as the coolness and dryness of vata, and the heat and oiliness of pitta. These often balance each other out or need balancing depending on the season.

Vata/kapha or kapha/vata

A dual-dosha type where either vata is dominant over kapha, or kapha is dominant over vata. If you are a vata/kapha type, you may have a light and slender build with an easy-going personality. You may be vulnerable to colds and flu, with feelings of unease during the winter months. You could be susceptible to suffering from anxiety. A kapha/vata person may have a robust and rounded build with lean muscles and fluctuating weight, or they may have a good balance of rest, relaxation and activity and creativity. In someone with these dual-dosha combinations, there will be an overlap in the quality of cold and so the effects of cold will be strong in this type. They have opposite qualities in the mobility, lightness, roughness and dryness of vata and the heaviness, stability, smoothness, and oiliness of kapha, so can be naturally balancing.

Pitta/kapha or kapha/pitta

A dual-dosha type where either pitta is dominant over kapha, or kapha is dominant over pitta. If you are a pitta/kapha type, you may have the well-proportioned body of a pitta with a good combination of drive and endurance. You are likely to have a sharp intellect with a more easy-going approach influenced by kapha. A kapha/pitta person may have a rounded face with a pointy nose, or perhaps you have a strong hunger and digest well but tend to gain weight easily. In someone with these dual-dosha combinations, there will be an overlap in qualities such as oiliness, but there will be the opposite qualities of heat, sharpness and lightness of pitta, and coolness, sluggishness and heaviness of kapha.

Tri-dosha type – vata/pitta/kapha

A varied combination of all three dosha types, with a near equal proportion of each dosha type. Quite a rare type that's blessed with a robust constitution. If imbalances in a tri-doshic type continue for a prolonged period, they can be difficult to manage.

Dosha imbalances

When a dosha becomes imbalanced or distorted from its natural state, it can go one of two ways. The dosha can either become aggravated or in excess of its normal state, or the natural state can be reduced and become depleted.

Generally speaking, it is when your dominant dosha becomes overstretched or increased that imbalances manifest. For example, a person with too much vata could have dry skin, constipation, cracked heels, cracking joints or insomnia. Too much pitta could lead to acidity, heartburn, skin irritations or ulcers. Excess kapha could lead to obesity, sinus congestion, asthma or depression. But similarly, a depletion in vata could lead to reduced mobility, appetite, energy, sensations, speech and vigour. Depleted pitta would result in loss of digestive fire, body fuel and glow in the complexion. Depleted kapha would result in dizziness, a feeling of emptiness, increased palpitations and dryness in the body.

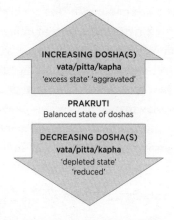

Two Directions of Dosha Imbalances

The rise of dosha imbalances

Even in a perfect world, we rarely remain in complete 'balance'; our job is to notice when things are starting to sway off kilter. We are prone to becoming imbalanced in the dominant dosha of our prakruti first, followed by the other doshas. When the doshas become imbalanced, we can start to experience psychosomatic discomfort. For example, if kapha is increased, this could be visible as excess mucus; if pitta is increased it is visible by heightened acidity; if vata is increased it is visible in the form of bloating. If this is left unresolved, over time it can lead to illness.

If you want to manage health both from a curative and preventative perspective, understanding the characteristics of the doshas can help you identify where your susceptibilities to physical, mental and emotional imbalances lie. Like increases like, and opposites can create balance. The goal is to keep your doshas in balance as close to your natural state as possible.

From the questionnaire you will have gained a sense of your prakruti and vikruti. When managing doshas, the key is to first normalise your vikruti (the imbalanced dosha). You can then stay aligned to your prakruti. The problem is that so many of us have been out of balance for so long that we think that our out-of-balance state is our nature. So, if you are unsure, consult an Ayurvedic practitioner for clarity.

In the meantime, here is an overview of how each dosha can get imbalanced, how to recognise the early signs, and the types of health issues that may manifest.

Vata dosha

Causes of vata imbalance

Vata is the most volatile of the three doshas and can easily get imbalanced. What happens when the natural qualities of vata become excessive beyond a balanced state in our body and mind? Too much air, dryness, lightness, coldness, too much movement? Vata types will be drawn to the qualities that are innate in them such as more movement, more activity, more irregularity, hence the imbalanced vata becomes out of control.

We can then start to identify this imbalanced state as being our nature, but this is not actually the case. Complexities in our lives today mean that we are all exposed to mental stress, and as a result we can suffer from prolonged worry, anxiety, fear, grief, shock and loneliness, but these are imbalanced states of the natural function of vata in the mind. Have you noticed how we start to use language that mirrors our imbalances and say things like, 'I feel spaced out' or 'I'm so scatty' or 'I'm feeling light-headed'? We are unconsciously revealing that our vata is out of balance.

Given that vata is dominated by mobile and irregular qualities, constant changes in life, frequent flying, travel by train and road, changes of time zones and irregular daily routines are going to aggravate vata, triggering displays of imbalanced vata symptoms and the natural gift of quick movement becoming excessive. A vata person who indulges in excessive physical and sexual activity, coupled with a lack of sleep and rest, will allow vata to spiral out of control.

The dry, cold and rough qualities of vata increase naturally during the autumn season; vata is also prone to increase at specific vata times – between 2 a.m. and 6 a.m. and 2 p.m. and 6 p.m. – and at the vata age of 55 and over. These imbalanced qualities will display themselves as dryness in the skin, cold extremities, worry, anxiety and fear.

Indulgence in vata-aggravating foods that are bitter, astringent, pungent, dry, cold, light and rough – for example, consumption of alcohol, black tea and coffee, popcorn, rice crackers, crisps and oatcakes – can increase vata too. Smoking cigarettes can have a similar effect. Too much air and dryness in the body will lead to dryness in the bowels and to chronic constipation over time.

Vata has an innate receptivity, so is prone to disturbance if you eat when you are feeling stressed and upset. This sensitivity of vata also means that overstimulation of your senses by things such as noisy environments and excessive talking can also provoke vata. Sensitivity is the gift of vata, but this compassion is easily defeated by anxiety when out of balance.

Suppression of creativity and emotions as well as suppression of your natural urges (eating, bowel movements, urination, passing of wind, sleep) can block vata's free-flowing nature. A diet and lifestyle consisting of qualities opposite to vata are necessary for balance.

Early signs of vata imbalance

When the space and air elements of your mind and body increase, early signs will present themselves. Take a look at this list of vata imbalance signals and see how many of them currently resonate with you. The more you identify with these, the stronger your vata imbalance.

❏ Easily fatigued and lacking energy
❏ Body aches, pains and muscle stiffness
❏ Joint pains, especially in lower back
❏ Cracking of joints
❏ Easily bloated, with excess gas and wind
❏ Explosive diarrhoea due to emotional stress
❏ Constipation and irregular bowel movements
❏ Indecisive and prone to forgetfulness
❏ Irregular appetite
❏ Loss of weight
❏ Amenorrhoea, or short and irregular menses
❏ Dry skin, hair and nails
❏ Restless sleep or insomnia
❏ Lacking coordination and feeling dizzy
❏ Constantly feeling cold; poor circulation
❏ Increased nervousness, anxiety, insecurity, shyness, self-pity, depression
❏ Tension headaches
❏ Shaking and tremors
❏ Dry throat and hoarseness of voice
❏ Restlessness, inability to sit still
❏ Emotional, irrational and reactive
❏ Impatient and quick to judge
❏ Lacking in confidence

❑ Overly active thinking
❑ Tendency to interrupt or easily disengage from conversations
❑ Tendency to be introverted and to procrastinate
❑ Feeling ungrounded and erratic

Common vata-driven disorders

• Muscle pain
• Arthritis and osteoporosis
• Tinnitus
• High or low blood pressure
• Chronic fatigue
• Premature ageing
• Prone to food allergies
• Mental disorders such as attention deficit disorder (ADD), obsessive-compulsive disorder (OCD), bipolar disorder

Pitta dosha

Causes of pitta imbalance

When pitta types are balanced, they are blessed with a sharp intellect; they have drive, clarity, joy and ambition. What happens when the natural state and qualities of pitta become increased? Too much heat, too much sharpness, too much lightness? Pitta types are naturally attracted to foods and habits that will increase pitta further, so opposite qualities to pitta are necessary for balance.

Pitta types, who are naturally emotional beings, can sometimes suppress their emotions, which can trigger an imbalance of pitta. The penetrating, sharp, driven qualities of pitta are aggravated by the eager and competitive streak, anger, jealousy, arguments and irritations. This can outwardly display itself as self-criticism and criticism of others and a sharp, aggressive tongue. Pitta types will use language such as 'he/she makes my blood boil' or 'I could punch his lights out'.

A balanced pitta is organised, efficient and decisive, but when rubbed up the wrong way they will become irritated, frustrated and display signs of perfectionism. Remember, these are not natural states of being but displays of imbalance. Drive can quickly become overdrive.

The natural and balanced heat of the pitta digestion will be fuelled out of control by excessive pungent, sour, salty, fried and processed foods, excessive intake of alcohol, black tea and coffee. Smoking cigarettes also exacerbates the imbalance. Skipping meals and eating while angry will fire pitta out of balance.

Pitta is susceptible to imbalance between the hours of 10 a.m. and 2 p.m. and 10 p.m. and 2 a.m. It is also susceptible over the most part of our adult life, from age 17 to 55, and to hot weather, direct sunlight and the summer months, when the body can get overheated.

Going to bed late, reading thrillers, watching TV late at night, overworking, being excessively competitive and overambitious in nature are all triggers for pitta. The excess of heat and liquidity in the body will become acidity and heartburn, and will show up as inflammatory conditions. Any condition that ends in '-itis' (for example, gastritis or tonsillitis) is an inflammatory condition, and pitta will have played a lead role, for sure.

Early signs of pitta imbalance

See how many of the below attributes relate to you. The more of these that resonate with you, the more you may have a pitta imbalance.

❏ Bad breath
❏ Profuse and odorous sweating; prone to fever
❏ Inflammation in the digestive tract, hyperacidity, gastritis, ulcers in the mouth and stomach

❏ Sore throat, tonsillitis, bronchitis
❏ Tendency towards bleeding (nose bleed; heavy menstruation in women)
❏ Excessive hunger and thirst
❏ Inflammatory issues of the eye, such as conjunctivitis, bloodshot eyes, sties
❏ Tendency to have loose motions or diarrhoea
❏ Yellow discolouration of skin, nails, teeth, urine and sweat
❏ Intolerance to heat
❏ Critical and judgemental attitude towards self and others
❏ Loss of clarity and rational judgement
❏ Tendency to put work first, becoming a 'workaholic'
❏ Argumentative, loud and domineering; inability to listen to others
❏ Overly intense personality
❏ Stubborn, egotistical and arrogant
❏ Disturbed sleep and agitated dreams

Common pitta-driven disorders

❏ Hypoglycaemia
❏ Haemorrhoids
❏ Hepatitis and other liver or gall bladder disorders
❏ Cystitis, burning urination
❏ Headaches and migraines
❏ Inflammatory conditions of the blood and skin
❏ Aggression, irritability, anger, arrogance, obsession, alcoholism
❏ Prone to energy depletion and 'burnout'
❏ Skin issues caused by inflammation, such as eczema, urticaria (hives), herpes, psoriasis

Kapha dosha

Causes of kapha imbalance

What causes the naturally stable, heavy, soft, cold, slow, oily and dense kapha to become imbalanced? Well, based on the theory of like increasing like, any food, thought or activity that shares the same characteristics will create sluggishness in kapha. The risk of kapha imbalance is that kapha types will be attracted to more inactivity and a more sedentary lifestyle, coupled with heavy foods, thus increasing the imbalance further.

The heavy, slow and dense qualities of kapha are easily triggered by a sedentary lifestyle, sleeping in until late morning and excessive sleep during the day, laziness, excessive indulgence in staying indoors watching TV and a lack of physical activity. Kapha people, when exposed to stress and who have become out of balance, will slow down significantly. They become dull, clouded, heavy and lethargic; over time, this becomes embedded and can lead to depression. When imbalanced, kapha types use language like 'I don't have the energy for that' or 'I'm so full' or 'I'm so sick and tired' while continuing to eat.

Similarly, indulgence in foods that are heavy, dense, moist and cold, like dairy, leftover meats or processed foods, and tastes that are sweet, sour and salty will drive kapha into a lethargic state. It goes without saying that overeating, emotional eating and irregular eating patterns will also add to the shortcomings of this dosha. The kapha body tends to immediately hold on to fluids and fat when it starts to become imbalanced.

The cold and heavy qualities of kapha are naturally prone to aggravation between the hours of 6 a.m. and 10 a.m. and 6 p.m. and 10 p.m., over the winter months and in cold and damp weather. Kapha naturally increases in childhood during the growth phase of life until 16 years of age. The loyal and stable qualities of a balanced kapha may mean that harbouring emotions for a long time could imbalance kapha.

Early signs of kapha imbalance

See how many of these attributes below relate to you. The more that resonate with you, the more you may have a kapha imbalance.

- ❏ Puts on weight easily
- ❏ Loves to take lots of rest and to sleep in
- ❏ Lethargy, heaviness and sluggishness in the body
- ❏ Poor circulation
- ❏ Water retention and bloating
- ❏ Prone to frequent colds, flu and sinus congestion
- ❏ Prone to increased mucus and phlegm in the body
- ❏ Low digestive fire and sluggish bowels
- ❏ Painful and swollen joints
- ❏ Aversion to change; procrastination
- ❏ Complacency and a lack of motivation
- ❏ Becoming greedy, possessive and attached to people and possessions

Common kapha-driven disorders

- Hypothyroidism
- Type 2 diabetes
- Polycystic ovary syndrome
- High cholesterol
- Obesity
- Asthma
- Yeast conditions, such as candida

CHAPTER 5

'Dis-ease' to Disease

'Natural forces within us are the true healers of disease'

Hippocrates

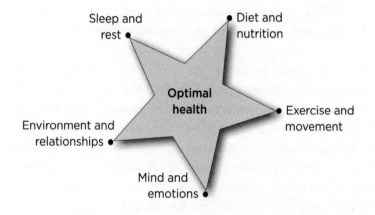

Ayurvedic Approach to Holistic Health

If it ain't broke, then why fix it? This is the mainstream attitude to health. We wait until the body is diagnosed with a serious illness such as cancer, diabetes or arthritis, yet by this point the disease has already been progressing for a long time. But if we understand the mind and body the way nature intended, and take preventative action, we may never need medicines, whether herbal or allopathic.

Causes of disease

Diseases don't just happen overnight, they take time to manifest. Knowingly or unknowingly, we can chip away at the complete health that we have been granted by living in disharmony with nature. Some of the ways in which we can set ourselves up for ill health include:

- Living against our constitution (our mind/body type)
- Undertaking inappropriate exercise
- Having a nutritionally inappropriate diet
- Being involved in troubled relationships
- Having an erratic schedule
- Holding negative or repressed emotions
- Being exposed to toxins, microbes and allergens

All of these causative factors can impact each and every cell of your body in a degenerative way, but what if you had more awareness of the triggers that unbalance you and of the signs that indicate this imbalance? A disease or condition can be caused by many factors, and the triggers can differ from person to person. In modern science we have names for thousands of diseases and these diseases are categorised by a collection of symptoms, but modern medicine often fails to identify the root cause of the illness, so we take a prescription to fix the symptoms. Though allopathic medicines have their place, the question remains: every time a condition pops up, are you going to keep taking another quick-fix pill? Our entire microbiome is connected by a network of channels, visible and invisible, so treating an organ in isolation will not bring the desired results. Each condition that presents itself is a symptom of an underlying fault in the ecosystem of your wellbeing.

Let's say you present symptoms of a skin condition, which your doctor diagnoses as psoriasis. She may give you a steroid cream to use externally to help relieve the irritated, dry, itchy, flaky, inflamed, cracked skin but these are just outward displays of an internal disturbance; while the cream may pacify the itch or calm the redness, the underlying issue continues to fester. We need an interconnected approach that is going to address the underlying imbalance and treat the root, so that you can be irritation-free for a long period and prevent similar outbreaks from occurring again. Ayurveda in this instance would look at cleansing the digestion, liver and blood but not without careful consideration of your prakruti and vikruti.

When doshas get unbalanced, the body is unable to cope with excessive exposure to the causative factors listed above. It is at this point that diseases can manifest, and can worsen, if these factors are continually ignored. This is why the focus of Ayurveda is on **swasthavritta**, the maintenance of personal health, which guides us on how to avoid the causes of disease and uphold a preventative approach to health, based on your mind/body type.

How diseases develop

Disease develops when a dosha (vata, pitta or kapha) enters a **dhatu** (body tissue) where there may be a pre-existing weakness in the tissue (due to lifestyle, wear and tear, trauma or heredity). The dosha begins to alter the structure of this tissue over time and cause disease.

Ayurveda's strength is being able to identify the six various stages of disease development, from early inklings to fully displayed manifestation, these stages are known as the **samprapti**. This means that as you get to know your mind/body type, you are also able to pre-empt which doshas are likely to become unbalanced and make lifestyle adjustments accordingly to prevent diseases from manifesting or progressing. If we catch conditions brewing in the early stages (stages 1–3), we have a stronger chance of nipping them in the bud.

The six stages of disease development are:

1. Accumulation (*chaya*)
2. Aggravation (*prakopa*)
3. Spread (*prasara*)
4. Localisation (*sthana samshreya*)
5. Manifestation (*vyakti*)
6. Complications (*bheda*)

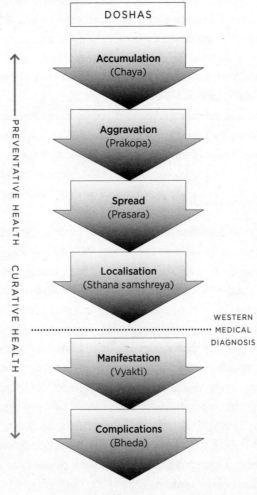

Six Stages of Disease Development

Stage 1: Accumulation

In this first stage, the early inklings of imbalance usually stir at the residing place of the dosha in the gastrointestinal tract (colon for vata, small intestines for pitta and stomach for kapha). Caused by either a weakened agni (digestive fire) or an accumulation of toxins (**ama**), at this stage the symptoms are more of a discomfort – a bloated tummy, sluggish motions, feelings of excessive hunger or lack of appetite. They are easily corrected by avoiding causative factors and listening to the body's inner wisdom.

Stage 2: Aggravation

If the increased dosha(s) is not pacified, it will increase further and discomfort will worsen – maybe causing mild abdominal pain or distension, indigestion, constipation, heartburn, nausea, or an increase in mucus, colds and coughs. These symptoms are aggravated by unbalancing diet and lifestyle choices, and we often ignore them or reach for a quick fix.

Stage 3: Spread

At this stage, if an accumulated dosha(s) is left unresolved it will move out of the gastrointestinal tract and start to circulate throughout the body. Symptoms for vata might include dry skin, cold hands and feet, tinnitus and heart palpitations; pitta would be displayed as intense heartburn, acne, skin irritations; and kapha as sluggishness in the body, water retention or clogged lymphatics.

Stage 4: Localisation

The moving, vitiated dosha(s) finds body tissues where there is weakness and calls it home. This is the beginning stage of a felt and visible disease. It is the starting point for degenerative diseases. The quality of the tissue starts to change, but it is still possible to reverse the condition at this stage. Vata at this stage may display cracking and popping of joints. Pitta may display increased heat in a specific body part. Kapha may display as a common cold.

Stage 5: Manifestation

At this stage, a clinical diagnosis would be given in Western medicine. The dosha(s) settles into the weakened tissue and causes further structural damage. An example would be osteoarthritis, where vata settles in the weakened bone tissue; or, if pitta is dominant, there will be an increase in inflammation; if kapha is dominant, perhaps a chronic common cold may manifest. Damage reversal becomes difficult at this stage.

Stage 6: Complications

Progress of the disease takes place if left unmanaged in stage five. Tissue damage becomes severe and irreversible in some instances. In osteoarthritis, vata completely breaks down the joint, requiring it to be replaced; pitta creates ulcerations and bleeding disorders; kapha triggers tumour formations. Here diet, lifestyle and herbs can serve only to manage the symptoms.

Sadly, conventional medicine does not recognise the early stages of disease development identified in Ayurveda, nor its associated symptoms. These symptoms are often those where we feel out of kilter, and yet the doctor is telling us everything is 'normal' or 'the feeling will pass'. Ayurveda pays close attention to these early warning signs, as they indicate an imbalance. If we learn to recognise these signs in the first three stages, Ayurveda can work its magic to prevent the progression of diseases and damage to our body's tissues. After all, this is the art of preventative health.

As we progress to the latter stages of disease development (stages 5–6), where there are clearly defined signs and symptoms, the time it takes to reverse the imbalance may be longer and, in some chronic cases, diseases may be incurable through diet, lifestyle treatment and herbs alone. At that stage, we would need to turn to Ayurvedic purificatory treatments (**pancha karma**) to manage the symptoms.

It is not all doom and gloom, however. Getting to stage five and six of a disease can take a number of years. If you catch a condition brewing in the earlier stages, there is a strong possibility you can achieve reversal and restore health.

Grasping this basic concept of disease development here will shed light on why Ayurveda gives the utmost importance to daily regimens, digestive health and dosha balancing.

We are what we digest

We literally become what we eat but, in Ayurveda, it's not only what we eat but how well we digest that matters. Have you ever stopped to think about how your body actually operates and functions? If you have, you will appreciate that your body is the most intelligent and dynamic piece of machinery that has ever been created. We put food in and excrete waste out, but the process that happens in between is not always fully understood. It can take 30–40 days to fully nourish all the tissues of our body using the food that we eat, and each meal takes on average 3–6 hours to fully digest depending on what it is and your digestive strength.

Food is broken down in the mouth by mastication (chewing) and mixes with salivary enzymes and travels to the upper digestive tract. The more broken down the food is, the better it is for the second stage of digestion. This first stage is the kapha stage of digestion.

The food is broken down in your stomach and small intestines by the **jatharagni** (the various enzymatic secretions from the liver, pancreas and stomach) and this is the pitta stage of digestion. The result is the initial formation of **ahararasa** (a nutrient fluid), similar to the concept of chyme in Western medicine, a semi-solid bolus of partially digested food. This ahararasa is transported through the liver, where it is further broken down and metabolised by the **bhutagnis** to form the five basic elemental nutrients (ether, air, fire, water and earth); these elements are now ready to take the journey around the body to nourish all the seven body tissues (**dhatus**). Each dhatu can be closely correlated to tissues known in modern science.

- **Rasa** (plasma)
- **Rakta** (blood)
- **Mamsa** (muscle)
- **Meda** (fat)
- **Asthi** (bone)
- **Majja** (bone marrow)
- **Shukra** (male)/**artava** (female) (reproductive tissues)

Once the nutrient fluid (ahararasa) is fully formed, the waste material is passed through the colon (the vata part of digestion) and excreted out. The more subtle nourishment of the tissues then starts with plasma, blood, muscle and so on.

Each of the seven tissues has its own individual agni (fire), called **dhatvagni**, which is responsible for the transformation of nutrients required for that particular tissue. The dhatvagnis transform the mobile form of nutrients into specific tissues. Since agni plays a critical role in the formation of healthy tissues, we must ensure that we maintain balance by having a suitable diet and a balanced digestive fire to form good ahararasa. If the dhatvagni is overactive, the tissue formation will be inadequate; if the dhatvagni is underactive, the tissue formation will be in excess. For example, if the agni associated with medas dhatu is weak this can lead to an accumulation of fat tissue. If ama (toxins) is present in the ahararasa, the tissues may also absorb the ama in the process of their formation. When doshas are in balance or as near balanced as can be, and all the digestive fires are strong, then you are in a good position to create healthy body tissues.

Malas – the waste matter of digestion

As established in our definition of health at the beginning of the book, the proper function of body processes is essential for good health – and this includes waste elimination. **Malas** are the metabolic waste products in the body which are formed as a result of the properly digested and metabolised food (plus water and air).

We have three primary types of body waste from food (**ahara**):

1. Faecal matter (*purisha*)
2. Urine (*mutra*)
3. Sweat (*sweda*)

When you eliminate malas naturally, by listening to your body's signals and urges, your body will remain free from undigested materials and toxins. Each of these malas has a fundamental role in your body: urine, faecal matter and sweat excrete metabolic toxins. Sweating also plays a role by helping your body stay cool and moistening your skin.

An imbalance in the doshas or dhatus can cause an excess or a deficiency in one of these three malas; they can also become susceptible to damage, which can lead to disease. For example, an accumulation of urine can cause bladder pain and bladder infections. Suppressing defecation or stagnant stools can cause abdominal pain, constipation and headaches. Skin conditions, such as fungal irritations, can be a result of excess or lack of sweating. This is why I always endorse the number one rule in Ayurveda: do not suppress your natural urges, whether it is to go to the bathroom, eat, drink water or sleep.

Your body channels

Your body contains a myriad of both physical and energetic channels or pathways. Known as **srotas**, they are your internal transport system for your body and mind to convey doshas, dhatus and malas to the right places in the body in order to carry out their functions. The obvious visible channels are the respiratory system, the gastrointestinal tract and the urinary tract, which carry nutrients, gases, air and liquids through the body. The more subtle channels include the lymphatic, circulatory and nervous systems and the channels of the mental faculties, waste material, reproductive channels and energetic channels. When your channels are open and clear, the body functions well and allows free movement of essential substances. Any blockages in the srotas can inhibit this function; for example, cholesterol in the arteries, or constipation, where faecal matter is blocked in the colon, causing diseases. Ama and increased doshas can accumulate in the srotas and trigger many diseases. Keep your channels clear by fine-tuning your diet and lifestyle to your body type and practising as many day-to-day cleansing rituals as you can. Treatment can be taken for more serious blockages to your srotas.

Western medicine follows a similar pathology to disease and recognises the body systems outlined in Ayurveda, but it doesn't recognise the involvement of the subtle energy channels. Ayurveda also considers the influence of the elements and the possible psychosomatic roots of diseases. The physical body systems are often considered as the gateway to the less obvious pathology of the subtle body. The **marma** points, the **nadis** and the **chakra** system recognised in Ayurveda allow us to work at different levels of our being.

Marma Chikitsa

Marma points are junctions in the body where two or more tissues meet, including muscle, arteries, veins, ligaments, bones and joints. The more commonly known Chinese acupuncture points are born of the system of marma chikitsa. Marma points are much more than just a meeting point for body tissues; they are vital energy points in the body – think of them like the doorways to the subtle body and, ultimately, to our consciousness. They are connected to the seven-centre chakra system, the vibrational energy centres located along the spine of your body. We have 107 marma points located throughout the body, and they can become vulnerable as your doshas become imbalanced. Energy flows through these points and when they become blocked, stagnation occurs, leading to physical and mental dis-ease and disease.

The ancient warriors and martial artists used the knowledge of marma to strike their opponents at these vulnerable places in battle. This art form, known as kalari, is still very much alive in southern parts of India. Today, the wisdom of marma is used in therapy. A skilled practitioner can gently work on these energy points to release any blockages and stimulate the flow of energy, both in the physical and astral body. You might feel a sensitivity or pain at these points, indicating a blockage. But working on these points can bring deep pain relief, reduce headaches, improve skin, clear toxins, improve organ function, stimulate neurochemicals such as serotonin, melatonin, oxytocin, dopamine and endorphins, and support the immune system.

You can even work on some marma points on yourself. I always encourage clients to use a strong circular clockwise motion in the very centre of the palm of the hand for about five minutes on each hand. The *talahridaya* point stimulates energy circulation to the entire body, benefiting your overall health and balance. You can use **ghee**, a medicated oil such as *mahanarayana* or a sesame-based oil. Rubbing your hands together vigorously also stimulates these points. Focus your mind on this point during meditation to release negative energy and stress.

Section 2:

Illness to Wellness

CHAPTER 6

Find Your Balance –
Create Your Zen

'The art of medicine consists of amusing the patient while
nature cures the disease'

Voltaire

Your prakruti is unique, so creating a lifestyle that is balancing
for your health also needs to be suitably personalised. Doshas
influence every aspect of your life, so in Ayurveda understanding
how to regain dosha balance is key to your wellbeing. Now that
you are able to identify the dominant dosha(s) in your prakruti,
you can make adjustments to your diet and lifestyle that are
aligned to your mind/body type.

If you are a single-dosha body type, the advice will seem
straightforward to follow. However, most of us are a dual-dosha
body type, meaning that we need to balance the characteristics of
two often dissimilar doshas. Factors such as the seasons, your age,
the time of day will all play a role in fine-tuning what works for
you. For example, for a vata/pitta prakruti, you can follow a vata-
pacifying regime in the changing seasons and in cool, dry months,
and a pitta-calming regime in the summer months. Furthermore,
if your presenting health ailments are displaying pitta dominance,
for example, then you will need to pacify this dosha first.
Addressing the main imbalanced dosha is the best place to start.
The three doshas also share certain characteristics, for example
the 'light' quality is present for both vata and pitta so balancing

this with grounding, stabilising and nourishing substances will pacify both doshas.

Over time this will become intuitive, and you will realise that the seasons will influence those doshas that are more active and need balance. For instance, if you are a vata/pitta type, you are more inclined to have warming and nourishing foods in the autumn, winter and spring months and pitta-pacifying cooling foods over the summer months.

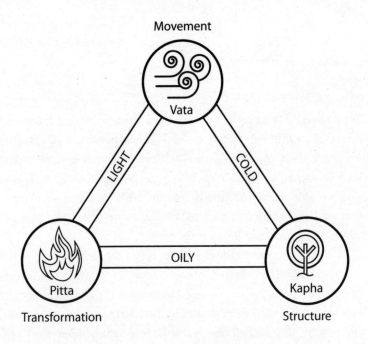

Principal Action and Shared Attributes of the Three Doshas

Dual-dosha balancing

Your prakruti	Seasonal conditions	Follow guidance for
Vata/pitta	Cool and dry. Windy weather, changing seasons (autumn)	Vata
Vata/pitta	Warm weather (summer)	Pitta
Pitta/kapha	Cool and damp weather (winter, early spring)	Kapha
Pitta/kapha	Warm weather (summer)	Pitta
Vata/kapha	Cool and dry. Windy weather, changing seasons (autumn)	Vata
Vata/kapha	Cool and damp weather (winter, early spring)	Kapha

Seasonal influences

Not only does Ayurveda recognise the intimate relationship between the mind, body and soul, but also the key influencing factors of the environment and seasonal changes (**rtu-charya**), which impact our health. *Rtu* means season and *charya* means moving or following. The science of Ayurveda places great emphasis on living in tune with nature so that we have the ability to adapt and stay healthy in an ever-changing climate.

Just as the trees shed leaves in the autumn and blossom in the spring, our bodies are designed to respond to the atmospheric changes in the same manner. Each season is influenced by a different dosha, and this changes as the seasons transition. Vata, pitta and kapha accumulate during seasons that share the same qualities. For example, vata increases and dominates when the climate is cool, dry and windy (autumn), pitta increases in the heat of the summer and kapha increases when it is wet and cold (winter). Should the doshas increase beyond a certain limit, aggravation begins and symptoms of imbalances and disease start to manifest. Our aim is to maximise the benefits from the seasonal changes and protect ourselves against the negative effects on our wellbeing by making suitable diet and lifestyle choices.

Traditionally, Ayurveda breaks the year into six seasons based predominantly on a tropical climate, but in the northern hemisphere and some countries in the southern hemisphere, we are more accustomed to four seasons.

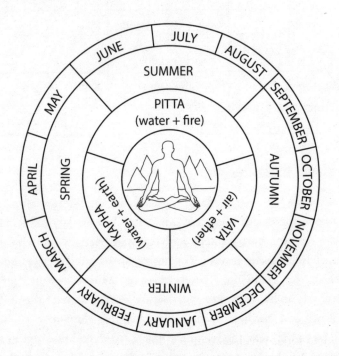

Seasonal Influence on Dosha Balancing

Season	Effects
Spring	Kapha is aggravated, pitta starts to increase
Summer	Pitta increases and becomes aggravated
Autumn	Vata increases and pitta can be aggravated
Winter	Kapha and vata increase

Here are some suggestions as to how you can adjust your diet and lifestyle to stay in harmony with each season and boost your immune system.

Spring

Spring marks the beginning of the new year as far as nature is concerned. Seeds start to germinate and flowers begin to bud, and life just seems to unfurl once again from the hibernation of winter. For me, spring is a season of transition and the most natural time for cleansing processes and a fresh start. January just feels so wrong for detoxification, and you will come to see why once you follow nature's lead.

Kapha increases over the winter months and over the spring it starts to liquefy through the heat of the sun, reducing agni and potentially giving rise to many diseases, often of kapha origin, such as colds, coughs, fluid accumulation in joints, and phlegm in lungs. Spring is influenced by kapha and is the start of the allergy season. Here is how to stay balanced in this season:

- Favour fresh (not raw), easily digestible and kapha-pacifying food; these can include barley, wheat, corn, millet, dried oats, chickpeas, beans, **kitchari** (a mixture of rice and mung beans, see p.146 for recipe), honey, fat-free meats, apples, and foods which contain less moisture
- Take warming drinks such as honey with warm water; this can help dry mucus

- Avoid dairy and foods that are hard to digest, cold, sour, sweet or fatty, and drinks that are cold; these can increase kapha dosha, which is already in excess
- Do dry powder massage or body brushing before a bath to increase stimulation
- Increase physical exercise, such as gardening, going to the gym, yoga, dancing, cycling etc.
- Avoid sleeping during the day
- Use nasal and emetic medications (**nasya**) and oil pulling (**gandusha**), see p. 267
- Follow the daily morning rituals outlined in chapter 16
- Have some dry wine, and dry, pungent, bitter and astringent spices

Summer

In the summer, kapha decreases and the sun reduces our strength, dehydrating the body, leaving us feeling exhausted and lethargic. Summer is the pitta season – the sun causes pitta to increase, and also vata, slightly.

- Favour sweet, bitter and astringent foods; light, cool, slightly fatty and liquid foods; all fruits in abundance
- Eat cool foods, such as leafy greens, okra, courgettes, watermelon, coconut, cucumber, coriander, asparagus, rice, wheat, amaranth, tapioca, milk, ghee, butter, cottage cheese, occasional ice cream
- Drink room-temperature or cool water and coconut water
- Drink plenty of fresh seasonal and sweet fruit juice; buttermilk is also healing for the digestion
- Consume restorative drinks that include grape juice, honey, dates, cardamom, liquorice, peppermint and fennel
- Avoid or limit foods/drinks that are salty, sour or pungent, including wines, Indian curries, chillies, sour fruit juice, vinegars and pickles

- Short naps during the day are acceptable on very hot days, as nights are shorter
- Choose shady environments and cool places to reside, and avoid too much exposure to direct sunlight (sunbathing)
- Wear breathable, loose and light clothing
- Take cool baths with cooling herbs such as sandalwood, aloe vera and rose
- Moderate sexual activity
- Exercise in the early morning, and ensure it involves only light physical exertion

Autumn

Autumn is another time of transition; in the northern hemisphere and predominantly European and North American countries, autumn means the winds pick up and the atmosphere becomes cold and dry. It is the vata season!

- Eat foods that are mildly pitta-pacifying and predominantly vata-pacifying
- Opt for foods such as soups and stews, wheat, tapioca, oatmeal, lentils, quinoa, fish, kitchari, carrots, root vegetables, cooked apples, avocado, asparagus, courgettes, almond milk, raw (soaked) nuts and nut butters
- Avoid vata-aggravating foods that are dry and gassy such as crackers, brassica vegetables, millet, dried fruits, beans, popcorn
- Take Ayurvedic enema treatments
- Indulge in oil-based massage and steam baths
- Increase exercise over these months to a moderate level
- Take nasal errhines to lubricate nasal passages
- Take **chyawanprash** to prepare for winter immunity

Winter

Agni is at its strongest in the winter months, hence the tendency to feel increased hunger, but this also means that your body strength improves too. Winter is a time for rest, reflection and hibernation. Vata and kapha dominate this season, so these doshas need to be balanced with a grounding and warming diet.

- Eat foods that are sweet, sour and salty in taste to help pacify vata dosha. Opt for oily foods, including nuts, oils, meats, fish, chicken, eggs, seasonal fruits, apples, pears, prunes, figs, dates, berries, root vegetables, rice, wheat, ghee, hot warming spice such as ginger, nutmeg, cinnamon, clove (sounds like a mulled wine is in order?)
- Drink sweet wines and warming liquors – they are fine in winter – and warm, nourishing milky drinks
- Drink warm/hot water to support digestion – herbal teas are great
- Try not to skip breakfast – opt for a porridge of oatmeal, barley, corn, quinoa or amaranth
- Opt for regular massage and steam baths and saunas
- Take plenty of exercise, preferably indoors, ideally between 6 a.m. and 10 a.m.
- Wear warm clothing made of natural fibres, such as cottons, silks and wools
- Take exposure to the sun as regularly as possible
- Take chyawanprash for winter immunity
- Indulge in regular sexual activity

Like increases like – opposites balance

We all have a unique proportion of all three doshas in our prakruti. We become imbalanced when we sway too far from our natural doshic state and this creates an environment where disease can thrive.

We have already learnt in the previous chapters that the dominant dosha of your prakruti is likely to get imbalanced more easily. For example, a vata type will be naturally drawn to being active, having irregular mealtimes and juggling many things. It's part of the vata nature. However, over time this type of activity can drive vata dosha out of balance. Regaining dosha balance means keeping your doshas as close as possible to the ratio of the natural prakruti you were born with. It does not mean an equal balance of vata, pitta and kapha.

Since everything that exists has inherent qualities, anything can be used as medicine, including food, drinks, herbs, treatments, lifestyle, environments, smells, tastes, colours, sounds, routines, job choices and more. This is the holistic approach and the beauty of Ayurveda. Choosing the 'medicine' that decreases your vikruti (aggravated dosha) due to its opposite qualities will bring you back to balance.

The next three chapters will help you grasp what brings balance to your prakruti. Just remember to consider the seasonal influences on your doshas.

Client story

'I had been waking up with nausea every day and having it throughout the day for about a year before I saw Geeta. I saw a variety of different doctors and specialists who couldn't help me, so my sister suggested I see an Ayurvedic doctor.

I desperately needed to find balance and sort out this problem of nausea that was consuming my day-to-day life and disturbing my usual activities and work life.

I adopted a diet for my dosha and made many lifestyle changes that have definitely helped. I have also found a solid balance since incorporating breathing exercises into my routine.

The abdominal treatment was a key tool in my recovery, and I found it shifted me in so many ways I did not expect. Drinking warmer liquids is also something that really has stuck with me.

When everything else I tried failed, Ayurveda was the only thing that actually helped me. I am more in tune with my body and it's unlikely I will rely on modern medicine or treatment again.

Nicky

CHAPTER 7

The Vata Way

Grounding		Slow down
Nourishing		Lubricating
Warming		Soothing
Regularity		Nurturing
Routine	Vata	Sweet-Sour

Key Words for Balancing Vata

When you visit a practitioner for a consultation, more often than not the first steps in treatment will include calming the vata dosha. Even if vata is not your dominant dosha, the strong mobility quality of vata will mean that it can play a lead role in triggering pitta and kapha out of balance. Managing vata alone can often be enough to calm many health symptoms, despite their dosha origin.

Vata-balancing lifestyle

Every action we take in one part of our life will have an effect on another part of our life; be it big or small, there is always an interplay of cause and effect. Bearing this in mind, we can appreciate that our lifestyle choices will contribute to our dosha balance and, ultimately, to our health.

Early signs of vata imbalances, such as body aches and pains, dry skin, constipation, disturbed sleep, anxiety and fatigue, are easily balanced by making subtle changes to our diet and lifestyle. The key is not to become overwhelmed and to start grounding vata where you can.

Settle into a routine

By its very nature and characteristics, vata is aggravated by specific circumstances: as we enter our later life (55-plus); as the autumn season arrives, where dryness is dominant; during afternoon time, generally between 2 p.m. and 6 p.m.; by travel; by loud noises; by cold and windy weather. When the dry, mobile, light, cold, rough and irregular qualities are dominant, it is essential that you take care to nurture and balance particularly at these times. Minimise travel and disturbance to your daily circadian rhythms.

By nature, vata is irregular and mobile, so regularity and routine are crucial to balance it. This includes your day-to-day patterns of eating, sleeping, working and exercising, essentially. If you maintain consistent timings to your day, your body will thank you for it. What's more, when you eat all your meals at a regular time each day, you will better manage your appetite and hunger, resulting in improved digestion and elimination.

Early to bed

Go to bed early and ensure you get enough sleep to balance the erratic energy and tendency for disturbed sleep. Sleep is particularly important for vata types due to the quality of sleep being light in nature. Encourage sound sleep with a cup of spiced hot milk (optional additions include nutmeg, cardamom, ground almonds and saffron). More on sleep in chapter 15.

Slow down

The airy and quick quality of vata is balanced by activities that are grounding and calming. Exercise should be inspired, fun and light. Make sure that you do not overexert yourself with physical exercise, which vata types have a tendency to do. Strenuous, competitive and high-endurance sports will increase air and exhaust the body. Instead, opt for gentle walking, swimming, hatha yoga with balancing and stabilising postures, tai chi and Pilates. Bring mental awareness to your exercise and slow it down a pace. Hatha yoga can be very grounding and stabilising for vata, especially when focus is kept on the breath.

Abhyanga

Daily self-massage helps nourish the dryness of the skin and feels nourishing and grounding for the mind and emotions. Cured sesame oil or a vata-balancing oil works really well. Ayurvedic treatments such as hot oil **abhyanga** massage and **shirodhara** are perfect choices for vata balancing and during the autumn and winter months. Stimulate warmth by taking a relaxing hot bath with oils or a steam bath with warming aromatics, such as cinnamon, ginger, cardamom, juniper, orange, geranium, patchouli and frankincense.

Cultivate creativity

Vata can quickly trigger stress and anxiety; keeping a healthy mind balance by getting your creative juices flowing can reduce stress. Carve out a little me-time in your – quite often self-made – hectic schedule to do something inspiring, like a cooking class, dancing, painting, reading or writing.

Silence the mind

Breathing and meditation is a central activity to managing your nervous system. It can bring instant calm and relaxation to the overactive mind. Using sound can add extra benefits, since vata types are sensitive and responsive to sound. Sitting quietly and connecting with nature really helps you calm the mind. Become aware of anything that makes your mind race. Slow down and be more present in each moment. This will help you to stay focused and grounded.

Nurture and be kind to yourself

Since cold is a strong quality of vata, opt for warmer, nurturing environments. Now, for me, this is just the excuse I need for a holiday in the sun and no doubt you will agree. Avoid exposure to air conditioning and wind. Wrap up with hats and scarves. Warmth can be created in other ways too – wear and surround yourself with earthy or warm pastel colours, such as yellow, ochre, orange, brown and green. Warm your emotions by spending time with people who are grounding and stable with direction (pitta and kapha types are ideal). Surround yourself with sweet scents, serene scenery and soothing music. Wear balancing gemstones, such as rose quartz, clear quartz, gold, citrine, jade, amethyst, green aventurine, aquamarine and yellow sapphire, as these are warming, nurturing and grounding.

Shirodhara

Shirodhara is one of the most effective treatments used in Ayurveda today, for bringing the deepest of relaxation and calmness to the mind. Warm herb-infused sesame oil is gently poured in a stream over the forehead. This treatment is known for its therapeutic effects on anxiety, stress, disturbed sleep and more, by working on rebalancing the pituitary and pineal glands situated deep in the brain. It is truly blissful and perfect for vata balancing.

Vata-balancing diet

How to eat the vata way

The vata person's appetite can be unpredictable, and digestion can potentially be the most volatile and weak of all the prakruti types, so how we eat is just as important as what we eat. By its very nature, vata can be erratic, excitable and mobile, so an eating environment that is peaceful, clean and clutter-free, and mealtimes that are free from distractions, will soothe vata. Focusing on mindful eating practices therefore can be hugely beneficial (see p. 133). This means a 100 per cent focus on being nourished by your meal. Avoid eating meals if you are feeling nervous or anxious, worried or distracted.

Since vata types may feel a strong hunger at times and no hunger at other times, regulating mealtimes and portions helps to stabilise the appetite. Vata types do best not to skip meals or overindulge in them. Increased frequency of meals is fine, as long as there is a genuine hunger and the previous meal is digested, usually within two to three hours. If you are vata-dominant, you are likely to get full quickly, so three to four moderate-sized meals can be suitable. Eating a balancing and energy-sustaining breakfast is more important for vata types than for the other dosha types.

Vata types tend to eat fast, so purposefully slowing down the time you take to eat your meal and chewing your food well will help you digest better and prevent the formation of abdominal discomfort and gas. Since the vata digestion is sensitive, it is best to avoid excess water before meals and sip only a little warm water during and after meals to aid digestion.

With our busy working lives, it can sometimes be hard to follow the ideal balancing diet. So, if you just remember that vata types thrive on a simple, well-cooked, easy-to-digest diet with foods, served warm, which are soft, heavy and unctuous, you should stay in the balanced zone. For me, simple home-cooked one-pot meals are the best option. Generally, fasting is not recommended for this dosha type and a simple kitchari diet would be more balancing and cleansing than any juice fasting. Similarly, it is best to avoid stimulants such as sugar, caffeine and alcohol.

Taste-balancing for vata

How do you like the idea of having dessert at the beginning of your meal? Well, the sweet taste pacifies vata and is the first taste to digest, so opting for the sweet element of your meal first is actually not a bad idea at all. In the same respect, a hot milky drink with some sweet spices at night time will help the vata mind to sleep soundly. Sweet foods, including root vegetables such as sweet potato, beetroot and carrots, work well to balance vata. Sweet foods also include most grains, eggs, nuts, seeds, oils, ghee and fruits; the table on pages 94-7 gives you more options for vata-pacifying foods. Sweet foods generally balance vata, as they are nourishing, grounding and build tissue strength. One thing to bear in mind: favouring the sweet taste does not mean you should consume large amounts of refined, sugary foods, which actually provide no nutritional value and can lead to blood sugar fluctuation. Fruits are a great option for vata types to consume the natural sweet taste. Ensure fruits are in season, ripe and ready to eat.

Stewed apples and pears and baked fruits also make a great dessert and snack. Lightly spicing fruits with cinnamon, cardamom and black pepper can aid digestion. Cooked fruits can be eaten twenty minutes after a meal, although waiting a little longer is always best.

Vata is also pacified by the sour taste and although not usually the main attraction, it lifts the entire meal and brings a flavour balance to the other tastes. The sour taste improves the digestion and moistens the food. Sour foods that pacify vata include oranges, grapefruit, grapes, lime, lemon, vinegar, cheese, miso, sauerkraut and sour cream.

The salty taste is also pacifying for vata – just by adding a little rock salt to your diet itself is usually sufficient. Salt is stimulating for the vata appetite and digestion and provides moisture and flavour to your food, giving support to healthy elimination. Just be careful not to overgrind that mill! A little can go a long way.

The pungent taste has a light, hot and dry quality and is best consumed in minimal amounts so that vata does not become aggravated. Limiting excessively hot dried spices and spicy ingredients, such as chillies, horseradish and raw onions, will ensure that vata doesn't dry out. Bitter foods also have light, dry and cooling qualities and so in excess can aggravate vata. These might include foods such as aubergine, kale and bitter melon. The astringent taste is the one taste that is totally drying to vata, leaving a chalky texture in the mouth. This is best minimised to avoid vata aggravation. That means avoiding those unripe bananas, cranberries and many members of the legume family. Also watch out for the brassica vegetable group (cauliflower, cabbage, sprouts) and peppers which can be gaseous – these are best limited. If you do have them, it is best to ensure they are well cooked, spiced and eaten hot.

Balancing foods for vata

Vata people thrive on moist, oily and unctuous foods as, by their very nature, they pacify the innate dryness of vata. Oils and fats are vata's best friends. Ghee, sesame oil and olive oil are great options for vata balancing. The oily and heavy quality of nuts makes them an excellent source of fat for nourishing vata types. Soaking nuts before eating them helps the oils to be utilised effciently. Roasting nuts destroys the beneficial oils that are volatile to heat. Vata types do well with foods that are well cooked and moist in nature, while they should limit their intake of dry foods, such as dry crackers, dried fruits, popcorn, and so on.

Though beans are a good source of protein, they can be gassy and airy and can often be a challenge for vata types to digest. Soaking lentils overnight and cooking them with spices such as cumin, ginger, turmeric and asafoetida can help make them more digestible. Mung beans are tri-doshic and can be digested by all dosha types. Splitting beans and removing their husks makes them easier to digest. Eat while hot, and chew well.

All dairy products are nourishing, grounding and pacifying for vata. Milk and ghee are the most beneficial for this dosha type. Vata types can be prone to lactose intolerance, but boiling milk prior to drinking helps remove the milk proteins, making it more digestible. Try it if you struggle to digest milk. Soft cheeses are better digested than hard cheeses. Foods such as cooked grains, vegetables and fruits work well along with plenty of digestible nuts and seeds.

So many people choose to go grain-free these days, but for vata types, cooked grains, especially with salt, ghee, ginger and natural sweeteners added to them, provide great balance, as they are grounding and have a sweet taste. Grains that are dry or puffed (for example, Rice Krispies) can be aggravating to vata, as they have light and dry qualities. Yeasted breads and pastries are best avoided, as they can be gassy.

Meats are heavy and nutrient-rich, so vata types do well to eat moderate amounts of meat, but if your digestive fire is disturbed it is always best to avoid them temporarily. If you do eat meat, it is best to have it in your lunch meal so that your body is able to digest it well as digestion is strongest at this time.

Warm food is the antidote for vata indigestion – this means warm in terms of temperature, as well as energetically. Use warming spices to balance the coldness of vata and stimulate digestion – see the table overleaf. In your diet, you can include ginger, garlic, asafoetida and black pepper. Just beware of excessively pungent spices that can be somewhat drying.

It is best to have vegetables lightly cooked, baked or steamed and eaten while hot, rather than consuming raw vegetables and salads. If you do want to opt for salads, go for a cooked salad – roast your vegetables and eat them with lettuce leaves at room temperature. Juiced vegetables, in moderation and balanced with ginger, can also be easier to digest for vata types. Vata types don't always do well with nightshades (tomatoes, aubergines, peppers and potatoes), so limit these in your diet if you have disturbances.

Eat minimal cold foods, including frozen items, iced or carbonated drinks, foods straight out of the fridge and those lunchtime classics such as sandwiches and sushi. If digestion is disturbed, then those raw fruits and vegetables can lead to bloating and gas. Stimulate warmth in the body by drinking plenty of warm water and herbal teas, such as ginger, lemon, cardamom, tulsi (holy basil) or fennel. Adding lemon to warm water is the best antidote for vata imbalance. Some red wine in moderation also gets the thumbs-up for vata types.

Eating-out tips for vata

- Avoid cold, icy drinks with meals; sip warm water or herbal teas during and at the end of the meal – you can also enjoy a little wine
- If you have dessert, go for the warm option
- Choose soup as a starter, over a salad
- Keep the meal simple, ideally one or two courses – too many varieties / sharing dishes become confusing for the digestive system

Vata-pacifying foods

Type of food	Favour	Limit
Vegetables	Asparagus, beetroot, cabbage (cooked), carrots, courgettes, daikon radish, fennel, green beans, leeks (cooked), mustard greens, okra, olives (black and green), onions (cooked), parsnips, pumpkin, squash (acorn squash, summer squash, winter squash, yellow crookneck squash), sweet potato, tomatoes (cooked), watercress Cooked vegetables	Aubergine, bitter melon (karela), broccoli, Brussels sprouts, burdock root, cabbage (raw), cauliflower, celery, collard greens, Jerusalem artichoke, kale, kohlrabi, leafy greens, lettuce, mushrooms, onions (raw), peas, peppers, radish, spinach, tomatoes raw, white potato Raw, dried vegetables; salads
Fruits	Apricots, avocado, bananas (ripe), berries, cherries, coconut (tender), dates, figs, grapefruit, kiwi, lemon, lime, mango, oranges, papaya, peaches, pineapple, plums, prunes, red apples, rhubarb, soaked raisins, strawberries, sweet melon Seasonal fruits eaten alone; cooked/stewed fruits; ripe fruits	Apples (raw), cranberries, persimmons, pomegranates, quince, watermelon Dried fruits, unripe fruits, excessive raw fruits

Type of food	Favour	Limit
Grains	Amaranth, cooked oats, quinoa, rice (basmati, brown, red, wild), spelt, tapioca, wheat, wheat or rice noodles	Yeasted breads; cold, dry, puffed cereals; barley, buckwheat, corn, dry oats (granola), oat bran, millet, muesli, rice cakes, rye, sago, wheat bran, white flour
Legumes	Lentils (black, puy, red), mung beans, mung tur dahl, split yellow	Aduki beans, black beans, black-eye beans, broad beans, brown lentils, chickpeas, kidney beans, lima (butter) beans, navy beans, pinto beans, soya beans, split chickpeas (chana dahl), split peas, tempeh, white beans
Dairy and eggs	All dairy is fine (but not cold) – butter, buttermilk (*takra*), cream, dairy milk, eggs, fresh cheese (paneer), ghee, goat's cheese, goat's milk, hard cheese (moderate amount), soft cheese, sour cream, yoghurt	Dried goat's milk, ice cream (in winter)
Meat and fish	All white fish (fresh and sea), beef, chicken, duck, goat, kippers, mackerel, tuna, turkey, salmon, sardines	Lamb, pork, rabbit, venison

Type of food	Favour	Limit
Nuts and seeds	All nuts in moderation, especially if ground or as milk; almonds (peeled and soaked), Brazils, cashews, coconut, hazelnuts, macadamias, peanuts, pine nuts, pistachios, walnuts All seeds, especially seed butters – chia, flax, hemp, pumpkin, sesame, sunflower	Almond skins, chocolate, popcorn, psyllium
Herbs and spices	All spices and herbs are beneficial – ajwain, allspice, anise, asafoetida, basil, bay leaf, black pepper, caraway, cardamom, cayenne, cinnamon, clove, coriander, cumin, dill, fennel, fenugreek, garlic, ginger, marjoram, mint, mustard, nutmeg, orange peel, oregano, paprika, parsley, poppy seeds, rosemary, saffron, salt, spearmint, tamarind, tarragon, thyme, turmeric, vanilla, wintergreen Pickles and chutneys	

Type of food	Favour	Limit
Oils and fats	All oils and fats are balancing – ghee, olive oil, sesame oil, sunflower oil, tahini	
Sweeteners	All natural sweeteners – agave syrup, barley malt syrup, brown rice syrup, fructose, honey, jaggery, maple syrup, molasses, rock sugar, stevia	Refined white sugar; honey in excess
Drinks	Almond milk, aloe vera juice, carrot juice, cow's milk, all natural sweet fruit juices (diluted with a little warm water) Warm herbal teas including liquorice root; warm chai and milky drinks	Alcohol, banana smoothies, caffeinated drinks, carbonated drinks, cold dairy drinks, cranberry juice, pomegranate juice, pungent teas, sour apple juice, wine Ice in drinks; too much hot chocolate

Meal suggestions for vata

Breakfast	Lunch	Dinner	Snacks
Oat porridge with mixed seeds, and almond milk (spiced with cardamom/ cinnamon) * Masala scrambled eggs on rye toast / any style eggs with wholegrain buttered toast * Upma (savoury semolina) * Spiced almond and date shake (spiced with cardamom, nutmeg, ginger)	Rice and vegetables (optional: oven-roasted chicken/fish) * Sweet potato and sweetcorn poha (flaked rice) * Spicy lentil dahl and rice with vegetables * Gnocchi with spiced oil-based dressing or pesto	Kitchari * Oven-roasted spiced vegetable tray bake with couscous/rice/ quinoa * Any vegetable/ lentil/meat soup * Root vegetable / vegetable stew	Sweet seasonal fruits * Warming herbal teas * Dates, soaked almonds * Sliced ripe avocado with lemon juice and cayenne pepper

CHAPTER 8

The Pitta Way

Cooling
Calming
Grounding
Stabilising
Relaxing

Pitta

Nurturing
Bitter-Sweet
Hydrating
Self-reflecting

Key Words for Balancing Pitta

Pitta folks in balance are intelligent, warm, generous, confident, courageous, thoughtful and enterprising. They don't like time-wasting.

Pitta-balancing lifestyle

'Cool, calm and collected' is the **mantra** for balancing the pitta person. Early signs of pitta imbalance, such as hyperacidity,

excessive hunger, irritability, skin irritations and mild inflammation, are easily balanced by making subtle changes to your
diet and lifestyle that are opposite in nature to pitta.

Be a little sun-shy

Since the fire element is in full power over the summer months
due to the heat of the sun, around midday, and in the major part
of our adult life, you need to be mindful at these times if pitta is
your dominant dosha, as it can easily become imbalanced.

Pitta types need to take extra care not to have prolonged
exposure to the fire element, especially the sun (sorry, bad news
for you sun-worshippers); remember, like increases like. This also
means you should avoid the steam rooms and saunas, as they will
overheat your body; instead, take tepid or cool-water showers or
baths. Hot showers are aggravating and will dry out your skin.
Daily self-massage with cooling oils such as coconut works well
for pacifying the pitta body.

Go within

Work in a calm and peaceful environment or, if you can't, ensure
you have some time away to spend in nature to balance yourself.
Often it is the directors and CEOs who easily suffer from pitta
imbalance. Keep the mind calm by engaging in calming breathing
exercises and meditation, bringing groundedness and coolness to
the mind and body. Rest is critical to pitta balancing. Immerse
yourself in calming music. Choose soothing classical or relaxing
instrumental music like the bamboo flute or sounds from nature.
Take time out from work and engage socially with relatives and
work colleagues, laugh and have light-hearted conversations
regularly. Avoid stressful situations and people; engage with people
who are creative, compassionate and grounded to expose yourself
to balancing energies.

Settle into a routine

Like vata, keeping a routine to your day will really help your cause, so go to sleep by 10 p.m. rather than going to bed in the pitta time between 10 p.m. and 2 a.m. Ensure you have a satisfying main meal at lunchtime.

Be playful

Avoid excessive or high-intensity exercise and do cooling and calming exercises, such as walking in parks, woodlands, by the sea, swimming and tai chi. Outdoor and water-based activities are best, and it's definitely worth engaging in relaxing yoga, such as hatha yoga or yin yoga, as well as breathing exercises such as **shitali** and **ujjaya** (see chapter 17 for instructions), which are great to relieve pitta aggravation, supported by meditation, which is the perfect antidote for increased mental pitta. Ultimately, pitta can be calmed down by prioritising some downtime, light-hearted fun and laughter.

Keep cool and calm in every aspect of your life, including the types of colours that you wear. Surround yourself with cooling colours such as blue, green, white, purple, grey and silver. Use cooling herbs, essential oils and aromatics, such as sandalwood, rose, jasmine, lavender and camomile. Wear or surround yourself with cooling and nurturing gemstones, such as yellow sapphire, moonstone, pearls, aquamarine, rose quartz, amethyst, purple agate, and silver.

Pitta-balancing diet

How to eat the pitta way

The fire element of pitta means that the pitta appetite will be strong and sharp. Like vata, regulated meals are essential so that pitta does not become aggravated and overactive. This especially means not skipping meals. So, ensure that you have three regulated and satisfying meals a day but do avoid late-night eating, as this can stimulate pitta at the wrong time. Alcohol, tobacco and caffeine can be overstimulating for pitta, so should be minimised or avoided where possible.

Eat a light, balanced breakfast and aim to have your main meal of the day at lunchtime (early if possible), as this is when pitta is the strongest and hunger can be ravenous. Opt for wholesome and nourishing foods; despite the fact that you have the capacity to digest most foods, an overindulgence can still lead to an imbalance in the long term.

Pitta types cannot escape the need for mindful eating patterns. Sit down and eat in a peaceful and relaxing environment, take the time to focus on your food and switch off from working. Do not eat if you are angry or frustrated. Business lunches, for example, can make you irritated. Adopt an attitude of calm and gratitude. Engage fully in the process of nourishing your body with the meal. Your body will fully register that you have eaten and it will leave you feeling deeply satisfied.

Taste-balancing for pitta

All natural sweet-tasting foods are fine for pitta types and, similarly to vata, it is highly balancing, but mainly because sweet foods can be cooling and heavy in nature for pitta and provide grounding, tissue nourishment and satisfaction for the appetite. This taste can also help pacify excess heat and inflammation in the body. Choosing sweet fruits works well and can be balancing; however, sour, citrus or unripe fruits can be unbalancing. Seasonal fruits are perfect for snacking. Root vegetables, most grains, milk and ghee are also sweet and nourishing for pitta. Honey has a heating and drying quality, so it's always best taken in moderation by pitta types. As described for vata, sweet does not mean a free rein to indulge in refined white sugary foods.

Bitter foods can be highly satisfying and balancing for pitta, as they improve the sense of taste and provide a cooling and drying effect. Examples include ingredients such as neem, cumin, turmeric, bitter melon and dark chocolate. Similarly, the astringent taste is beneficial due to its drying and cooling nature. Legumes are astringent, and the bean family is easily digested by pitta types, as are apples, broccoli and pomegranate for example.

Avoid foods that are pungent, as these can be too heating for the pitta person due to their hot and light qualities. Radishes, raw onions and chillies are a few examples.

Sour-tasting foods such as vinegars, citrus fruits and fermented produce aggravate the liquid part of pitta due to their hot, penetrating and sharp qualities. Excessive consumption of sour foods, which can also include fried and processed foods, may result in excessive thirst, inflammatory conditions and burning sensations in the chest for pitta types.

The salty taste is the third taste pitta types need to limit as, like the sour taste, it is hot and light, as well as unctuous in nature, and it can intensify inflammation, high blood pressure and stimulate premature ageing and greying of hair.

Bitter, sweet and cooling vegetables are a great choice for pitta balancing. Pitta types can digest cooked and raw vegetables easily, since their digestive fire is usually strong. Nutrients are metabolised quickly, so opt for mineral- and vitamin-rich foods.

Balancing foods for pitta

Unlike vata, pitta-dominant people require foods of a cooling quality, as digestion tends to be naturally strong. This means that if your digestive system is working well, you are able to digest raw vegetables and salads as well as cooked foods. Opt for foods that are cooling in nature, such as coconut and coconut products, aloe vera, milk, root vegetables, mung, mint, coriander, sweet fruits and salad leaves. Pitta types can snack on raw fresh fruits and vegetables without having too much of an issue.

Limited digestive spices and cooling herbs are suitable for pitta. Though pitta people typically will be drawn to spicy foods, they will then have to deal with the aftermath.

Pitta types need a healthy dose of protein to stabilise and ground their hunger, but most meats are too heating or too fatty. Due to their heating, rajasic (see p. 186 for more details on rajasic foods) and oily nature, meats should be limited in pitta diets. Red meats, egg yolks and saltwater fish are the biggest offenders. Poultry and freshwater fish are fine, or you can opt for a plant-based protein.

Consider the benefits of takra (buttermilk), which is a great neutralising drink for pitta (see recipe on p. 207). Wholesome dairy such as ghee, milk and soft cheese can be nourishing and cooling for pitta, with the exception of salty cheese, sour cream and curds. Room-temperature or cooling water work best for pitta, as do cooling drinks such as coconut water, aloe vera juice and bitter-sweet fruit juices such as pomegranate.

Since pitta is light in nature, heavy, balancing and stabilising foods are what will ground pitta types. Grains are generally balancing and grounding if they are cooling in nature – for example, rice, quinoa and wheat. Corn, millet and rye are some of the grains that have a mild heating effect on the body.

Most legumes are a great source of protein; it is always best to pre-soak legumes to kick-start their digestibility, as does adding spices to them during the cooking process.

Less is definitely more when it comes to oils for pitta, since pitta is naturally oily. Light cooling oils are the best choice, especially ghee, coconut and olive oil.

Most nuts are too oily and heating to balance pitta, so pitta types should limit themselves to blanched and soaked almonds, as well as coconuts and sunflower seeds.

Eating-out tips for pitta

- Opt for clean, good-value eateries that aren't too loud and noisy
- Opt for restaurants that serve Japanese, Italian and Middle Eastern food; avoid Mexican, Indian and Thai restaurants
- Have a salad as a starter
- Avoid alcohol with meals

Pitta-pacifying foods

Type of food	Favour	Limit
Vegetables	Artichoke, asparagus, bitter melon, broccoli, Brussels sprouts, burdock root, cabbage, carrots, cauliflower, celery, collard greens, corn, courgette, cucumber, fennel, green beans, Jerusalem artichoke, kale, leafy greens, lettuce, mushrooms, okra, parsnips, peas, peppers (sweet), pumpkin, squash (butternut, spaghetti), sweet potato, watercress, white potato (in moderation)	Aubergines, chilli peppers, garlic, horseradish, leeks, mustard greens, onion (raw), peppers (hot), radish, spinach, tomatoes (raw), turnips
Fruits	Avocado, banana, coconut, dates, figs, grapes (black or red), green papaya, lime, mango, melon, pears, pomegranate, prunes, raisins, sweet apples, sweet apricots, sweet berries, sweet melon, sweet oranges, sweet plums, watermelon	Cranberries, grapefruit, kiwi, lemons, papaya, persimmon, sour apricots, sour berries, sour cherries, sour grapes, sour oranges, sour pineapple, sour plums, tamarind, unripe banana

Type of food	Favour	Limit
Grains	Barley, couscous, oat bran, oats, quinoa, rice (basmati, white), rice cakes, sago, spelt, tapioca, wheat, wheat bran	Amaranth, buckwheat, corn, millet, polenta, rye, white flour, yeasted bread
Legumes	All beans and most lentils are fine – aduki beans, black beans, black lentils, black-eye beans, broad beans, brown lentils, chickpeas (garbanzo beans), kidney beans, lima (butter) beans, mung beans, navy beans, pinto beans, puy lentils, red lentils, soya beans, split chickpeas (chana dahl), split peas, split yellow mung, tempeh, tofu, white beans	Black lentils (urad dahl)
Dairy and eggs	Buttermilk, cottage cheese, egg whites, ghee, goat's cheese, goat's milk, ice cream, milk, paneer, unsalted butter	Egg yolks, feta, halloumi, hard cheese, salted butter, sour cream, yoghurt
Meat and fish	Chicken, freshwater fish, prawns, turkey, venison	Beef, duck, lamb, pork, salmon, sardines, seafood, tuna
Nuts and seeds	Coconut, soaked and peeled almonds, pumpkin seeds, psyllium, sunflower seeds	Most other nuts are imbalancing to pitta in excess. Chia, flax, sesame, tahini

Type of food	Favour	Limit
Herbs and spices	Black pepper, cardamom, cinnamon, coriander, cumin, curry leaves, dill, fennel, fresh basil, fresh ginger, hibiscus, jasmine, lemongrass, mint, neem, orange peel, parsley, rose water, saffron, spearmint, tarragon, turmeric, vanilla, wintergreen	Ajwain, allspice, amchoor, anise, asafoetida, bay leaf, caraway, cayenne, clove, dry ginger, fenugreek, garlic, hawthorn, horseradish, juniper berries, mace, marjoram, mustard, nutmeg, oregano, paprika, poppy seeds, rosemary, star anise, sage, thyme
Oils and fats	Avocado, coconut, ghee, olive, sunflower, walnut	Almond, corn, sesame, safflower, vegetable oil
Sweeteners	Agave syrup, barley malt syrup, brown rice syrup, fructose, fruit concentrate, maple syrup, rock sugar, stevia	Honey, jaggery (in excess), molasses, refined white sugar
Drinks	Almond milk, aloe vera juice, coconut water/milk, cooling herbal teas, cow's milk, date shake, goat's milk, grape juice, mango juice, milky drinks, prune juice, pomegranate juice, sweet berry juices (diluted), sweet orange juice	Alcohol, banana smoothies, black tea, caffeinated drinks, carbonated drinks, chocolate drinks, coffee, cold dairy drinks, cranberry juice, orange juice (in excess), pineapple juice, pungent teas, salted drinks, sour apple juice, tomato juice

Meal suggestions for pitta

Breakfast	Lunch	Dinner	Snacks
Buckwheat pancakes with mixed seeds and flaked coconut	Asparagus and soya bean risotto	Kitchari	Fresh seasonal fruits (banana, coconut, mango, sweet berries)
*	*	*	*
Avocado on spelt or wholemeal toast	Mild Mexican vegetarian chilli and rice	Roasted sweet potato and mildly spiced puy lentil salad	Cooling herbal teas (mint)
*	*	*	*
Sweet and spiced quinoa porridge with coconut milk	Coconut-based chicken and vegetable curry and rice	Middle Eastern mezze platter	Dried fruits and nuts (dates, walnuts, almonds, sesame snaps)
*	*	*	*
Hearty, seasonal fruit salad	Chicken and vegetables with wholewheat pasta and coriander pesto dressing	*Rajma* (kidney bean curry) and basmati rice or flatbread	Crudités and hummus, tzatziki or beetroot dip

CHAPTER 9

The Kapha Way

Stimulating
Warming
Drying
Movement
Lightness

Kapha

Variety
Flexibility
Bitter-Pungent
Detachment

Key Words for Balancing Kapha

Kapha individuals are very calm, relaxed and content. They are generally loyal and hardworking, and nothing bothers them too much. They are graceful, compassionate and tolerant.

Kapha-balancing lifestyle

The earth and water elements make kapha stable, and this means that the susceptibility to illness is lower than that of the vata and pitta types. Good health and longevity is the natural advantage for kapha types. However, modern conveniences and a sedentary lifestyle are an attraction for kapha types, and these can often aggravate kapha. By its very nature of heavy, unctuous and cold qualities, kapha is increased between 6 a.m. and 10 a.m. and 6 p.m. and 10 p.m., in the wintertime and during the adolescent growth phase of life, so be careful of your diet at these times.

Get a move on

If you want to balance kapha, you should encourage qualities in your lifestyle that are opposite in nature to kapha, such as lightness, warmth, mobility, and so on. So, for kapha types it is essential to increase physical activity and exercise to help maintain weight and strengthen agni. Regular body movement is necessary to balance kapha, so take regular gentle walks after meals. In general, you should opt to walk briskly, take the stairs rather than the lift and do regular stretching away from your desk if you have a desk job. Exercise such as mountain climbing, long-distance running, hiking, ashtanga and vinyasa flow yoga are all good options.

Stimulate the mind

Clear the mind and stagnant energy through regular breathing and meditation practices. Stimulating breathing exercises such as **kapala bhati** (skull shining breath) can be great for their immediate effects (see chapter 17 for instructions). Active meditation such as a walking meditation can be beneficial for kapha types. Kapha needs to be invigorated and stimulated, so relieve the monotony of your day-to-day life by having variety in your foods and activities. Spend time with people who are creative, energetic and go-getting. Listen to stimulating music that encourages you to move and dance. Nasya is the treatment of choice for kapha cleansing and stimulation, see p. 268.

Embrace the sun

Generate warmth and heat in the body by taking regular exposure to the sun and opt for the outdoors rather than air-conditioned environments. The heat will balance the cold and damp qualities of kapha within, as will regular hot-water showers and baths. Saunas are great to stimulate heat in the body.

Curb your sleep

Sleep is the beloved friend of kapha but too much sleep can quickly aggravate it, so it is best to limit sleep to 7 to 8 hours maximum. Avoid sleeping during the day and especially after food, as it makes the body feel even heavier.

Declutter and detach

Get into the habit of regularly decluttering your life; kapha types tend to have an attachment to possessions and hoard items, so clear out your cupboards and drawers often. Focus your energy on detachment to people and possessions. You're open and generous in nature, so pay attention to strike a balance between being kind to people and pushing back so that you are not being taken advantage of.

Variety of life

Stimulate and invigorate every aspect of your life with gemstones and metals that balance kapha, such as ruby, blue sapphire, copper, garnet and carnelian. Wear and surround yourself with bright and vivid colours, such as orange, red, gold and purple. Balance any nasal blockages with inhalation of a bowl of steaming hot water with stimulating essential oils, such as eucalyptus, tea tree, myrrh and cedar.

Kapha-balancing diet

How to eat the kapha way

When it comes to kapha, how you eat will determine how food digests and how kapha stays in balance. Kapha types do best when they focus on a controlled and lighter diet plan, where meals are packed with high-prana foods (vegetables, legumes and fruits), smaller in portion size, less frequent, eaten only when genuine hunger is present, and chewed well to aid digestion. Kapha types can happily skip breakfast and opt for a juice or herbal tea, and meals are best taken between 10 a.m. and 6 p.m. Two low-fat and high-protein meals a day support kapha well, so don't feel the need to force down the conventional three meals. A small piece of freshly grated ginger, a pinch of rock salt and a dash of lime can help kindle the digestive fire before lunch and dinner. Since kapha types can have an indulgent nature, discipline is key when it comes to food, and snacking between meals should be minimised or cut out completely, and lunch should feature as the main meal of the day.

By virtue of this dosha, kapha types are already flowing in water so kapha types do well to minimise water at mealtimes, drinking only enough to moisten food and best taken warm. In between meals, drink only when thirsty and, when you do, focus on warm spiced drinks (ginger tea or chai). Coffee and black teas are fine for kapha and a coffee after the lunch meal can actually aid digestion. A hot lemon or ginger tea is a great start to the kapha day.

Kapha types are prone to look to food for emotional support (if nervous, anxious, depressed, worried or distracted) and can overeat, binge and graze, so mindful eating habits are all the more important. Be mindful of those indulgent food traps, particularly sweets, breads, cheeses and late-night kitchen raids.

Fasting is recommended for kapha as it helps regulate the agni, since the digestion can often become sluggish. A liquid fast once a week is usually sufficient to give the digestive system time to rekindle and realign (see p. 147), while a longer mono diet of kitchari can also be supportive for the kapha digestion.

Taste-balancing for kapha

Getting familiar with the tastes that balance kapha will mean that you don't need to memorise long food lists, just allow your palate to navigate you to the right foods. For kapha balancing, favour foods that are bitter, astringent and pungent. This means that, apart from salt, you need not shy away from any of those wonderful spices. Spice up your foods to your heart's desire! The pungency of spices helps to liquefy and dry out excess mucus/secretions (for example, a runny nose) and stimulate heat in the body and digestion. The rough, dry and light quality of the bitter taste supports the absorption of moisture, fat and lymph which are prone to increase in kapha types. Bitter foods are cooling in nature, so they need a little balance with some punchy pungency. The astringent taste, like bitter, is light, rough and drying, so for kapha types, these foods can be taken without too much concern (pomegranate, broccoli, cauliflower, beans, apples, crackers, rice cakes). For the kapha person, astringency helps to tone the body tissues and absorb excess fluids.

Contrary to vata, kapha types need to reduce foods that are sweet, sour and salty in taste. Opt for fruits that are less sweet and heavy and keep it seasonal. Light fruits such as apples, pears and pomegranates work well. Limited dried fruits can be a good option for snacking if necessary.

The sweet taste, by its cold, heavy, moist and oily nature, will in large quantities imbalance kapha so should be limited. In excess, it can trigger a surplus of mucus, heaviness, lethargy and increased weight, as well as foster coughs and colds. Raw honey is the rare exception, as it has the property of heating and *lekhana*, a scraping effect on the body that helps to remove hardened toxins from the body channels, so a maximum one tablespoon a day is fine.

Sour foods, such as vinegars, citrus fruits and cheeses, stimulate the water element in kapha and in excess can lead quickly to water retention or swelling. Likewise, salt can increase the moisture in the body so it's best used in moderation by kapha types.

Balancing foods for kapha

Since kapha is generally dense and heavy in nature, opting for foods that are light and airy will counterbalance this dosha both in terms of weight and density. Vegetables are easier to digest when cooked and most are suitable for kapha. Limit heavy and sweet fruits and vegetables such as root vegetables and avocado, but tuck into vegetables that are grown above ground and flourish with green freshness. Vegetables and most foods are best eaten cooked and warm, but some light salads are OK, with a warming dressing (ginger, garlic or a little balsamic).

Heavy foods tend to be kaphas' weakness and are best avoided, especially cakes, breads, nuts, desserts and fried foods. Dairy is also a food group that should be moderated for kapha types due to its heavy and cold quality. Dairy can quickly and easily increase mucus and lead to respiratory congestion. Milk when boiled and spiced with cardamom or nutmeg can be more digestible. A little ghee can aid digestion, as can takra (buttermilk) in a limited amount.

Instead, settle for warm water and stimulating hot herbal teas such as chai, made with ginger, fennel, cinnamon or cardamom to prevent accumulations, improve digestion and cleanse body tissues. Avoid cold and carbonated drinks. Moderate intake of coffee can aid kapha digestion.

Warming foods can nullify the coldness of kapha both in temperature and in spice levels. Cold leftovers or foods straight out of the fridge can quickly imbalance kapha.

Maintaining body mass is not a challenge for kapha types, so you do not need meats to sustain energy. Meats are heavy and often slow to digest, so a limited serving is fine and more suitable in the winter months. If you do eat meat, don't forget to spice it up and opt for white-fleshed meats such as chicken, turkey and fish.

Plant-based foods such as lentils, tofu or beans are a great low-fat source of protein. They can still be demanding on the digestion, so they should be eaten warm and spiced, just like for vata types. Many lentils and beans, with their astringent taste and dry quality, are balancing for kapha.

Most grains are starchy, moist and heavy and, much like meat, kapha types do not require grains in abundance. Moderate measures of corn, millet and buckwheat can be good options. Grains that are flaked, puffed or come in a dry form are best. Sprouted grains can also be nutritious.

Heavy and oily in nature, most nuts and seeds are not so suitable for kapha types, although pumpkin and sunflower seeds can be fine in moderation. Only light oils are recommended for kapha such as sunflower or, in some cases, ghee when used in moderation.

Eating-out tips for kapha

- Opt for a hot soup or broth for a starter
- Enjoy hot meals
- You can have a little red wine
- Opt for Mexican, Thai and Indian foods that are light and healthy but have a kick
- Opt for a vegetarian meal in the evening
- Avoid rice and wheat at dinner and limit meal portion sizes
- Avoid desserts
- End the meal with a herbal tea

Kapha-pacifying foods

Types of food	Favour	Limit
Vegetables	Artichoke, asparagus, aubergine, beetroot, bok choy, broccoli, Brussels sprouts, burdock root, cabbage, carrots, cauliflower, celery, collard greens, daikon radish, fennel, garlic, ginger, green beans, horseradish, Jerusalem artichoke, kale, kohlrabi, leeks, lettuce, mustard greens, okra, onions, peas, peppers, radish, spinach, turnips, watercress	Courgettes, cucumber, parsnips, pumpkin, tomatoes, spaghetti squash, swede, sweet potato, white potato, winter squash
Fruits	Apples, apricots, berries, cherries, cranberries, dry figs, green papaya, lemon, lime, peaches, pears, persimmons, pomegranate, prunes, raisins, strawberries	Avocado, banana, coconut, dates, fresh figs, grapefruit, grapes, kiwi, mango, melon, oranges, papaya, pineapple, plums, rhubarb, tamarind, watermelon
Grains	Amaranth, barley, basmati rice, buckwheat, dry oats (limited granola), millet, oat bran, polenta, quinoa, rice cakes, rye, sago, tapioca, wheat bran	Cooked oats, pasta, spelt, wheat, white flour, yeasted breads Limited rice (white and brown)

Types of food	Favour	Limit
Legumes	Aduki beans, black beans, black-eye beans, broad beans, brown lentils, chickpeas (garbanzo beans), hot tofu, lima (butter) beans, mung beans, navy beans, pinto beans, puy lentils, red lentils, split chickpeas (chana dahl), split peas, split yellow mung, white beans	Black lentils (urad dahl), cold tofu, kidney beans, soya beans, soy products, tempeh
Dairy and eggs	Buttermilk, eggs, ghee (limited), goat's cheese, goat's milk	All cheese, butter, cream, ice cream, paneer, sour cream, yoghurt
Meat and fish	Chicken, freshwater fish, shrimp, turkey, venison	Beef, duck, lamb, pork, salmon, saltwater fish, sardines, seafood, tuna
Nuts and seeds	Flax, popcorn, psyllium, sunflower and pumpkin seeds	Minimal or no nuts recommended; also avoid sesame and hemp
Herbs and spices	All herbs and spices in abundance	Salt, tamarind, vanilla
Oils and fats	Small amounts of almond, corn, ghee, mustard, sunflower oil	Avoid all other oils or fats
Sweeteners	Raw honey, limited fruit juices	Agave syrup, barley malt syrup, brown rice syrup, fructose, jaggery, maple syrup, molasses, refined white sugar, rock sugar, stevia

Types of food	Favour	Limit
Drinks	Apple juice, black tea, carrot juice, coffee, fresh diluted fruit juices (moderate), hot and warming herbal teas, spiced milk, vegetable juice	Alcohol, cold drinks or ice, cold milk, hot chocolate, salted drinks, sour juices and smoothies

Meal suggestions for kapha

Breakfast	Lunch	Dinner	Snacks
Rye toast with wilted spinach * Stewed fruits with spices * Small glass of diluted vegetable juice or smoothie * Hot cereal of barley or millet with honey	Vietnamese rice noodles and green vegetable pho (chicken optional) * Lentil and vegetable soup with rye bread * Hot chickpea, roast vegetable and quinoa salad * Cauliflower, broccoli and leek bake	Kitchari * Lentil and vegetable soup with cornbread * Spinach and lentil curry with barley, millet or basmati rice * Spiced sweet potato, chickpea and spinach stew	Herbal teas * Rice crackers * Popcorn * Limited fresh fruits * Snacking is not advised for kapha

CHAPTER 10

Relight Your Digestive Fire

'Let food be thy medicine and medicine be thy food'

Hippocrates

Health starts with a healthy gut. I want to take you on a little journey to the epicentre of Ayurvedic healthcare – your digestive fire, or your agni.

The main source of energy for your body and mind comes from the food that you eat. What you consume is of course important and we discuss that in the coming chapters, but if your digestive system is out of whack, then it can lead to the formation of toxins, known as ama. When ama is present, you are no longer able to optimally digest, absorb and assimilate nutrients.

A strong balanced agni – a **sama agni** – is at the core of optimum health. Agni refers to our body's capability to digest and transform what we consume as food and drink to simple substances that can be assimilated by the body.

Ayurveda perceives all human experiences as 'food'. What is unique to Ayurveda is the theory of energetics and how all this food or 'information' from the environment is transformed into your biochemistry; this includes your thoughts and what you digest through your five senses. Paying close attention to this process gives us many indicators to the cause of illness.

The efficiency of your digestive fire plays an important role in how you are nourished from what you eat. Agni maintains both your body strength and immunity. It is also responsible for destroying disease-causing microorganisms. Agni is required for all functions in the body and so it stands to reason why this subject deserves special attention. For most practitioners digestion will be the focal point of a consultation.

Agni plays a role at three stages in your body: firstly there is the jatharagni in the digestive tract, which is your main digestive fire. The ingested food is broken down into nutrients that are digested further by elemental fires (bhutagnis) and finally the dhatvagnis, the fires responsible for forming each of the dhatus (seven bodily tissues). By following daily habits aligned to your prakruti, your digestive fire can stay in a balanced state. When agni is in balance (sama agni), the food and drink that you consume is optimally assimilated and provides nourishment to your tissues, and as a result you prosper in good health.

'Agni is responsible for life span, complexion, strength, health, enthusiasm, corpulence, lustre, immunity, energy, heat processes and prana. Agni is the root cause of both health and disease'

Charaka Samhita

The characteristics of a sama agni are light, clear, hot and pure, a brightly burning fire. When your agni is balanced, your digestive fire is transforming and converting all food and sensations into nutrients that your body subsequently uses as energy and information for your body to function.

So, what is a healthy agni supposed to look and feel like? A healthy agni can be felt with lightness in the body, easily passing stools, a distinct feeling of hunger and thirst, radiant skin, good levels of energy and vitality. Does this sound like you? With our varied and highly processed diets nowadays, few people actually experience a balanced agni. A change in the state of agni is the trigger for ama (toxins) to accumulate and the root cause of most disease in the body. Agni can become imbalanced in three ways.

Vishama agni is influenced by the unpredictable airy qualities of vata flaring up or putting out the agni. 'Vishama' means irregular and those with this type of agni will tend to have a mix of intense or no hunger, and a sensitive digestion with a limited digestive capacity. Regulation of meals and eating patterns and a vata-pacifying diet is key to bringing this type of agni back to balance.

Tikshna agni is affected by the fiery qualities of pitta. 'Tikshna' means penetrating or sharp. This type of agni displays an excessive appetite with a fast digestion. The ability to handle heavy or difficult-to-digest foods is a typical sign of this type of agni. A pitta-pacifying diet would be suitable in this case.

Manda agni is influenced by the kapha qualities in digestion where there is sluggishness. Those with a manda agni will gain weight easily even from small portions of food. A kapha-reducing diet would be most suitable here.

Do you identify with any of these? The more you identify with one of these types, the stronger the imbalance of agni.

Agni	Characteristics
Sama agni (balanced agni)	Able to digest moderate portions in all seasons. Able to adjust to and tolerate seasonal changes. Timely appetite, balanced digestion and regular elimination. Ama is not present and there is general equilibrium and vitality.
Vishama agni (vata)	Variable appetite and digestion (quantity and timing), flatulence and bloating, constipation, dark coating on tongue, dry mouth, underweight, insomnia, mental restlessness.

Tikshna agni (pitta)	Strong appetite, prone to acid reflux, food digested quickly, burning sensations, thirst, diarrhoea, yellowish coating on the tongue, sour taste in mouth, moderate weight, impatience, irritability, anger.
Manda agni (kapha)	Prone to low appetite, slow digestion, a feeling of heaviness, overweight, lethargic, sleepiness after eating, excess salivation, white coating on the tongue, mucosal stools, mental dullness, depression.

How ama develops

If you continue to eat foods that disrupt your digestion – such as heavy, cold, excessively spicy, raw or fried foods – or if you consume incompatible food combinations or medicines, undertake excessive fasting, experience emotional upset or stress, have erratic eating patterns or eat when no hunger is present, your agni becomes weakened and imbalanced. When the strength of your agni is not adequate, the food you consume remains undigested and unabsorbed by the intestinal tract; this toxic substance that is formed as a result is called ama and has no supportive function in the body. This foul-smelling, thick, heavy and sticky ama ferments and clogs the intestinal channels of the body. It provides an internal environment that supports a breeding ground for bacteria, yeast and parasites. If ama is not taken care of, it can lead to what has commonly been labelled as the 'leaky gut' syndrome. In this scenario, the ama irritates the gut lining, creating microscopic holes in the intestinal walls and causes the ama to 'leak' out of the intestinal wall. In extreme cases, it can lead to complications such as food intolerances and compromised immunity.

Your brain is in continual dialogue with your digestive system, so mental and emotional as well as sensory disturbances can put a strain on your digestion. Your digestive enzymes can either be inhibited, resulting in reduced digestion and absorption, or there can be an excess of enzymes, causing irritation and burning. Ama prevents the nutrients from your food from being fully converted into the energy and information that enables your body to function optimally.

How to spot if you have ama

Any one of these would indicate some level of digestive toxins in your system:

- Coated tongue (whitish or yellowish)
- Poor appetite
- Sensitive digestion/indigestion
- Bloating and wind with bad odour
- Irritable elimination/sluggish, sticky bowel motions
- Foul-smelling or sinking/sticky stools
- Undigested particles in stools
- Fatigue/lethargy
- Bad breath/sticky mouth
- Unusual or foul body odour
- Generalised body ache/heaviness
- Headaches and migraines
- Lacking lustre in eyes and skin
- Depression
- Low immunity and recurring infections
- Waking up feeling unrested, even after good sleep
- Constipation
- Emotional volatility, lack of attention and memory

When your digestive fire is low and your dietary choices and patterns are destructive on top of that, ama will start to accumulate, stagnate and ferment.

Unhealthy eating habits that cause ama accumulation include the following and should be avoided where possible:

- Eating when you have indigestion
- Consuming incompatible foods
- Overeating
- Consuming heavy or indigestible foods
- Eating raw and uncooked foods
- Consuming foods and drinks that are too cold
- Eating unclean/contaminated foods
- Drinking too much water with food
- Suppressing natural urges (belching, passing urine, wind or stools)
- Eating when you are under intense emotional stress
- Eating when there is no real hunger, having irregular diet habits
- Eating dry, fried or dehydrated foods in excess
- Eating excessive amounts of processed/packaged foods
- Eating when constipated
- Eating before your previous meal has been digested
- Drinking fruit juices with meals

Sometimes it is hard to believe that these small factors can have such a significant impact. Of course, ama doesn't form after the occasional offence. Disease is the result of a collective and cumulative pattern that allows ama to become present over time, and thrive.

Unless you have a strong reaction to a specific food, your body goes through several stages before food triggers imbalances and develops into a health issue or disease. I explain the process of disease development in chapter 5. Whatever your gut does not digest properly can become toxic waste for your body, and this starts with ama.

Digestive stimulation

Natural substances that kindle the digestive fire and strengthen appetite are called **deepana**. To rekindle the digestive fire (agni) in the absence of ama, you can opt for foods that have a pungent, sour, salty and bitter taste, as these are stimulating. Foods that are cooked and easy to digest will ensure that your agni doesn't have to work so hard. Ingredients with these tastes help to ignite and strengthen the digestive fire.

The best pungent herbs for increasing your fire include ginger, black pepper, long pepper, cinnamon, asafoetida, clove, mustard and cayenne. If your constitution is more vata or pitta, then these may be too pungent or drying, in which case you can opt for seeded spices that work to ignite agni in a much softer way. These include cumin, coriander, fennel, dill, ajwain and fenugreek. Bitter tastes can also be beneficial (see p. 178).

Clearing digestive toxins

Substances that neutralise toxins and ama in the body are called **pachana**. The stimulating bitter and pungent tastes can help to 'burn off' the ama. While the pungent tastes 'burn' or 'digest' toxins, bitter herbs help to 'scrape' toxins from the tissues and channels. Since the role of the liver is to detoxify and preserve the blood from any toxic contamination, the health of your biggest organ is imperative. Cleansing the liver and enhancing its function is a key component of any Ayurvedic detox. With the consumption of indigestible foods, chemicals, alcohol and drugs in today's world, it is easy for our liver to become overloaded and overworked. Bitter herbs can also work wonders for your skin, and their cooling nature also helps reduce any conditions of inflammation. Turmeric is an obvious choice for a bitter herb (see p. 220). Agni deepana and ama pachana foods, herbs and spices are usually light, heating and drying in quality.

Keeping ama at arm's length

Preventing ama from forming and clearing accumulated ama is the mainstay of Ayurveda. Following the conscious eating practices outlined and using specialist herbal remedies, you can easily ensure your digestive fire stays strong and that ama is kept at bay. No matter what your health issue, the process of disease management will always start with strengthening and maintaining a healthy agni while destroying ama. This is always my main focus with clients. In addition to healthy eating practices (see p. 127), here are a few quick reminders and tips to help you clear ama and fire up your agni:

- Maintain regular meal patterns, but ensure hunger is present; no hunger, no food. Snacking between meals weakens agni
- Choose light, fresh, easy-to-digest meals to prevent ama from forming
- Scrape your tongue twice a day to reduce oral toxins from being reabsorbed into the gut
- Avoid kapha increasing foods (see p. 116); they can often be synonymous with ama formation
- Loosen toxins of the body, such as in the skin, by doing regular self-body massage
- Drink hot water, hot lemon water or herbal teas with warming spices such as ginger, cinnamon, fennel, black pepper, cayenne and long pepper
- Take regular exercise that is suitable for your body type, including yoga
- Practise **pranayama** breathing exercises to stimulate agni such as kapala bhati and bhastrika pranayama (see p. 279)
- Opt for foods and spices with sour, salty, pungent and bitter tastes to stimulate agni; since agni is dry, light, hot and penetrating, anything with a similar nature will stimulate it
- Clear ama with bitter and pungent tasting spices, such as

turmeric, ginger, long pepper, black pepper, ajwain, fenugreek, *trikatu* and *hingwastak*

- An occasional fast of a mono diet (kitchari) and a seasonal cleanse can keep agni healthy

Healthy eating habits

It's not only what you eat, it's how you eat that contributes strongly to keeping agni fired up and ama at bay. Listen to your natural instincts and follow these simple guidelines.

Observe good hygiene

Are you mindful of hygiene at mealtimes? We are touching phones, handles, computers and shaking hands constantly these days, and these places are a hidden breeding ground for bacteria and microbes. Next time you grab a sandwich for lunch at your desk, just ask yourself, how germ-free are your hands before you take a bite?

Keep a calm environment

Eat in a calm and relaxed environment – that means no TV, phones or heated discussions. Take your time and enjoy your meal, preferably around a dining table. Your emotions speak directly to your appetite and digestion. Do not eat when you are angry or upset. Keep a peaceful and pleasant mood while eating.

Sit down

Always take time to sit down to eat. Yes, this actually means that you need to step away from your computer and desk. Ensure that you are not eating while you are standing, driving or walking. Sitting down to eat ensures that your stomach is in a relaxed state.

It sounds crazy, but so many people don't sit down properly. It actually doesn't take that long to eat. So, it is worth taking the time out!

Many Asian cultures choose to sit on the floor, cross-legged (*sukhasana*) which helps the blood flow to the abdomen. The slight bend forward to eat from your plate on the floor and back to swallow increases the secretion of stomach acids and engages the abdominal muscles, which results in improved digestion. This way of eating helps to control overconsumption of food, as the upper part of the stomach naturally gets compressed, reducing the capacity to overeat.

Focus on your food

Be present and give your full attention to your meal. Engage all your senses in the process of eating. Since food sustains your life, don't you think it's worth giving it 100 per cent of your attention? The food is being converted into information and essential energy for the body, so allow your brain to fully register the process of digestion. Don't divert the pleasure that your brain takes in processing all the tastes, textures and smells. If your mind is focused on anything other than eating, the body and brain do not fully register the digestive process. So, it is worth making the effort to eat away from your workspace.

Are you really hungry?

Eat to live but don't live to eat – be mindful of your cravings and indulgences. This does not mean that you shouldn't enjoy tasty wholesome food, but only eat when you're hungry. How often do you grab breakfast or lunch just because 'it's time' or because your colleagues are ready to eat? If you're not feeling genuine hunger, this means that your digestive enzymes are not ready to work and your food will not get digested properly. This is a key rule to eating in Ayurveda. Wait until you feel a genuine hunger. Your system can be stimulated and trained to eat at the right intervals. You can use a simple combination of a teaspoon of freshly grated ginger, a pinch of rock salt and a dash of lime taken as a paste with a little warm water 15 minutes before your meal to encourage your agni to fire up.

Only eat after your previous meal is digested. If you eat when you're still in the process of digesting your previous meal, it confuses your system. Half-digested foods get mixed with new foods, leading to the formation of ama.

Unless you feel hungry, avoid mindless snacking in between meals. If you do feel hungry, then opt for fresh fruits or a handful of nuts and seeds.

Pace yourself

Eat at a sensible pace. Not too fast, not too slow. Eating in a hurry will trigger indigestion, bloating and possibly abdominal pain. If you slow down your meal, it gives you a chance to engage your sensory organs and supports the metabolism of nutrients. Chew your food well – thirty-two times according to self-proclaimed diet expert, Horace Fletcher, in the 1800s. This will ensure that your food is mixed with saliva and broken down enough for your stomach to digest it well. The mouth is the primary starting point for the process of digestion. Our food won't run away, so take smaller mouthfuls. The oral cavity is able to break down foods in a way that is not possible by the digestive enzymes in the stomach and intestines (largely due to saliva and teeth). Proper chewing can help limit indulgences and help the body and brain to feel sufficiently satisfied. Savour every bite!

Portion control

Stop eating when you feel satisfied. Portion control is key. Only fill half of your stomach with food. One-quarter of your stomach's capacity should be left free for the liquid portion and the other quarter for space for the digestion to take place. If you cup both of your hands together, the amount of food that fits in your hands is your personalised portion size – one **anjali**. Everyone's hands vary, so eating a full meal just because that is what is served to you does not mean that it is the right amount of food for you.

Kindle a strong digestive fire

Kindle your digestive fire by eating warm meals. Cooked foods eaten fresh and hot are easier to digest than cold or raw meals. Favour a plant-based diet. Kitchari is an ideal food for a strong agni. Avoid ama-producing foods such as dairy, heavy meats, raw foods and incompatible food combinations.

Timing is everything

Eat regular and timely meals. This helps the agni to stay regulated and fired up to break down and absorb nutrients to sufficiently support your health.

Lunch should be the main meal of the day, when your digestive fire is optimal. Eat your evening meal ideally by 6.30 p.m., avoiding heavy foods. Follow the principles of the seasonal and daily rhythms.

Avoid exercising or taking a bath after eating your meals. Again, your system is focused on digestion and the body gets confused if it needs to direct energy elsewhere. Have you noticed that you can often feel cold after a meal? This is because your body's energy is focused inward on digestion and not on keeping your body warm.

Do not sleep immediately after eating a meal. Your body is focused on digestion and this process is interrupted if you sleep, triggering indigestion. It is also a distraction to the tissue repair and rejuvenation that happens during your sleep. Always try to allow 2 to 3 hours between your last meal and bedtime.

Don't over-hydrate

Avoid drinking too much water before, during and after your meal, as this can weaken your agni. Drinks at mealtimes should be just enough to moisten your food and not douse your digestive fire. Too much water will put your fire out, although a little wine is fine or even a little home-made buttermilk. Similarly, you should avoid drinking fruit juices and cold or icy drinks. Drink most of your fluids in between meals.

Digestive aids

Favour foods that balance your prakruti and where possible include all six tastes (sweet, sour, salty, bitter, pungent and astringent) at every meal. Use herbs and spices to aid digestion. Supportive herbs for digestion would include: trikatu, ginger, cinnamon, black pepper, *amalaki*, cumin, coriander, turmeric, ajwain, fennel and more. I always suggest to my clients to include at least one seeded spice in every meal if not more. As mentioned, ginger is also a great digestive stimulant, as is ghee. If ama is present and agni is to be rekindled, your practitioner may advise on various fasting methods, digestive herbs and even pancha karma therapies to get you back on track.

Fresh breath

Chewing fennel seeds, sesame seeds, roasted coriander seeds, dill seeds or betel leaves helps to freshen the breath, encourage digestion, prevent flatulence from forming as well as cleanse the oral cavity. The combination of these seeds as a digestive aid is known as *mukhwas* in India and will often be given to you at the end of a meal in an Indian restaurant.

Client story

'I started to experience stomach issues that left me feeling very weak after carrying out strenuous exercise. I had a series of tests for months and even an endoscopy, but doctors couldn't find anything. I was prescribed omeprazole and was written off as having acid reflux. This episode also left me feeling very emotional, as I could feel that something was not right internally but no one could find the cause.

In January 2015, I paid a visit to Geeta, who diagnosed me as having a navel imbalance. From there on, I had a round of four treatments where Geeta helped to bring my navel back into balance. She advised me on the foods I should be eating for my body type (predominantly vata) and advised on exercises I should be doing to keep my navel in balance. Soon after my first treatment, I started to feel my energy return and my emotional self become stronger. The treatments were strong, and I needed rest, but I stayed positive and had patience with Ayurveda.

I now have hot water with honey and turmeric every morning. I do a self-abhyanga once a week and practise yoga twice a week. My diet is mostly vata-based and I now choose food depending on the season.

Ayurveda is a huge part of my life now, and it has inspired me to think about natural alternatives to medication to achieve a balanced life, both mentally and physically. This process has given me a new life.'

Joey

Conscious eating

Good digestion depends just as much on your emotional state as it does on your physical agni. By learning to listen to your body and having an awareness of your nutritional requirements, you can tailor a diet that is perfect for your needs.

Engaging all your sensory organs in the process of eating can enhance the way your body digests your meal. What does your meal look like? Is it appealing and appetising to you? Take time to look and observe your food colours and textures. If you are not appetised, your mind will register this and send signals to your gut, which can subsequently reject the food. What are the pleasant aromas coming from your food? Food smells can stimulate salivation immediately, so take a moment to allow yourself to observe them to enhance the initial stage of digestion in the mouth.

Traditionally in the East, meals are eaten using the right hand. We have the energy of the five elements in our fingertips and so we are drawing this collective energy into each morsel. What's more, eating with your hands allows you to further explore the texture of your food through the sense of touch.

Take time to eat slowly, taste the flavours and feel the textures in your mouth. Take small bites and chew properly to ensure that you give your digestion the best chance to fully break down and absorb the nutrients in the food. At this point, you can also use the sense of sound to notice the texture – is it slurpy, crunchy or chewy in texture? Does your food have a balance of all six tastes? We will look at the significance of taste in chapter 12.

Conscious eating may sound a little obvious, but so few of us actually practise this, and I can assure you, the more you slow down, the more you will notice a difference in your satisfaction with your meal. What's more, you are able to control the portion size based on what is right for you. We often feel so full at the end of meals because we feel pressured to finish what is served up, and by the time our brain registers that we are actually full, it is usually too late.

Conscious-eating exercise

Take a whole piece of fruit. Any fruit! Take a few minutes to observe the look and feel of it as a whole fruit. Does it have a smell? You can take a moment to give gratitude for having this piece of fruit that you are about to eat.

Prepare the fruit by first cutting it into chunks or slices, depending on your preference. Then notice again the look, texture and smell. As you take a small piece into your mouth without biting or chewing, observe how your mouth salivates and what flavours you are getting. Is the flavour as you imagined it would be? Then, after at least one minute, start to bite down and chew on the fruit slowly and purposefully, with 100 per cent of your attention on eating. You can do this for the remainder of your whole fruit. What are the flavours, textures, smells, changes you observed? At the end, pause, sit and notice how you feel. How is your belly responding?

You don't have to eat all your meals this slowly, but the practice of giving 100 per cent attention and slowing down the pace by half of your normal speed will work wonders for your digestion, your connection to your food, not to mention your waistline.

Traditional digestive preparations

There's an encyclopaedia's worth of traditional herbal preparations in Ayurveda, from powders (churna), tablets, oils, tinctures and decoctions, to medicated ghees, juices and pastes and more, which can be consumed for all sorts of ailments. I just want to draw your attention to a few herbal compounds that are useful for your digestive health. These are available predominantly in powder, capsule and tablet form from most good health food stores near you or from reputable online suppliers.

Triphala churna

Ingredients: *amalaki, bibhitaki, haritaki*

Triphala is by far the most popular herbal compound going in the Ayurvedic arena. The three-fruit powder or capsule gently enhances appetite and digestion, and it is the safest way to cleanse the bowel and relieve constipation. It is a **rasayana** or rejuvenative, nourishing the nervous system and strengthening the blood and muscle tissues. It protects the heart and contains antiviral and anti-inflammatory properties. It regulates metabolism and improves liver function, while balancing all three doshas.

Avipattikar churna

Ingredients: *dry ginger, black pepper, long pepper, amalaki, bibhitaki, haritaki, musta, vidanga, cardamom, bay leaves, cloves, trivrut, rock sugar*

A great combination to remove excess pitta from the gastro-intestinal tract. This compound clears inflammation and toxins out of the system, and can be a powerful aid for loss of appetite. It balances the digestive fire and reduces excess acids that cause hyperacidity, heartburn, gastritis and constipation. It can have a useful effect on skin issues and pitta-type headaches and urinary problems. It is a great digestive aid for pitta types.

Hingwastak churna

Ingredients: *asafoetida, dry ginger, black pepper, long pepper, rock salt, cumin, black cumin, ajwain*

This is good for disturbances such as abdominal distension, rumbling wind, gas and indigestion. Hingwastak is useful in increasing the digestive fire, and relieving cramping and abdominal pain. It gently burns away toxins and increases absorption of nutrients. This should be avoided in pregnancy and if high pitta conditions are present. This powder can be added to curries and other foods in the cooking process. This is an extremely helpful compound for vata types.

Trikatu churna

Ingredients: *black pepper, long pepper, dry ginger*

This pungent trio works in synergy to stimulate a sluggish digestion, increase agni, absorb nutrients and clear ama. It is helpful for kapha-type digestive disturbances. Trikatu supports weight management and reduces cholesterol levels and excess mucus. This combination rejuvenates the lungs and can be useful in asthma. It should be avoided if high pitta symptoms are present. This is not suitable in pregnancy, during heavy menstrual flow or in high acidity conditions. This is good for kapha types.

Consult a practitioner for specific advice on dosage and administration of herbal preparations for your specific digestive and health issues.

CHAPTER 11

Detoxification

'Each morning we are born again. What we do today is
what matters most'

Siddhartha Gautama (Buddha)

Some of my clients are vastly out of balance and they come to me
in search of a 'detox' programme. Every now and then you need
to pause to check in with yourself beyond the day-to-day, for a
deeper cleanse. After all, we are not all yogis living in the
mountain, with a perfect diet and lifestyle; we are exposed to a
multitude of toxins in our urban lives and increased levels of
stress. However, I am a firm believer that the more you take care
of the day-to-day, the less there is a need for vigorous detoxing.

What does 'detox' mean to you? Is it being 'good'? Fasting?
Going on a crash diet? Refraining from alcohol for a week or two?
Staying off the sugar? Stopping the smoking? Being less indulgent
after your holidays? Everyone's idea of a detox is different.

Client story

'I spent two years being bloated, unhappy in my own skin, gaining weight when actually eating very little, and I became depressed because it felt it wasn't me or my body, even a glass of water would make me inflate. I felt bad, grumpy, tired. My body was suffering without having a recognised Western illness. Why would I pile up fat around my belly when I've never had this in my life, and despite the fact that I was on a diet, eating well and going to the gym four times a week?

I consulted with allopathic doctors, who told me that I was stressed, without offering any relief or explanation. They told me that it was my age (forty-two) and it was "normal". But why wasn't I digesting properly or losing weight, considering the effort I was putting in? I wanted to lose weight to be myself again.

After the initial struggles to stick to a new Ayurvedic routine in my busy schedule, I started doing what I could. I learnt that there is no need for drastic measures or extreme diets. Instead, changing a few small yet significant things according to my dosha has helped rebalance my body gently.

I learnt how to cook simple vegetarian dishes and have cut out meat almost entirely from my diet, since it didn't digest well. I stopped drinking coffee, which seemed impossible at the time, and replaced it with ginger, lemon and honey tea in the morning. I finally started to digest and enjoy eating again, by being more mindful of my food. The herbs also helped me digest and evacuate. It felt great to not be bloated after eating.

Then the miracle happened: I did lose some of that weight that didn't belong to me, but more importantly I started to like my body and love it for what it is. A very significant shift. From my experience, I now understand how much the mind and body work together. Ayurveda has helped me focus on myself more, look inward and listen.'

Eve

I want to break down the subject of detox into a few key areas:

- Physical body detox
- Sensory detox
- Environmental detox
- Occupational detox
- Relationship detox
- Emotional detox

Everything we are and do is interrelated; nothing is isolated, and so our approach to health must not be viewed in isolation, but rather in the context of the entire macrocosm. Small changes can bring profound shifts to our overall wellbeing. Physically manifested diseases can be born of an emotional or mental seed, and physical ails can also disturb our mind and emotions.

Physical body detox

> 'The body is your temple. Keep it pure and clean for the soul to reside in'
>
> B.K.S. Iyengar

Traditionally, Ayurvedic detoxification (**langhana**) follows two paths. The first is **shamana** (palliative treatment), meaning calming or pacifying the imbalanced doshas to normalcy and clearing the accumulated ama. This involves strengthening the digestive fire and eliminating ama, which I discussed in chapter 10, as well as the practices of fasting and exercise. Over an extended period, this method of detoxification can be highly effective for lifestyle-related conditions.

The second path, **shodhana** (purification), is a specialist area of therapy designed to eliminate disease-causing imbalances from the root. This path requires careful preparation and monitoring by an Ayurvedic practitioner and is ideally carried out as a residential retreat. Here, the deep-seated imbalanced doshas and toxins are loosened and guided from the sites where they have become lodged back into the gastrointestinal tract and then naturally eliminated by pancha karma, the five cleansing actions:

- *Vamana* (emesis)
- *Virechana* (purgation)
- *Basti* (enema)
- *Nasya* (errhines/nasal administration)
- *Raktamokshana* (bloodletting)

In this chapter, we will focus on the palliative form of detoxification, shamana. If your health concerns are deeper than the scope of this book, I suggest you consult a practitioner for more guidance on lifestyle changes, suitable cleansing, herbs and treatments.

If you are suffering from ongoing conditions such as headaches, indigestion, frequent colds and flu, constipation or IBS, outbreaks of mild skin conditions, disturbed sleep, excess weight, sluggishness, fatigue, PMS, asthma, general aches and pains, recurrent annual hay fever, joint stiffness and pain, then a home-based Ayurvedic detox could just be what you need to put the bounce back into your step. Longer-term Ayurvedic lifestyle changes can then be implemented to prevent further imbalances.

I generally recommend my clients to wait for the next transitional season of either spring or autumn to undergo a detox process. Your digestive fire becomes stronger over the winter, so you tend to eat more and your bodily channels contract; this makes it difficult for your system to naturally release the toxins, which does not support detoxification processes.

Over the spring season, the accumulated toxins and doshas start to liquefy and become mobile, as your digestive fire starts to weaken; this makes it easier to expel toxins from the body and so it's an ideal and natural time for a deeper cleanse. Autumn is another great time for cleansing and preparing your body for winter wellness; in this season you can cleanse the accumulated heat from the summer and balance vata as it starts to increase.

Eliminating toxins

Ama is potentially harmful to the body, as it weakens your defences, generates free radicals that cause tissue damage and opens you up to various degenerative diseases, not to mention speeding up the process of ageing. What's more, ama prevents the breakdown and absorption of the beneficial nutrients that we eat. (See p. 123 for signs of ama.)

We all suffer from some level of ama accumulation, even if it is just from environmental pollutants. Before we can fully absorb the nutrients from our foods, the ama first needs to be cleared. The same principle applies when we want medicinal herbs to have an effect on the body in detoxification, and for this reason creating the right digestive environment is critical.

Benefits of detoxification

- A feeling of lightness is engendered by eliminating toxins in the body and the mind
- Your immune system is strengthened and your resistance to illnesses is increased
- You gain peace of mind and deep relaxation
- Better self-care is inspired
- Your clarity and concentration are increased
- Your digestion and elimination function properly
- You feel more connected to the natural rhythms of life
- A sense of creativity and enthusiasm is fostered

Get set for detoxification

When we detox Ayurvedically, there is no single fix or one herbal antidote to do the job. Careful attention is given to our dosha balance, strength of digestive power and clarity of channels.

Prior to and during detoxification it is important to observe the following processes:

- Sleep – Since your body rejuvenates and replenishes tissues overnight, you must ensure you get enough rest
- Breathe and meditate – Reduce stress by balancing emotional and mental triggers. Increased oxygenation will increase prana, your life force energy
- Keep moving – Gentle exercise and yoga will ensure that you keep circulation in flow and help clear toxins out of the body
- Self-body massage – Abhyanga is a focal point in Ayurvedic detox. This aids circulation and helps loosen toxins lodged in the peripheral body and directs them to the digestive tract as well as via sweat for elimination
- Digestive care – Make sure your digestion is nicely fired up (see p. 125)
- **Prajnaparadha** – We already know the recipe that causes toxins in the first place, yet we still take actions against our better judgement. Refrain from having coffee, alcohol, sugar, late nights, irregular eating etc., and avoid the causes of ama (see p. 126)

Detoxifying diet

This detoxification diet is designed to prevent ama from forming and clear any existing ama.

- Foods that are heavy, greasy, stale or old – such as cheese, pork, lard, refined flours, white sugars, raw foods – tend to clog the body channels and should be avoided
- Water intake should be limited before, during and after meals
- All meals should be taken between 10 a.m. and 6 p.m., with the main meal at lunchtime
- The meals should be light and easy to digest and approximately one anjali in portion size

- Foods should be freshly cooked and eaten warm – for example, kitchari or mung bean soup
- Generally, vata types can undergo an ama-reducing diet for a period of approximately two weeks, pitta types for about one month and kapha types for longer

To clear toxins efficiently and gently from your internal system, two processes always need to take place (usually simultaneously), both agni deepana (rekindling the digestive fire) and ama pachana (clearing toxins). See p. 125 for details of digestive stimulation and digestive toxin clearance.

While dietary herbs gently detox the body, taking herbs in a medicinal dose should be done under the consultation of a practitioner. My favourite and regularly recommended bitter herbs are turmeric, aloe vera, fenugreek, neem, *manjistha*, *guduchi*, milk thistle, dandelion root and burdock root. Other herbal compounds to help detox the digestive system include trikatu, triphala, hingwastak and avipattikar (see pp. 135–6). To increase their effectiveness, herbs are prescribed for different times of the day, before, during and after food or on an empty stomach to achieve a desired outcome. Herbs are also taken with an **anupana**, a carrier substance used to increase the effectiveness and absorbability. For example, for balancing vata, an oil-based anupana such as ghee works well; for pitta, a sweet or a cool anupana such as milk is suitable; and for kapha, a warming or dry anupana such as honey or warm water works well.

Toxins are eliminated from three main channels of the body – the bowels, the urinary tract and the skin. For example, allowing the body to sweat by means of warm medicated oil massage, fomentation and exercise can increase blood circulation and the flow of lymph. By drinking teas made from herbs and spices such as coriander, fennel and mint, the urinary tract also eliminates toxins. Lastly, the bowels are able to clear the bulk of toxins to bring digestive calm, increased energy and immunity.

Food preferences for Ayurvedic cleansing

Type of food	Favour	Avoid
Fruits	In small quantities and preferably sour and astringent fruits such as cranberries, grapefruit, lemon, lime and pomegranate	Sweet fruits such as bananas, pears, persimmons
Vegetables and herbs	All vegetables can be eaten cooked or steamed. Prefer green vegetables: alfalfa, coriander, leafy greens, parsley and spinach	Mushrooms, potatoes Raw vegetables, tinned vegetables
Grains	Whole grains for longer diets Kitchari, quinoa, rice, barley Wheat and oats to be taken sparingly, if at all	Breads, crackers, pastries, white flour
Legumes	Mung beans	Avoid most beans, as they cause gas
Nuts and seeds	Small amounts of pumpkin, sesame and sunflower seeds	Most nuts are heavy and mucus-forming
Dairy	Buttermilk (limited)	Avoid dairy, especially cheese and yoghurt
Meat and fish	Chicken and turkey (only if absolutely necessary)	It's best to avoid all meats
Oils and fats	Flaxseed, ghee, mustard	Most other oils

Type of food	Favour	Avoid
Sweeteners	Honey	White sugars
Spices	All spices are good	Excess salt, pickles, vinegars, wines, chutneys
Drinks	Warm water, black tea, herbal spiced teas (ginger, cinnamon, cardamom)	Cold drinks, ice, coffee

The herbal wonders of triphala

My family and friends know that triphala is my go-to formula for herbal healthcare and an integral compound to any detox programme.

Triphala is a trio of herbs consisting of *Emblica officinalis* (amalaki), *Terminalia bellerica* (bibhitaki) and *Terminalia chebula* (haritaki) and is known as the 'three fruits'. It's the panacea of Ayurvedic medicine for gastrointestinal health and a powerful modulator for the human gut microbiome. It is light and dry in quality and a perfect component for protecting the liver against free radical damage.

Triphala is known to be useful for stimulating the appetite and reducing hyperacidity, and for its mild laxative action, antioxidant, antibacterial, anti-inflammatory, carminative, antispasmodic and immunomodulating properties. It is considered a rasayana, or a rejuvenative, in Ayurveda, especially when taken with honey and ghee. The best thing about triphala is that it is tri-doshic, so suitable for all prakruti types, since it contains a balance of five of the six tastes, excluding salt.

It is a safe compound and can be taken on a longer-term basis. A recommended dosage would be around 500–1,000mg twice daily.

· ·

Detox dish: Kitchari

This simple, nutritiously wholesome Ayurvedic recipe of rice with split green mung beans (mung dahl) is suitable for all doshic constitutions, and my clients love it.

Serves 2

Ingredients:

3–6 tsp ghee

2–3 tsp mixed whole seeds, such as cumin, coriander, fennel, fenugreek (cumin alone is also fine)

1 small onion, diced (optional)

½ tsp ground spices, such as cumin, coriander

½ tsp turmeric

1 tsp rock salt

2 cups vegetables, diced into 1cm cubes, such as carrots, peas, cabbage, kale, spinach, sweet potato, green beans, broccoli

2 tsp fresh ginger, grated

½ cup basmati rice, rinsed

1 cup split green or yellow mung dahl, rinsed

4 cups boiling water (you may need to add more)

Freshly squeezed lemon juice to taste

Coriander to garnish

Method:

Heat the ghee in a medium-sized saucepan until melted, then add the whole mixed seeds, allowing the aroma to release, then stir in the onion (if using). Allow to soften for 2 minutes.

Add the ground spices, turmeric and salt. Allow the aromas to release for 10–15 seconds.

Add the vegetables and ginger and sauté for 2 minutes.

Add the rice and mung dahl and stir in for 1 minute until fully coated, then add the boiling water and reduce to a low heat. Cover and cook for 25–30 minutes or until the vegetables and mung dahl are cooked and tender. Stir every 5–6 minutes. Add more water as needed. The final consistency should be like a risotto.

Allow to stand for 2–3 minutes. Add lemon juice to taste and garnish with coriander. Serve while hot.

Ready for some fasting?

In many cultures and religious practices, ritualistic fasting has been an age-old tradition, an act of devotion to the divine, a time for quiet reflection or undertaken during seasonal transitions. I do believe that the underlying sentiment for fasting in most cultures was for the benefit of health.

The aim of fasting is to enable the body to eliminate metabolic waste and unwanted body fat and allow a digestive rest. Fasting should never feel stressful. Long-term fasting is not recommended but a regular fasting day, once a week, is far more effective. The purpose of fasting from a health perspective is to give the digestive system time to rest so that your appetite and digestion can recalibrate. By fasting, you should see a visible reduction of any white coating on the tongue, your body should feel light, refreshed and energised and you should feel mentally more alert. Your fast should be supported by a restful mind so that your body can focus on eradicating toxins and stimulating the digestive fire. Sipping warm water throughout the day is essential.

Although you can fast all year round, spring is the best season for this type of cleanse, as the sun starts to put in more of an appearance and the body naturally wants to remove excess kapha from the body. Fasting does not mean complete abstinence from food, but rather a simplified and reduced diet suited to your prakruti, so that your digestive fire is not overstrained. A plan for fasting is as personalised as your lifestyle changes.

Fasting can really highlight our hunger patterns. Having genuine signs of hunger is a great indicator that the detox is having a positive effect.

I recommend fasting safely under the consultation of a practitioner. Based on your prakruti, here is how fasting should be approached.

Vata fast

Vata types may struggle with fasting, so you must ensure you don't feel weak from fasting. A simple kitchari-based fast works well for one to two days, as it will both cleanse and nourish without debilitating the body. See p. 146 for the recipe. You can omit the vegetables to simplify this dish further.

Pitta fast

Pitta types have a naturally strong hunger, so excessive fasting would increase pitta and make you irritable. The best type of fast for the pitta type is a liquid-based diet of fresh fruit, vegetable juices and smoothies, or you can add psyllium husks, ground oat or wheat bran to juices to provide bulk. You can also opt for a simple fruit-based diet or lightly cooked vegetables. Remember, bitter and sweet tastes are perfect for pitta so carrot with spinach would be a good base.

Kapha fast

It is almost like fasting was designed for the kapha person. Not only can you tolerate fasting, it is great for kapha-type conditions such as obesity, excessive mucus, excess toxins and water retention. A clear fluid-based diet is most suitable for kapha types. Lots of warm water, stimulating herbal teas and abstinence from all solid foods. You can do this fast for up to three days. Kapha types should avoid sweet and sour juices.

Short periods of fasting suitable for your body type on a regular basis can be beneficial. Fasting for more than three to five days at a time can be counterproductive and can unbalance the doshas, and weaken the digestive fire. So, fasting one day a week is the best option to introduce fasting into your routine. If you are new to fasting, then start with the vata fast and then adjust according to your dosha type.

A simple trio of lemon, ginger and honey makes a great detox tea. See below for a detox tea that is suitable for your body type.

If you undergo a fast, break it gently by introducing light and easy-to-digest foods in a moderate-sized meal, preferably vegetarian. It is not the time to indulge in a meal that you have been craving all day – that may be too heavy to digest and can reverse the effects and hard work of fasting. Soups, broths or kitchari with vegetables and spices would be a great start.

....

Home-made detox tea recipes

Detoxifying tea for vata
Ingredients:
1 litre water
1 tsp fresh ginger, grated
1 tsp mixed whole seeds, such as fennel, cardamom, ajwain
   (fennel alone is also fine)
½ tsp raw organic sugar, such as jaggery or agave (optional)
Freshly squeezed lemon juice to taste

Detoxifying tea for pitta
Ingredients:
1 litre water
1 tsp mixed whole seeds such as cumin, fennel and coriander
5–6 fresh mint leaves or rose petals
½ tsp raw organic sugar, such as jaggery or agave (optional)
Freshly squeezed lime juice to taste

Detoxifying tea for kapha
Ingredients:
1 litre water
1 tsp fresh ginger, grated
1 small cinnamon stick
1 tsp mixed whole seeds, such as black pepper, cumin, coriander
Freshly squeezed lemon juice to taste

Method:
Boil the water with the other ingredients for 2 minutes. Remove from the heat and steep for 2 minutes. Sweeten according to taste. Strain and drink, or store in a flask to drink throughout the day.

. . . .

Tri-doshic detoxifying mung bean soup
This is a perfect recipe for detoxifying as it's light, easy to digest and great for removing toxins and cleansing the digestive system. See p. 202 for the healing benefits of mung.

Serves 4
Ingredients:

1 tbsp ghee	2 tsp fresh ginger, grated
⅛ tsp asafoetida	(adjust to 1 tsp for pitta type)
1 tsp cumin seeds	5 cups boiling water
½ tsp fennel	1 tsp lemon juice to taste
½ tsp turmeric	¾ tsp Rock salt
1 cup whole green mung beans, washed thoroughly and soaked overnight	Black pepper to taste (for vata and kapha types only)
	Coriander leaves to garnish (optional)

Method:
Bring the ghee to a light sizzle in a heavy-based pan, add the asafoetida, cumin, fennel, turmeric and sauté lightly for 10–15 seconds. Then add the drained, soaked beans and ginger and sauté for 1 minute further.

Add the boiling water and bring to the boil, then gently simmer until the mung beans are soft (approximately 30 minutes). Add the lemon, salt and pepper to taste. Stir and cover, checking now and then, adding more water if necessary.

If you have a hand blender and like it smooth, you can give the soup a blitz. Garnish with coriander if desired.

. . . .

Caution for fasting and detoxification

I strongly recommend that you do not fast if you are pregnant, menstruating, are debilitated or underweight, have diabetes, heart conditions, acute health conditions, cancer, hypotension or are a child or over the age of 75. It is best to consult your Ayurvedic practitioner about the suitability and safety of fasting and detoxification for your body type. During a period of illness, a reduced mono-diet is best or at least until your natural hunger resumes. Start by introducing mung bean or rice water (kanji), then well-cooked rice with ghee and ginger, followed by kitchari.

Sensory detox

'The world is full of magic things patiently waiting for our senses to grow sharper'

W.B. Yeats

We don't just digest through our stomach; we also digest all information that comes through our sensory organs. It is the impressions of our sensory stimuli that have the power to cultivate our mind. What we absorb and digest through our eyes (sense of sight), ears (sense of sound), nose (sense of smell), skin (sense of touch) and tongue (sense of taste) can be either healing or keeling. I'm not saying that a little sensory indulgence every now and then is going to do any serious damage, but if you are constantly overindulging in something that unbalances your doshas, it can be potentially harmful to your health over the long term. Everything in moderation is my motto.

Today, with our exposure to social and mass media, we are bombarded with information; our senses are overloaded with impressions, and this is very unnatural. We are constantly looking externally for the next thing to stimulate us. Not to mention that our total immersion in and obsession with social media means that we are losing touch with our own reality and lives. I am just old enough to remember life before the explosion of mobile devices and email, and while it revolutionised the way in which we communicate, from my experience I can say that my social relations felt much stronger before the smartphone (which became an indulgence in itself), because the relationships were deeper than just virtual. Please be my guest to take a moment here to ponder this in your reality.

Sensory indulgence could include, for example, late-night horror movies that can trigger negative perceptions. Such impressions can be disturbing to your sleep and emotions and cause imbalance to the release of melatonin, the hormone responsible for sleep. Blasting loud music every day on your headphones can disturb your energy and sense of hearing over time. Of course, there are times where we cannot control what comes into our sensory field, but we can at least consciously, where possible, absorb more positive impressions and connect more with nature. Neuroscientific research indicates that stimulants affect our consciousness. We can take care of our physical body, but we pay little attention to the types of impressions we digest.

A great way to connect with your senses is through silence. Meditation can help you connect with your inner wisdom and give your sensory organs the much-needed conscious rest and rejuvenation they need. I am a morning person, but that doesn't mean I jump out of bed, have a coffee, turn on the radio or TV and check my social media feed, and I certainly don't like to engage in too much conversation first thing in the morning. This is my sacred time and space to check in with myself. Give yourself the 'me' space that you deserve.

Having clear and pleasant aromas in your environment can help stimulate positive responses in your olfactory receptors, which are situated deep in your nasal passages. These receptors are connected to the limbic system, the part of the brain that governs your emotions, behaviour and long-term memory. Your sense of smell is linked more to your memory than any other sense. For this reason, your associations with smell can evoke pleasant and healing benefits. It can lower your stress levels, bring a sense of awakening, induce sleep, improve concentration and make you feel good about yourself.

The sense of smell would have been more powerful in humans during the primitive age because of the way in which it was used for survival and hunting. Although you won't be needing your sense of smell to go hunting for your food anytime soon, what remains is your associations to various smells and the effect on the body and brain. It is on this basis that aromatherapy is established.

One way of healing all your senses is to connect with nature. I love to connect with nature, no matter the season or location – whether it's the flower gardens of Regent's Park in the summer, the rain in the muddy countryside in Northern Ireland, a long walk along a sandy beach with the salty sea breeze in Goa or the wonder and awe when you reach the summit of that mountain climb in Peru. Each time I connect with nature, it brings me back to the present moment and connects me to my inner self.

Practical exercises for sensory detox

- Digital detox! The simplest and easiest way to create peace and balance is to refrain from using digital and electronic devices for a short period of time every day – 15–20 minutes a day to start, more if you can. This will reduce exposure to electromagnetic radio waves. Just notice the difference it makes. Practise this every day for the next week and make a note in your journal. Better still, try it for a whole day a week.
- Take some silent time for yourself. Try it for a day or two; after the initial anxiety, your mind will settle and become clearer and you will start to feel a sense of peace within.

- Pop down to your local health shop and have a smell of the vast array of essential oils; see which ones you connect with and feel pleasant to you. Maybe they possess properties that can bring balance to your life. I adore burning scented candles, incense and essential oils for this very reason.
- Why don't you take a moment to remember the last time you truly connected with nature and make it a regular practice? Take a walk in the woods, on the beach or up the mountains.
- Maybe a couple of days at a quiet countryside retreat could be just the holiday that your soul craves. It will give you a chance to focus on all of the above.

Environmental detox

'The environment is everything that isn't me'

Albert Einstein

Whenever I go through a declutter of my home and workspace, it seems to bring with it a real sense of physical and mental clarity. Less really is more! The truth is, we need very few possessions in our lives, yet we have become experts at hoarding. Energetically, when you get rid of possessions that no longer serve a purpose in your life, you create space for newness.

Your environment includes any space that surrounds you, from your car, office, home, gym, places you travel and ultimately the entire universe. There is no doubt that your environment influences your health. Whether you are in the process of a detox or not, being in or as close to nature as possible will bring holistic healing as well as a lift in your mood. There is nothing wrong with bringing a little piece of nature into your workspace. I do this all the time, especially since our workplaces have become breeding grounds for potentially harmful positive ions generated by industrial lights, computers, TVs, electrical equipment, printers and photocopiers.

A scientific relative of Ayurveda known as **vastu shastra** is the ancient Vedic science that explores the connection between humans and our dwellings. *Vastu* is the science of architecture based on directional alignment, the five elements and energy flow. This science teaches us how to align ourselves to our space to bring health, prosperity and harmony to our lives. A vastu consultant will suggest how to design your rooms based on astrology and how to position the various contents within the room to maximise positive energy, as well as clear the negative energies in the home. It is a fascinating science and I for one want to learn more.

You can choose bedroom colours that balance your mind/body type. For example, earthy colours balance vata, cooling colours balance pitta and warm and vibrant colours balance kapha. Of course, when you share a space with a partner with the opposite prakruti, you may need to compromise or find some common ground that balances you both.

Practical exercises

- In the summertime, if you have an outdoor green space, take the opportunity to walk barefoot or stand and meditate on the fresh dewy grass. I do this when I am feeling particularly disconnected and I find it really grounding and awakening.
- Declutter! How do you feel when you have had a good old spring-clean? Are you ready for newness? What do you want to create space for in your life? Time to clear out all the old energy.
- Perhaps you might create a space where you have pictures of loved ones, flowers and plants, candles, incense, crystals, and so on – a sacred space for yourself that makes your

environment feel warm and cosy. Buy yourself a plant or flowers for the home or office.

- Is it time for a little bedroom decoration? Bring some balancing colours, freshness and a peaceful ambience to your sacred spaces.

Occupational detox

Do what you love or love what you do! How much satisfaction, enjoyment, happiness or peace does your job bring you? If you say a lot then perhaps you have found your vocation in life and that is great. Are you in your job simply because you have to pay the bills or because it's just comfortable, or is it because that is all you have ever done or known? Or don't feel you have the skills to change and feel stuck in a rut? Or perhaps you are still not sure what is your life purpose?

Since we spend most of our adult life at our place of work, it is one of the most influential factors that can disturb our emotions and mind. If we lack job satisfaction or even passion, it can lead to imbalances that can affect our health in the long term.

More recently, I have been seeing many clients who are not happy in their workplace and complain of stress, sleeplessness, weight increase and depression. At this point you can take time to figure out what your passions are for work or as a hobby. Journaling is a great tool.

I feel truly blessed to be able to have found a perfect marriage of passion and life purpose with Ayurveda. Though it wasn't the easiest transition and took several years to get there, it all feels worth it now. I just remember sitting at my desk in my job one day feeling that the work that I was doing was not what I was put on this earth to do and, although I enjoyed my job in the most part, there was a sense of deep dissatisfaction. Soon after I decided to take a leap of faith and quit, I spent several months travelling and landed in New York where I was committed to start a course in

Ayurveda. Turns out, the course was not right for me and I was back in London with my tail between my legs, not knowing what I should do or whether I should simply go back to an office role which just didn't feel like the right path. After a few months, I found another UK-based course in Ayurvedic medicine with incredible doctors and teachers for whom, to this day, I hold the utmost respect and gratitude. I haven't looked back since. Though I spent the best part of four years in classrooms, even at the weekends, the risk I had taken to pursue this journey was worth every minute. Ten years on since setting up my clinic, I continue to help clients on their journey of wellness with Ayurveda, helping them to grow and evolve at a pace that feels right for them.

Not everyone will want to turn their passions into a career but nothing is impossible. If you believe it, you can create it. People are ever-ready to judge, criticise and push back on your dreams but the only opinion that truly matters is your own. Can you nurture your passion into a sustainable hobby that encourages deep satisfaction and joy which can offset any dissatisfaction in your work?

Your mind/body type will certainly shed a little light on the type of work that you may be naturally suited to. Vata types are naturally drawn to creative roles such as teaching, writing, acting, communication, the arts etc. However, it is worth remembering that irregular lifestyle patterns such as travel and late nights can quickly imbalance vata types. Even in your job you need to stay balanced and grounded by sticking to routines and having meditation practices. Pitta types are natural-born leaders with their organised, intelligent and focused minds, and are great in the fields of law, finance and politics. Pitta types need to guard against becoming competitive, critical and dominating in the workplace. You can stay balanced by exercising your listening and compassion skills. There is more to life than people meeting pitta's high expectations and standards. Kapha types are relaxed, stable and methodical in their approach to work. These people are great in a job where love and compassion are central, such as nursing and horticulture. For kapha types you need to be aware of when people are taking advantage of your good nature. Ensure you exercise assertiveness with your colleagues and take breaks to move your body and freshen your mind from being too static.

Journaling exercise

Here are some questions you can answer in the private space of your journal if you feel that you are in need of an occupational detox:

- Is your passion something that you can turn into a career?
- What is your life purpose?
- What is your personal mission in this lifetime?
- What are your special gifts and talents?
- What have you come here to contribute?
- Are you getting in your own way?
- Perhaps you can look at courses and classes that awaken your passions, whether it is dance, yoga, health sciences or creative writing.

Relationship detox

'Spiritual relationship is far more precious than physical. Physical relationship divorced from spiritual is body without soul'

Mahatma Gandhi

Your relationships are instrumental to the quality of your health. We grow and expand in love and contract in loneliness. A healthy balance of time alone for self-reflection and time spent with loved ones is essential. It is in the presence of others and especially close romantic relationships that we can truly grow. Sure, it is going to bring up challenges and sometimes you may feel like running away, but all relationships exist to teach us something. Your ability to self-reflect and stay flexible within a relationship will enable you to be the best version of yourself. The truth is, as humans we are born social beings, and interaction is a natural part of our daily life.

In my clinic, I see many clients who present physical health issues that stem from difficulties in their relationships, either with their spouse, parents, siblings or work colleagues. On a physical level, this is reflected by issues surrounding sleep, weight gain, stress, anxiety and depression. What is important is how you accept yourself, how you prioritise your soul's needs and how much love and respect you have for yourself.

The healthiest relationships are the ones where you accept yourself, the good bits and the bad bits, and practise self-love and self-care. Only then are you able to express love for others in a genuine way. Healthy relationships set people free, but I see so many people who feel bound and restrained in their relationships. Healthy relationships are a balance of giving and receiving in all senses of the word. If you struggle to receive love from another, then it is possible you may have limited self-love.

Now, I am no love doctor, but if you understand the energetics of human needs and desires then you can certainly grasp what constitutes healthy relationships. While romantic relationships are exciting and lustful in the beginning, an element of this excitement should remain throughout your relationship. Someone once told me that you have to feed the relationship in order to help it grow. In the happiest relationships I have seen, there is always mutual respect, support, space and comradery. Healthy relationships have longer periods of constants among a few ups and downs, and not the other way around. How does your relationship measure up?

It is equally important to recognise when relationships of any nature are no longer serving you. No two relationships will ever have the same dynamics. This doesn't just refer to romantic relationships but also to relationships with your parents, siblings, children, friends, clients, students and colleagues. Here are some things you can do to nurture healthy relationships with those around you:

- Accept people for who they are and not who you want them to be. Everyone walking this earth's plane is on a different journey.
- Don't sweat the small stuff. If it's not going to matter in years to come, don't let it matter now.
- Are you really listening? We often listen just to be able to give a smart answer back. Sometimes people just need to be really heard without the need for a quick response or an opinion.
- Laugh it out. Bring lightness and humour to serious situations. Laughter really is the best medicine.
- Patience is a virtue. Allow the person to evolve in their own way, at their own pace. Despite your frustrations, remember it is not your journey.
- Be authentic both with yourself and others. Truth will always prevail.
- Do not immediately see ill intention behind another person's actions. You are not the sole focus of another person's actions, despite what your ego may think.
- Take responsibility for your thoughts, emotions, actions and reactions. As hard a pill as it is to swallow, no one can ever 'do' anything to us unless we allow it. While we cannot control another's actions, we can however control our actions and reactions. Always opt for the mindful path.

These are not easy guidelines to live by, but we can at least try our best.

Emotional detox

Letting go and true forgiveness are life's hardest challenges. Somewhere deep down in your being resides a bank of accumulated emotions, some of which may be very old and negative. Pain, regret, guilt, anger, hurt, fear, loneliness, grief, hate, worry ... the list goes on. Not only can harbouring negative emotions hold us back from our life's full potential, but it can have a harmful impact on our health. You know, the type of health issues that seem such a surprise and don't have a clear pathogenesis?

We cleanse our body in various internal and external ways and, in this book, I also talk about techniques to cleanse the mind. We take time to rest and eat warming and nurturing foods when we have a cold or flu. But what about care for your emotional body? Do you go on pushing through the pain of negative emotions? Sure, there are moments in which we need to stay strong, but being authentic and giving yourself permission to feel your feelings, accept them, work through them and let them go if they don't serve you is the only way to truly cleanse your emotional self. This is, unfortunately, rarely acknowledged.

The truth may be ugly or painful, but nevertheless it is the truth. For me, honesty really is the best policy and, by that, I mean be honest with yourself. What are you feeling? Are you open about your feelings? Finding ways to numb the pain won't resolve the issue in the long term, even though in the short term it may seem like the only option.

Are you freely able to express your pain and emotions? Crying is not a sign of weakness, it is a physical form of expressing deep-seated emotions and creating the space to let go. Sometimes a good cry can be all the therapy that is needed. It is a way for your soul to shed the 'old' emotions and patterns.

The art of 'letting go'

Detach from what is going on around you for a while to give yourself space to reflect and feel. Distractions may seem like a great answer, but they are exactly that – a distraction from addressing what is truly going on within you. Turn off your phone if you need some time out. Take a break and go for a walk as a start. Minimise non-essential activities so you can focus on emotional healing and spiritual connection to your higher self.

Physically allow yourself to increase oxygen, hydration, exercise and rest as a way to connect to your emotional body. Aside from dietary and lifestyle changes, meditation, pranayama and spiritual knowledge can help wash away those pains. There is a myriad of disciplines out there and hundreds of experts who can help you work through your deep-seated emotional pain in a way that suits you best; we are all unique, so different techniques will resonate for different people. There are also some incredible books that will inspire you to drop the emotional baggage and set yourself free. Much of the focus is on a shift in your perception and belief patterns.

If you ever decide to have rules for yourself let your first one be:

To be gentle and kind to yourself.

It is from this point that your journey of emotional healing can begin.

If you want to begin the healing process yourself, then keeping a journal is a great starting point. It can help you identify negative emotions and where they might stem from, in a safe and confidential place. Journaling helps you to be really honest with yourself – you don't need to hide, and once it is written down and out of your mind, you can even ceremonially burn it if you want to. Techniques such as affirmations and the emotional freedom technique (EFT) can be effective tools for self-healing. EFT, also known as 'tapping', is a technique whereby you can gently shift your belief structure and mindset by using your fingertips to tap on the end points of energy meridians that reside under the skin while making statements about a particular emotional blockage – for example, a fear around public speaking or a fear of heights or an inability to break a habit such as coffee or sugar. Theta healing, sound healing, reiki, hypnotherapy, angelic healing, energy healing and prayer are some of the wonderful tools to help you connect to your deeper being and create shifts that can bring joy, freedom and inner peace.

Affirmations

Affirmations are a powerful and simple tool to create and support positive wellbeing. They are statements that you can make about anything in your life to create a positive shift in your conscious and subconscious mind. These sentences will energise and motivate, as well as purify your thoughts – after all, we are what we think. Clearly affirm what you want to experience as if it is already granted.

Here are some examples of affirmations:
- My body is healthy, my mind is clear, my soul is peaceful
- Today, I let go of unhealthy habits and embrace healthy new ones
- Every cell in my body vibrates with energy and health
- I nourish my body with healthy food and positive thoughts
- I sleep peacefully and soundly, feeling rested and energetic when I awake
- I send love and healing to every organ of my body
- I wake up in the morning feeling happy and enthusiastic about life

Rasayana: rejuvenation and healthy ageing

'Our bodies are our gardens – our wills are our gardeners'
William Shakespeare

Rasayana is a rejuvenative therapy that helps your body and mind to regain strength after detoxification, and a specialist area of Ayurveda dedicated to delaying the negative effects of ageing. If you are recovering from a cold or flu or have completed a detox, your body can become vulnerable; the idea of rasayana is to replenish your body and mind with supporting (**brmhana**) foods and herbs so that you can rebuild your resilience and immunity to external factors that cause stress in the body. After an Ayurvedic cleanse, I recommend that you also give yourself some time to reconnect to the flow of life and to nourish and nurture yourself.

The rasayana process and its supporting herbs are particularly useful if you are in old age, pregnant, recovering from an illness, have recently given birth, feel run-down or debilitated, or have anaemia. It is also helpful for children.

Ayurvedic rejuvenation can:
- Protect the body from premature ageing
- Slow down ageing and restore your youthful looks
- Strengthen your ability to fight disease
- Enhance the quality of your body tissues
- Protect your body from free radical damage by taking herbs with antioxidant qualities
- Improve mental alertness and memory
- Boost ojas – your life force energy

Rasayana works best on a well-cleansed system. I do not advise undergoing rasayana if you still have ama in the body, are overweight or are experiencing allergies or acute illness.

In order to follow a rasayana diet, a strong digestive fire is important since these foods can often be slightly heavy in nature.

Without good digestive strength, the body tissues will not be suitably nourished and ojas, which is the essence of all body tissues, will not be sustained.

Life-enchancing herbs

There's an abundance of wonderful plant-based herbs that can nourish and strengthen our ojas and immunity and slow down the process of ageing, as well as protect us against the harsh environment that we live in.

Below are some of my favourite single herbs and herbal compounds, which are easily available in good health food stores or online.

Aloe vera	The inner gel of this plant is a great anti-inflammatory due to its cooling and soothing action. Aloe delays ageing, improves the function of the liver and spleen, and supports gut flora. It can be applied externally to heal wounds and burns. Useful in increased pitta conditions.
Amalaki	An excellent antioxidant that protects against toxic invasion. One of the main ingredients of chyawanprash and triphala, this herb is great for a weakened body, especially one suffering anaemia. It helps to regulate blood sugar and enhance digestion and absorption. It promotes growth of new tissues, hair and nails, and delays the ageing process.
Ashwagandha	A fantastic nervine tonic, giving strength and power to the body and reproductive tissues (an aphrodisiac). Great for degenerative conditions and ageing when taken with milk and ghee. It has a sedative effect so can be effective as a sleep aid. It improves resilience to stress and anxiety.

Brahmi	As an adaptogen and nervine tonic, this is a great herb for mental and physical longevity. It helps to calm and clear mental disturbances, and is a rejuvenative for the brain. It has anti-inflammatory properties.
Chyawanprash	A sweet and sour herbal jam packed with nutritive herbs. Suitable for children, older people and anyone who has debility. Suitable for all dosha types. An energy and immunity tonic.
Guduchi	One of the best immune-boosting herbs, it increases energy and vitality and reduces the premature greying of hair. It enhances digestion and liver function and relieves acute respiratory infections. It helps resilience to stress and acts as an antioxidant.
Shatavari	A great female tonic, it regulates menstrual flow, and supports pregnancy, menopause and hormones. It brings nourishment and strength to the tissues, and soothes digestive inflammation. It is an adaptogen that enhances immunity and mental clarity.
Triphala	This is the best rejuvenative for the colon. It improves digestive fire, increases appetite, reduces constipation and regulates metabolism. It has antioxidant and antimicrobial properties.
Yastimadhu	Liquorice root is a great rasayana for complexion, voice, hair, eyes and nerves. It helps to relieve respiratory congestion. It has mild laxative properties, stimulates bile flow, reduces cholesterol and protects the liver. It has immune-boosting properties and increases resistance to viruses.

Rasayana foods

Certain foods are considered to have powerful rasayana qualities for the body, bringing back strength and nourishment to your body tissues. Some of these foods I will discuss in chapter 13; however, in the context of rasayana I want to highlight some useful foods that you can feature in your diet when you are in need of some extra va-va-voom.

Ghee increases ojas and is an elixir to health. Something about ghee just makes me feel that it is edible ojas in a jar. It is a nourishing tonic to the nervous system and the brain, especially when taken internally or through nasya (nasal errhine). It improves perception, clarity and memory. Ghee nourishes, supports and improves the function of the eyes. It can be used as drops or as a therapeutic bath (*netra tarpana*). Read more about the benefits of ghee on p. 195.

Cow's milk is strengthening for ojas and useful if you are feeling weak and malnourished. It supports cellular regeneration, brings mind clarity and joy, and boosts strength and immunity. Goat's milk is great for combating ageing, as it is light and easy to digest. In addition to milk, buttermilk (chaas) improves digestion, reduces fatigue, cleanses channels and increases appetite for food.

Ingredients with a natural sweet taste help to build body tissues. Jaggery is a raw cane sugar packed with minerals. Natural syrups, molasses, rock sugar and honey can all be beneficial but should be moderated considering our modern-day sugar-loaded diets. Honey has a great rejuvenating effect on the eyes, voice, complexion and intellect. Honey helps to gently remove excess waste matter from the body.

Healthy oils from raw nuts and seeds, and their butters and milks, improve vitality and nourish the nervous system. Almonds, cashews, pine nuts, walnuts, coconut and sesame seeds are all excellent nourishing options.

Spices such as ginger encourage the digestive fire; cardamom is good for respiratory support; cinnamon can be used for supporting reproductive tissue; garlic is useful as a cardio tonic, aphrodisiac and to stimulate the mind. So, gentle spices are always welcome rasayana ingredients.

Most grains, including wheat, oats, millet, rice, red rice and barley are nourishing and strengthening. Kitchari is the food of choice, since it is suitable for all doshas, light and easy to digest, not to mention delicious.

Black gram, red lentils and mung beans (sprouted or made into a dahl) are considered the best options in the legume group. This food group is more suited to pitta and kapha types.

Most meats promote muscle strength by their very nature. They have an aphrodisiac and nourishing quality. Meats can include goat, buffalo, chicken, partridge and pork. Meat in the form of soup is nourishing and easier to digest. A moderate amount of fresh- and saltwater fish can increase strength and agni, and nourish your body tissues.

Sweet and seasonal fruits are best for rebuilding tissue strength. Dates, raisins, figs, grapes, mangoes, bananas and pomegranates are all rejuvenating. Fruit should always be fresh and ripe.

Opt for grounding and sweet vegetables. Root vegetables are ideal, especially if cooked with ghee.

When I think of rasayana and simple dishes that incorporate a balance of tastes that nourish the body yet are simple and easy to digest, aside from fresh soups made using ghee, kheer pops into my mind. This sweet creamy rice pudding has all the ingredients to get your ojas pumping.

Spiced rice kheer

One of the most common desserts is a very simple preparation of milk and rice, better known as Indian rice pudding. It is a wonderful, nurturing dessert for the winter months, at the same time being wholesome and vata-pacifying.

Serves 3–4
Ingredients:
3 cups whole milk
½ cup basmati rice
½ tsp cardamom seeds, crushed
2 tbsp almonds, blanched and sliced
1 tbsp pistachio nuts, skinned and chopped
Pinch saffron
1 tbsp raisins (optional)
3–4 tbsp jaggery, sugar or honey to taste
1 tsp ghee to finish

Method:
Soak the rice for 10 minutes and drain.

Heat the milk, rice, and cardamom in a medium pan and bring to the boil, then simmer gently and keep stirring to prevent lumps. Cook until the rice is soft and starting to break, around 20–25 minutes.

Add the sugar and raisins (if using) and simmer for a further 4–5 minutes. If you are using honey, add at the time of serving – do not heat it.

Remove from the heat and serve while warm. Drizzle with ghee and garnish with almonds, pistachios and saffron.

CHAPTER 12

Food as Medicine

'When diet is wrong, medicine is of no use. When diet is correct, medicine is of no need'

Ancient Ayurvedic proverb

If your gut microbiome is not working adequately, you won't only struggle to digest the bad foods but also the good foods too, and this is my focal point in clinic. When it comes to your health, you have total control over how you nourish, balance and heal yourself through food choices.

It's not just about what you're eating, but what is eating you? Everything on this earth can be medicinal and healing, but the same substances taken inappropriately can also make you imbalanced and can lead to disease. Let's take milk, for example. A cup of boiled and spiced milk can be nourishing for your body, but a glass of cold milk if you are suffering from a cold can significantly increase mucus.

As a necessity of life, food brings people together through its diverse flavours, textures and cultural depth; and is a huge subject we all just love to talk about. Well, I certainly do! Cooking and mealtimes were once the focal point of family life, but somehow we have lost this magic, as we are constantly rushing around – having meals on the go and often eating out in the evenings; we grab a salad or a sandwich, eat at our desk, while we continue to work or browse the internet.

The food we eat comprises the same five elements as our body.

Having an awareness of what elements are present in our food can help us make better decisions to eat foods that balance our dosha and to limit those foods that can cause imbalances.

Food in Ayurveda is traditionally classified in terms of its energetics, such as taste (**rasa**), quality (**guna**), potency (**virya**), post-digestive action (**vipaka**), action (**karma**) and sometimes a special effect (**prabhava**), on the doshas rather than balance in terms of carbohydrates, fats and proteins. It is at this level that you can carefully sculpt the shape of your health. The Ayurvedic approach to nutrition is ingenious. Food is understood in terms of the taste and qualities that are experienced when we eat. Food is a central focus to healing in Ayurveda, not just an ancillary aspect, meaning that food is just as medicinal as medicines themselves.

One diet does not work for all

No one food is intrinsically good or bad for you, as everyone reacts differently to foods. So, there is no one ideal diet for people to follow. Remember, you are unique, and so should your diet be. Various considerations need to be taken into account when working out the personalised diet that is right for you. Choosing a suitable diet is essential to preventing and treating disease.

Just because we live in the Western world does not mean we are immune to malnutrition. Our bodies are overfed, yet we are starved of essential nutrients. Our diets lack the variety of natural, colourful and 'prana'-rich foods that are too often replaced by processed foods that bring convenience. Despite the welcome surge of global cuisines now available, the diversity and quality of day-to-day basic food intake for the majority of us has diminished over the years and in my opinion, limits our exposure to essential nutrients.

Food should nourish, build and repair every cell in our body. A balanced diet also nurtures the subtle energies of our body, mind, senses and spirit, providing strength, vigour, glow and emotional healing.

Knowing when to eat and when not to eat is key to keeping the digestive health strong. While we should not ignore hunger, we should be able to differentiate between a genuine hunger and a mental craving. We can often mistake thirst as hunger too. So, try having a herbal tea and see if your hunger dissipates.

I often see clients who consume foods when no hunger is present, even at mealtimes, indicating that the digestive enzymes are not ready to work. We want our body to feel hunger at the right time.

Give yourself a couple of weeks to notice the patterns of your genuine hunger and honour that. Eventually you will establish a good pattern with timings that suit your body type and lifestyle.

Diet is central to your health

A wholesome diet is central to health, and no other science details food and its properties as thoroughly as Ayurveda. Without it, there is no true health and healing, no matter how many pills you swallow.

Now, while I am almost certain that at the point of eating you will not be thinking about how your food converts and nourishes your body, it is still worth bearing in mind that a healthy and wholesome diet should:

- Be satisfying to the palate and the body
- Increase body strength and provide sufficient energy
- Maintain the regular functions of the body and tissue nourishment
- Increase longevity
- Stimulate the digestive fire, increase vitality and immunity
- Be eaten while hot and unctuous, and not dry or cold
- Be a suitable portion size
- Be suitable to the climate and season
- Be suitable to the dosha

As discussed in chapter 10, how your body is able to digest is central to optimal health but a wholesome diet alone does not guarantee good health.

An unhealthy diet does not just comprise unwholesome foods – there are certain habits that can weaken the agni and imbalance your doshas:

- Mixing healthy and unhealthy foods
- Overeating or undereating
- Having imbalanced tastes in a meal: if you only eat foods of a single taste – for example, the sweet taste – it can cause an imbalance
- Eating foods that are excessively pungent, sour, astringent or salty
- Eating foods that are not suited to the climate of residence
- Eating foods that are not suitable for the season
- Eating foods that are of poor quality
- Eating foods that aggravate your mind/body type
- Eating foods when your digestive power is weak
- Eating incompatible foods
- Eating excessive amounts of raw foods
- Eating foods that are processed, stale, cold, old, fermented or heavy to digest
- Eating foods at irregular hours. Midnight munchies get the spotlight here!
- Not eating when hunger is present and eating when hunger is not present
- Eating foods that you are not habitually accustomed to

In the ancient days, each and every food and ingredient was considered by its taste and quality. In food preparation, knowing which foods will nourish the body tissues and balance the doshas was the true essence of food being medicine and medicine being food. A balanced meal according to Ayurveda will be simple, tasty and nutritious and will include all six tastes in suitable quantities.

Your relationship to food

Changes to your diet and lifestyle will depend on your commitment, your strengths and weaknesses, the scale and speed of change, and your attitude towards how you eat. I suggest making changes slowly, so that you can ensure they stick in the long term. Following the Ayurvedic path is more than calorie counting! Your state of mind, state of agni and the energetics of the foods you consume all have an impact on your health.

We have lost the art of eating, and, in many cases, we have become overly restricted by following diets that are deemed to be 'healthy'. Food is, of course, functional and needs to be wholesome, but it is also designed to delight the palate. So, there is a fine art to choosing foods that are nourishing for your body, senses and emotions. Any substance consumed in excess is capable of creating an imbalance. The same is true for the time of day a food is eaten. For example, a heavy meal eaten in the evening will not digest as well as it would if eaten at lunchtime. Eating hot, spicy foods in the summer will aggravate the fire in your body and lots of dry foods in the latter stages of life will create an increase in vata.

Balancing six tastes

Dosha	Balancing tastes	Imbalancing tastes
Vata	Sweet, sour, salty	Bitter, pungent, astringent
Pitta	Sweet, bitter, astringent	Sour, salty, pungent
Kapha	Pungent, bitter, astringent	Sweet, sour, salty

Not everyone enjoys food and tastes in the same way. One person will have a really sweet tooth, and another may love the saltiness of a food. The same food may taste spicy to one person and not at all to another. Your perception of taste is very personal, and certain tastes are more suitable for you, once you start to understand which tastes are balancing for your mind/body type. Taste is nature's way of telling us what is good for us and the effect it will have on our body's physiology. Listen to your body. This is the essence of living in tune with nature.

Every food and ingredient has a unique taste profile – rasa. As we know, there are six tastes – sweet, sour, salty, bitter, pungent and astringent – and each has a different quality and different actions on the doshas but all are important in satisfying our overall health.

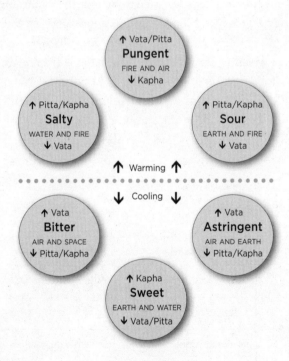

Six tastes in Ayurveda

Taste	Increasing effect (↑) and decreasing effect (↓) on dosha	Qualities	Action in body	Food source examples
Sweet	↑ Kapha ↓ Vata/ Pitta	Cold Heavy Moist/ oily	Builds tissues, increases strength, calms nerves, increases weight, brings comfort, moistens digestive system, awakens mind	Beans and lentils, cardamom, cinnamon, coconut, fats, fennel, grains, milk and dairy products, oils, rice, root vegetables, sweet fruits including dried fruits, wheat
Sour	↑ Pitta/ Kapha ↓ Vata	Hot Heavy Moist/ oily	Cleanses tissues and increases appetite, aids absorption of minerals and maintains mineral balance, moistens, increases fluids, soothes nerves	Cheese, chutneys, fermented foods (wine, vinegar, sauerkraut, soy sauce), pickles, sour fruits (apples, berries, citrus, pineapple, plum), tamarind, tomatoes, yoghurt

Salty	↑ Pitta/ Kapha ↓ Vata	Hot Heavy Moist/ oily	Improves taste of food, lubricates tissues and stimulates digestion, dries and removes ama, clears congestion in channels	Anchovies, fish, natural salts and sea vegetables (sea kelp, seaweed), pickles
Bitter	↑ Vata ↓ Pitta/ Kapha	Cold Light Dry	Detoxifies, de-blocks and lightens the tissues, dries ama and mucus, opens channels and eliminates blockages	Aloe vera, bitter melon, coffee, dandelion greens, dark chocolate, fenugreek, grapefruit, green vegetables (green cabbage, spinach, kale), neem, olives, tea, turmeric
Pungent	↑ Vata/ Pitta ↓ Kapha	Hot Light Dry	Stimulates digestion, metabolism and burns ama	Black pepper, chilli peppers, clove, garlic, ginger, horseradish, mustard, onions, radish, rocket, wasabi

				Artichoke, asparagus, broccoli, coffee, cranberries, green veg, marjoram, old honey, pears, pomegranate, quinoa, red wine, rye, tannins in tea, turmeric
Astringent	↑ Vata ↓ Pitta/ Kapha	Cold Light Dry	Absorbs water, strengthens tissues, dries fats	

Sweet taste (**madhura**)

Elements: earth and water

Who doesn't love something sweet? Over the last few decades, our concept of what is 'sweet' has evolved significantly and we are now accustomed to associating it with refined sugar. However, the real and natural sweet taste has a very important function in nourishing and fuelling the body with its cooling, heavy and unctuous qualities. This taste relieves ravenous hunger, brings strength, growth and development to all body tissues, increases vitality and, of course, increases body mass. 'Sweet taste' refers to foods that have a natural sweetness to them and can include milk, grains such as rice and wheat, and root vegetables.

Sweet-tasting foods bring joy to your senses and emotions, as well as vitality to the body, and should form the bulk of your diet. The result of having a balanced sweet taste in your diet is lustrous-looking skin and hair.

An overindulgence in the consumption of foods with a sweet taste will reduce the digestive fire and can lead to excess weight, feelings of lethargy and heaviness and blood sugar imbalances. Kapha can easily increase if the sweet taste is taken in excess, so kapha types should moderate their intake of this taste.

Sour taste (**amla**)

Elements: earth and fire

Sour-tasting foods are generally stimulating and refreshing for the body and mind. This is a necessary taste to increase appetite, relieve thirst, improve digestion, absorb foods, and stimulate circulation and elimination. Like the sweet taste, it helps to build all body tissues except the reproductive tissues. This taste sharpens our senses and supports heart function. This taste is balancing for vata types since it is warming and is useful in stimulating the digestive fire.

In excess, this taste can increase heat. The pH balance of the gut can get upset and lead to acidity, indigestion, heartburn, and over time skin problems, ulcers and burning sensations in the chest and bladder. The heavy quality of this taste can also lead to increased kapha if consumed in excess, so kapha types should not overindulge in this taste, although a little is beneficial and stimulating to kapha. Pitta types also need to moderate the sour taste due to its heating qualities.

Salty taste (**lavana**)

Elements: fire and water

A flavour dear to my heart, as most people who know me well will know. Salt brings out the flavours of all our foods and increases our appetite, digestion and absorption of food. It lubricates the body tissues, supports elimination of waste and detoxifies the body. It can have a grounding and calming effect on the nerves and reduce cramps and spasms. With its penetrating effect, salt can help to open blocked channels by liquefying mucus and can support the action of other ingredients – for example, when taken with warm prune juice, it can increase the effectiveness in relieving constipation. Rock salt and sea salts are the preferred salts in Ayurveda.

Vata individuals can be balanced by this taste, but an excess of salt, especially for pitta types, can increase heat, acidity, high blood pressure, inflammation and skin irritations. It can lead to fluid retention in the body, it can weaken the muscles and it can contribute to premature ageing and the greying of hair. For kapha types, excessive salt intake, due to its damp and heavy nature, can lead to swelling and obesity.

Pungent taste (**katu**)

Elements: air and fire
Foods that pack a bit of a punch get my thumbs-up, as they can burn off ama, destroy bacteria and parasites, and strengthen agni, thereby improving appetite, digestion and absorption. With its penetrating properties, this taste can clear the body channels, improve circulation, reduce cholesterol and detoxify by promoting sweat and stimulating the mind.

If your mind/body type is kapha-dominant, then this taste can be very beneficial, but for the fiery pitta types who are the ones who usually love spice, an excess of this taste can be unbalancing. It can create heartburn, ulcers, diarrhoea, dry skin, skin rashes and the depletion of reproductive tissues. Due to its drying effect, vata types should moderate their intake of this taste too.

Bitter taste (**tikta**)

Elements: ether and air
The light, cool and drying properties of this taste are highly detoxifying and cleansing for the mind and body. Of course, this taste is not always pleasing to the palate and that is why we say, 'a bitter pill to swallow'. This taste has the ability to reduce cravings; therefore, this is the taste of choice in weight loss and fat reduction. With its drying quality, it can reduce mucus, excess water and sweat, while keeping skin firm. Bitter-tasting foods can balance digestion, clear ama from the digestion and support liver cleansing and the flow of bile.

This taste is highly beneficial for pitta and kapha types, but in excess it can aggravate vata, triggering constipation, anxiety and insomnia. This taste only needs to be eaten in a small to moderate quantity, as bitter foods are generally quite strong in taste and action, and can help balance all the other tastes.

Astringent taste (kashaya)

Elements: air and earth

This cooling, light and dry taste makes your mouth pucker and feel dry or chalky, so really it is more of a sensation than an actual taste. Imagine what your mouth feels like when you consume an unripe banana, the skin of a grape or a high-tannin red wine. Astringency reduces the saliva in the mouth and dries out other secretions such as mucus.

The astringent taste can help tone and protect the mucosal lining of the digestive tract from inflammation, irritations and infections. It is great for ulcerations, colitis and gastritis. This taste is usually taken in minimal amounts and can be balancing for pitta and kapha but aggravating for vata in excess, as it can be drying and blocking.

Ideally, every meal should include all six tastes in balanced quantities, in the order as stated above. For example, the sweet taste includes carbohydrates, sugars, amino acids and fats and should dominate your plate, as these are the most nourishing foods. If you are prone to suffering from certain health issues, you can use the principles of taste to choose foods that will be more balancing. Variety of foods is key to ensuring you get a good balance of tastes in your diet. Remember, serious illnesses do not manifest by eating one unbalancing meal; the cumulative effect of continually irregular meals is what leads to a dosha imbalance and, eventually, to health issues.

The qualities of food

In addition to the concept of tastes in Ayurveda, all foods and herbs are assessed on their qualities or attributes, known as gunas. They fall broadly into ten pairs of opposite qualities. Ten are brmhana (nourishing) and ten are langhana (lightening).

Nourishing (brmhana)	Lightening (langhana)
guru (heavy)	**laghu** (light)
sheeta (cold)	**ushna** (hot)
snigdha (oily)	**ruksha** (dry)
manda (dull)	**tiksna** (sharp)
sandra (solid)	**drava** (liquid)
mrdu (soft)	**kathina** (hard)
sthira (static)	**chala** (mobile)
pichilla (viscous)	**visada** (clear)
sthula (gross)	**sukshma** (subtle)
slaksna (smooth)	**khara** (rough)

As we know, like increases like, so a vata person, for example, who consumes foods that have the same qualities as vata dosha, such as dry, light and cold, will increase their vata into an imbalanced state. Foods that have opposite qualities to the doshas can be balancing. So, if a vata person consumes heavy, hot and oily foods, they will remain balanced. Understanding the simple qualities of food means that you do not need to stress about memorising long food lists.

In everyday clinical use, we usually focus on six main gunas: heavy, light, hot, cold, dry and oily. If you pick any food, you can ask yourself which of these six qualities does this food have, what is its dominant taste? Does it balance or unbalance you?

Guna	Increasing effect (↑) and decreasing effect (↓) on dosha	Action on body
Guru (heavy)	↑ Kapha ↓ Pitta/Vata	It nourishes the body tissues, increases waste
Laghu (light)	↑ Vata/Pitta ↓ Kapha	It reduces weight, clears channels, improves digestion
Ruksha (dry)	↑ Vata ↓ Kapha/Pitta	It has a negative effect on body tissues, absorbs moisture, reduces excreta
Snigdha (oily)	↑ Kapha/Pitta ↓ Vata	It builds, lubricates and tonifies body tissues
Ushna (hot)	↑ Pitta ↓ Vata/Kapha	It has a mild heating effect on the body, increases metabolism and acidity
Sheeta (cold)	↑ Vata/Kapha ↓ Pitta	It decreases metabolism, reduces body temperature, produces a pleasant feeling

The potency of food

Every food has either a heating or cooling effect on the body. Depending on the health issues you are trying to balance, knowing the heating or cooling potency (virya) of foods can influence your food choices. Unless there is an imbalance of the pitta dosha, freshly prepared warm foods are generally the best option, as they are easier to digest than cold foods. The body is able to easily break down and metabolise the food. Cold foods require more energy in the process of digestion, taking away energy from other body functions.

Sweet, bitter and astringent tastes are all cooling, while sour, salty and pungent tastes are heating. You need a balance of these energies for good digestion and you should be led by your mind/body type.

Post-digestive effects of food

The six tastes are converted during the digestion and assimilation process. This transformed taste at the end of digestion is called vipaka and this can have a specific action on the body. A practitioner may often direct you to certain foods for their post-digestive effect on the body to balance various health issues. Here is how the tastes are converted post digestion and their effects:

Taste (rasa)	Post-digestive taste (vipaka)	Action on body
Sweet	Sweet	Aggravates kapha. Promotes tissue growth. Laxative and diuretic effect
Salty		
Sour	Sour	Aggravates pitta. Depletes body tissues. Laxative and diuretic effect
Bitter	Pungent	Aggravates vata. Depletes body tissues. Aggravates constipation
Pungent		
Astringent		

Food and the mind

Food affects our mind and emotions just as much as our physical body and we often refer to our relationship with food in the language that we use – for example, 'left a bitter taste', 'sour grapes', 'couch potato', 'cool as a cucumber'. Tastes affect our emotions in the following ways:

- Sweet taste promotes love, warmth and affection, pacifies the overactive vata mind and cools the pitta mind
- Salty tastes are soothing for the vata mind but intensify the pitta irritations
- Sour tastes sharpen the mind and senses, but can aggravate anger in pitta types

- Bitter tastes can clear the foggy minds of kapha types and cool the emotional pitta mind
- Pungent tastes awaken the kapha mind but can quickly heat the pitta mind and cause it to become aggressive
- Astringent tastes can stimulate fear and insecurity in vata types

Pure foods equal a pure mind

Sattvic foods

Why is it that certain foods leave you feeling dull and others leave you feeling clear and light? As mentioned earlier, your mind is influenced by the qualities of sattva, rajas and tamas. In order to keep your mind clear, focused and alert, foods that are pure, vibrant and full of life are the best choice.

Ingredients that have these qualities are considered sattvic in nature and optimally nourish your mind and should dominate your plate. Sattvic foods eaten in a balanced way do not aggravate the doshas and are considered the best for healing, increasing vitality and clarity.

Rajasic foods

In instances when you are feeling sluggish and dull, you need to have some rajasic foods that have a stimulating effect on the mind; but choose only those that are natural and purposeful for health and healing. Avoid those foods that are unnatural and over-stimulating, as they often lead to negative states of being such as anger, jealously, agitation, restlessness and excessive energy. Even sattvic foods can become rajasic and tamasic in nature if they are over-cooked, spiced, fried, old or cold.

Tamasic foods

Tamasic foods are those foods that are lifeless, poor quality and dull in energy, such as processed, fried, old and stale foods. They generally do not create energy for the mind or body, and they often require more energy in order to digest. If you have a habit of overeating or eating late, this can also increase tamas. Tamasic foods can be nourishing in a grounding and stabilising way but, like rajasic foods, only if they are kept pure and natural.

See the table below for examples of foods that are considered sattvic, rajasic and tamasic.

Type of food	Sattvic	Rajasic	Tamasic
Vegetables	Most fresh seasonal vegetables, carrots, sweet potato	Aubergine, broccoli, cauliflower, garlic, onion, potatoes, radish, spinach, tomatoes	Fried vegetables, potato crisps and chips, mushrooms
Fruits	All sweet seasonal fruits, dates, figs, raisins	Fruits with a sour quality, such as green apples, guava, grapefruit	Avocado, watermelon
Grains	Barley, quinoa, rice, rice milk, rye, tapioca, wheat	Buckwheat, corn, millet	Brown rice, pasta, wheat
Legumes	Mung beans, sprouted lentils	Aduki beans	Black beans, black gram, pinto beans
Herbs and spices	Black pepper, cardamom, coriander, cumin, fennel, fenugreek, ginger, rose, saffron, turmeric	Asafoetida, chillies, cinnamon, clove	

Type of food	Sattvic	Rajasic	Tamasic
Nuts and seeds	All nuts, especially almonds, cashews, pistachios, flax seeds	Peanuts	
Dairy and eggs	Butter, buttermilk, fresh cheese (paneer) in moderation, ghee, lassi, milk	Eggs, sour cream, yoghurt	Hard cheeses, ice creams
Sweeteners	Honey, raw cane sugar		Refined sugars
Salt	Rock salt	Sea salt	
Other food and drinks		Alcohol, caffeine (tea, coffee), chocolate, pickles and chutneys, vinegar. Fish and meat such as chicken, salmon, shrimps, tuna	Carbonated drinks, fermented foods, fried foods, microwaved foods, most meats and fish, old or stale foods, processed foods

If you are suffering from health problems where you lack clarity, concentration, poor memory or other mental health issues, please seek out an Ayurvedic practitioner who can guide you for your specific condition and prescribe medicinal herbs to give you extra support.

CHAPTER 13

Eat Yourself Healthy

'Leave your drugs in the chemist's pot if you can heal the patient with food'

Hippocrates

Energy at your fingertips

In the West, we are used to eating with a fork and knife; in the East, food is eaten with the hands, and there are practical reasons for this. Your sense of touch is awakened by feeling the texture and temperature of the food, so your mind and body can prepare itself for what is about to be consumed. Our five fingers represent the five elements, earth, water, fire, air and space. Using our hands enables us to infuse this collective energy into every morsel.

An insight into food combining

Our gut was not designed for overly complex varieties of food in one meal, as it can overwork our digestive system. The notion of correct food combining is geared to supporting the reduction of ama and ensuring agni stays strong. When foods are eaten correctly or separately, they can aid digestion. When we combine certain foods that require a conflicting digestive process, the digestive fire gets disturbed, slows down and can start to produce toxins in the system.

Not only can incompatible foods remain in the stomach for several hours, but combining foods improperly can cause indigestion, fermentation, putrefaction and gas formation. When foods are combined improperly over a prolonged period of time, it can lead to toxemia and to various other diseases.

Eating bananas with milk, eggs with fish, radishes with milk, lemon with yoghurt, melons with any other foods, raw foods with cooked food, and fruits with grains are just some examples of incompatible food combinations. What happens when we eat lemon and milk, for example? If you squeeze lemon in hot milk, it would instantly curdle and it's the same in your gut. The digestive enzymes that digest lemons cause the milk to curdle due to the sourness. This type of constant digestive confusion can be the cause of many diseases, especially respiratory or skin conditions.

An Ayurvedic practitioner will be able to offer you suitable dietary guidance, taking into consideration nutritional value, constitution, season, age and any disease condition. The key to all of this is to start slowly – take one thing at a time, such as beginning with separating fruits from other foods.

Incompatible foods

Ingredient	Incompatible with
Eggs	Fish, all fruit, cheese, meat, milk, yoghurt
Fruit	Any other food, particularly dairy
Honey	Toxic if boiled or used in cooking (for example, honey roasting)
Lemon	Cucumbers, milk, tomatoes, yoghurt
Melon	Dairy, fried foods, grains, starches. Melon is best eaten alone
Milk	Banana, fish, meat, melon, salt, sour fruits, yeasted bread, yoghurt

Nightshades	Other nightshades (aubergine, peppers, potato, tomato), cucumber, melon, milk, yoghurt, and all fruit
Radish	Banana, milk, raisins
Raw foods	Cooked foods
Grains	Most fruits
Yoghurt	Cheese, eggs, fish, hot drinks, mango, meat, melon, milk, nightshades, sour fruits

Some obvious incompatible food combinations we find in the Western diet include: fruits with yoghurt, cheese and grapes, melon and Parma ham, berry cheesecake, cheese omelette, bacon and sausage with eggs, cheese and tomato (toasties, pizza and pasta), fish pie, banana smoothie, orange juice with milk-based cereals, and fruits after meals. How many of these sound familiar to you?

Mealtime mantra

Saying a short prayer before each meal enhances calmness in the mind, with attention and intention focused on the food. For example:

'Brahmapanam brahma-havih, brahmagnau brahmana hutam,
brahmaiva tena gantavyam, brahma-karma-samadhina'
                                                    Bhagavad Gita

A simple translation of this would be: 'What I take comes from the divine, what I have to offer is to the divine, what I offer is the divine itself, I offer this food to my body, for I am also divine and the divine lives within me.'

There are no rules around how you pray or what you say, but what is important is that you pause before your food and connect with your meal with gratitude. Just notice the difference it makes as soon as you start.

Client story

'I had been suffering from acid reflux and low energy levels, and I hadn't been able to find a good solution. I was initially overwhelmed after my first consultation, but I decided to start small – it was easy to quit coffee, and I added the turmeric shots in the morning, and started cooking with coconut oil and ghee; I began taking herbal supplements like triphala, limiting some specific foods and eating aligned to my dosha. In a few weeks, I saw a very good result and felt excited to keep adding more things, using some of the recipes Geeta shared, like kitchari, trying self-massage with warm oil, tongue scraping, coconut oil pulling, and so on. I feel more energetic, I hardly have any reflux now, my bowels are working amazingly well and I felt better in general. The healthier diet makes me feel great, which is very satisfying. Of course, some things are still a work in progress.'

Aline

Your Ayurvedic staples

Fruits

Fruits are easy to digest and are generally considered to be a sattvic food, promoting clarity, lightness, harmony and intelligence. Most fruits are alkalising, cleansing and cooling, and great for people with mental stress, excess heat or who are physically overworked. Due to their natural fructose content, they are best eaten alone and make a great substitute for refined sugar foods, since they also contain valuable fibre, enzymes, vitamins and minerals. The whole fruit eaten in a natural form brings synergistic benefits. The problem with fruits nowadays is that they are too often force-ripened, which means that these fruits may not contain all the health benefits of natural sun-ripened fruits that have a sweeter quality. It's no wonder that fruits on holiday in tropical locations taste so much fresher and sweeter and leave us wanting more. Force-ripened fruits can also retain an acidic quality. So fresh, seasonal fruits are always preferred.

Choosing fruits based on your body type is helpful to staying in balance. But a purely fruit-based diet can create kapha or vata disturbances and trigger issues such as candida and blood sugar imbalances.

Fruits are not ideal in the morning, between 6 a.m. and 10 a.m. (kapha time), so offset raw fruits by adding spices to help digest them, such as cardamom, ginger, black pepper, clove or nutmeg. Cooked fruits are also neutral to digest.

Vegetables

There is such a wide range of vegetables available in each season of the year. Warm, cooked, hearty root vegetables in the winter provide strength and nutrition, and leafy green vegetables in the summer contain lots of vitamins, minerals and cleansing properties. The preparation of your vegetables and your prakruti will determine how well you will digest them. Vata types need cooked or steamed vegetables, as do kapha types, with some spices. Pitta types can eat lightly cooked and raw vegetables. Like fruits, fresh, local, seasonal vegetables are a vital component of your daily diet and are considered sattvic. Canned, processed, precooked and, to some extent, frozen vegetables don't have the same energy and are considered tamasic. Vegetables are great when combined with grains, and provide complete nourishment to the body.

Grains

These days, so many people are going low-carb, carb-free, gluten-free. But this does not make grains an evil food family – quite the contrary. We have unfortunately not had exposure to the wide variety of grains that are able to sustain life. Grains are essential for human development as they provide energy, calm the nerves, promote elimination, encourage clear thinking, induce deep sleep, and enhance memory. There are a multitude of grains, such as amaranth, millet, buckwheat and rice. Grains always need to be cooked and are best eaten warm. The digestion of grains is dependent on how well we chew and mix them with saliva. This action triggers the digestive tract to function appropriately. I am referring to whole grains here, and not the processed and highly refined varieties that are readily available in our supermarkets as flours and breads, and which can be nutrient deficient.

Legumes

This source of vegetarian proteins helps to regulate sugar, and the metabolism of the body. Legumes support the proper growth and development of the body and brain. Many people find them difficult to digest, but if they are properly cooked and prepared with spices and eaten warm with the right food combinations, they form a great staple. They are a balanced source of fat and carbohydrates, calcium, iron, potassium and several B vitamins. When we combine a grain with a legume, it is possible to get all the essential amino acids without the need for a meat-based protein. Lentils and beans are a staple in my meals since I have a plant-based diet; rice and dahl or kitchari leave me feeling totally nourished and full of beans.

Nuts and seeds

Nuts and seeds are oil-rich and a great source of vitamin E, an essential immune booster, antioxidant and nerve protector. Raw nuts and seeds are a rich source of protein and contain innumerable essential fatty acids required by the body. Vitamin E also plays an important role in your liver function.

Most nuts and seeds contribute to giving strength, weight and tone to the body. Nuts are best eaten when soaked, so they can be better digested, or opt for nut butters and oils.

Nine essential ingredients for health

1. Ghee

I love the nutty popcorn smell of ghee as it bubbles away in preparation. Ghee is the cooking oil of choice in Ayurveda. If you choose only the best quality organic butter made from grass-fed cows to make your ghee, you can create golden magic in a jar!

By clarifying butter, most of the milk proteins are removed, leaving a virtually lactose-free cooking fat which is free from hydrogenated fats and trans-fatty acids and protective against free radical damage.

Ghee has a high smoke point and can be used in cooking in place of butter and oil, as it does not easily burn. It is extremely versatile, as it is the most heat-stable fat for cooking. It is easy to digest, aids digestion by stimulating stomach acid secretions and aids absorption of nutrients.

The special gift of ghee is its catalytic properties and its ability to carry the medicinal properties of herbs to all the tissues of the body without interfering with the action of the herb. The medicinal properties of ghee increase as it ages. Ghee helps to pacify vata and pitta, and, if taken in small quantities, kapha too. Ghee supports the suppleness of the body and lubricates the connective and nerve tissues, as well as protecting the bone marrow. Ghee plays a role in the promotion of immunity, fertility, intelligence, vision, liver, kidney and brain function, and enzyme function in the intestines. Ghee is used therapeutically for ear, nose and throat problems and it makes a good base for herbal ointments.

You can, of course, use shop-bought ghee nowadays, but home-made is the best and super-easy to make – you can follow the recipe below. Please note, ghee should be used with caution in cases of obesity, high cholesterol and high ama conditions.

Client story

'I now prepare ghee for myself and my husband, and we love it. We use it in kitchari, and it feels like what my body needs – it feels so easy to digest.'

Ioana

• •

Ghee (clarified butter)

Ingredients:
1lb unsalted organic butter

Method:
Add the butter to a medium-sized heavy-based saucepan, and bring it to a low boil over a low to medium heat.

Turn the temperature down until the butter is just at a simmer and gently cook for approximately 25 minutes. It will bubble and splutter, and a white foam will form at the top. This will disappear as the ghee processes.

Whitish sediments will form at the bottom of the pan and will let off a sweet, popcorn-like smell.

As the ghee forms, it will become a clear golden colour – ensure that it does not burn. With a clean spoon, check that the ghee is clear through to the bottom.

When the colour is golden and it has stopped spluttering, take the ghee off the heat and allow it to cool.

While the ghee is lukewarm, pour it through muslin or a cheesecloth into a clean, airtight jar.

Throw away the sediments that are in the saucepan.

Store the ghee in a dry place – it does not need to be refrigerated.

• •

2. Almonds

Technically, almonds are actually a 'seed' rather than a nut. Almonds are a sattvic food and are a relative of the peach and apricot fruit. Almonds are one of the most nutritious nuts of all. They contain a high level of monounsaturated fat, which is known to reduce LDL cholesterol levels (the 'bad' cholesterol), as well as being a rich source of protein, fibre, vitamin E, omega-3, omega-6, magnesium, calcium, iron, potassium and zinc – so, packed with goodness!

The sweet taste of almonds pacifies the vata dosha, and almonds are the least acid-forming of all nuts. They are supportive for all body tissues, right down to the reproductive tissues. However, almonds can be quite difficult to digest. The skin of almonds contains tannins that can be enzyme-inhibiting and can aggravate pitta in the blood, so it is best to eat them blanched and soaked overnight, which allows the release of nutrients.

Almonds are a protein source that helps stabilise blood sugar and lower blood pressure. They are also known to increase memory and nourish the nervous system. My mum always used to say that a handful of almonds would make us brainy!

3. Water: the elixir of life

We always hear the advice that we should drink more water, but should we? What does Ayurveda say about water? Since over 70 per cent of the earth's surface is water-covered and our bodies are predominantly water, it is of course a key element to sustain life, and one of the five elements that constitute the human body. The fluidity of water provides a medium for all of our body's processes and functions.

Cold water has the capability of reducing the intoxication of alcohol, fatigue, vomiting, increased pitta symptoms, and of quenching thirst. However, as a general rule, Ayurveda favours hot or warm water over cold or iced water which can slow down metabolism. Warm water has increased therapeutic benefits, it has the capacity to stimulate hunger, aid digestion, soothe the throat, cleanse the body channels, including the bladder, relieve hiccups and flatulence and pacify increased vata and kapha. It is most useful in easing the symptoms of colds, coughs and fevers, and flushing toxins out of the body through urine and stools.

A regular intake of water will:

- Keep the skin hydrated through to the deeper layers and prevent wrinkles from forming
- Support the digestion of food, the absorption of nutrients, and the elimination of waste products
- Reduce the chances of becoming constipated
- Keep the mind hydrated and alert
- Flush out toxins from the body, reducing outbursts of acne
- Reduce the likelihood of the body mistaking thirst for hunger – drinking a little warm water 20 minutes before meals can help prevent overeating

Sip warm water throughout the day but minimise your drinking just before, during and just after mealtimes.

How do you know if you are drinking enough water? Simple: check the colour of your urine. If it is pale and clear, you are sufficiently hydrated. If it is yellow or darker, get some more water down you. This is your best indicator for hydration.

Water intake should be led by your thirst, which is your body's natural urge. Just be careful not to over-douse the body with water, as this can kill your agni and create an environment that gives rise to toxins. I have seen this several times in clinic, where clients have been fixated on drinking several litres of cold water each day to ensure they were 'hydrated', yet they suffered with symptoms of indigestion, bloating, abdominal pain and gas after food. On these occasions, the digestive system was not able to break down the food, as the agni was completely put out to the point that even healthy food choices were not being utilised by the body.

In this instance, I asked my client to reduce their water intake and we focused on stimulating the digestive fire with herbs, while limiting foods to an easy-to-digest, hot-food, vegetarian-based diet. After one or two weeks, the symptoms completely subsided, the appetite started to return to a normal pattern, regular elimination patterns resumed, and we saw a shift in energy, a reduction in toxins and a much happier client.

The magic of a copper vessel

When I was growing up, I recall my grandmother drinking water from a copper vessel that she had filled the night before. Turns out, Ayurveda promotes drinking water that has been stored in a copper vessel for around eight hours at room temperature; this ionic water helps balance the pH of the body. Our bodies cannot synthesise copper, so we need to extract it from our foods and drinks. Copper positively charges water and is an essential trace mineral for the body. Two to three glasses a day is as much copper water as you need, and early morning is a great time for drinking it. Copper water is balancing for all three doshas, so it's suitable for everybody.

Copper can reduce inflammation, strengthen our bone tissue, aid our brain function, assist in weight loss and fight cancer. There are now some great copper bottles available, and drinking water from these can ensure the water is free from harmful microbes and bacteria.

Bring a little zest back into your life

By adding the juice of half a freshly squeezed lemon to a glass of hot water and drinking it first thing in the morning on an empty stomach, you can gently cleanse your digestive system on a daily basis. Although lemons are acidic on the palate, the post-digestive properties turn to alkaline, which allows the body, and especially the liver, to detoxify. The antibacterial properties of lemons can also prevent the build-up of toxins and bacteria in the first instance.

Drinking fresh lemon with water can also enhance digestion and reduce sluggish and bloated feelings, and aid daily elimination. What's more, lemons are high in antioxidants, so you can help combat free radicals and give your skin a radiant glow.

Other natural waters used medicinally in Ayurveda are also getting a lot of airtime at the moment, including rose water for its anti-inflammatory properties and kewra water for its high antioxidant and anticarcinogenic properties, as well as its ability to calm and soothe the mind. Coconut water has taken the supermarkets by storm, and it is packed with beneficial electrolytes, minerals and hydrating properties.

4. Salt

We need salt in our diet to balance the electrolytes in the body, as well as other critical functions. The salty taste, lavana as it is known in Ayurveda, has the ability to heat, increase salivation and stimulate digestive activity, absorption and assimilation. It can clear obstructions in the bodily channels, such as relieving blocked bowels or arteries and pores. It has a penetrating quality, enhancing the properties of other herbs and spices, and is also responsible for the lubrication of the body as well as producing sweat as a metabolic waste product. According to Ayurveda, the water and fire elements of the salty taste increase pitta and kapha dosha if taken in excess, but can be balancing and calming for vata dosha.

In classical texts, Ayurveda outlines five types of salt, including sea salt, black salt and rock salt. Seawater has eighty-four naturally occurring minerals which are also beneficial for our bodies. No wonder we feel naturally refreshed by the sea breeze! Other natural sources of salt can be found in seaweed and samphire. Rock salt pacifies all three doshas and is traditionally considered the most beneficial form of salt in Ayurveda, as it has a high mineral content and a cooling action. A pinch of rock salt can act as a catalyst when taken with a teaspoon of freshly grated ginger before a main meal, acting as an appetiser to get the salivary and digestive juices flowing.

Excess salt intake in our diets today is a result of the salt hidden in processed and pre-prepared foods. This excess consumption of usually 'bad' salts can lead to health conditions including high blood pressure, water retention, dehydration, premature ageing and hair loss, and can hamper our taste buds.

Regular table salt is chemically cleaned and left with only sodium and chloride; prepared at high temperatures, the structure of the natural form of salt has been altered. An intake of this salt leaves our body deprived of essential trace minerals, leading to imbalances.

5. Honey

Natural honey has been widely used for thousands of years and daily consumption of honey always gets a vote in Ayurveda. Honey improves digestion and supports your complexion, eyes and heart, acts as a natural detox agent and cleanses the body channels.

As a sweetener, honey is an ideal substitute for sugar and a great source of energy. Though it contains slightly more calories, spoon for spoon, honey in warm water helps to break down fats and cholesterol stored in the body, as it contains many essential vitamins and minerals not present in other, refined sugars. Honey can be used as a weight-control measure when combined with cinnamon or lemon.

Honey is a wonder substance for wound-healing due to its antibacterial, antifungal and antimicrobial properties, but there are also a number of other common Ayurvedic uses.

Fat reduction/blood purification

Cleanse the bowels and burn fat by taking 1 tsp lemon juice with 1–2 tsp honey in a glass of warm water in the morning before food. Honey encourages the liver to break down and metabolise fat.

Asthma/cough

For a persistent mucus-based cough, take a pinch of black pepper with a tsp of honey and lick the mixture with a spoon after meals. For relief of phlegm, a cough, sore throat, runny nose or chest congestion, mix 2 tsp honey with an equal quantity of fresh ginger juice to help expel mucus from the chest and ear, nose and throat area.

Common cold

For a severe cold, take 1 tbsp honey with ¼ tsp cinnamon powder daily for three days. This will help clear the sinuses, strengthen the immune system and protect the body against bacterial and viral attacks.

6. Mung beans

This queen of legumes in Ayurveda is highly nutritious, wholesome and tri-doshic, making it suitable for everybody, no matter what your body type. As it contains protein, carbohydrates and fibre, it is a complete food source that nourishes the body tissues, yet is still light in quality, which is rare. It is the main component of my all-time favourite Ayurvedic dish, kitchari (see the recipe on p. 146). A simple version of kitchari was traditionally given to someone who was sick because it was easy to digest.

In the West, mung is not so widely known or used, and this is a real shame.

In the Indian culture, a combination of mung dahl and rice is very common and considered both auspicious and complete, due to all the sattvic and medicinal properties that it possesses. Mung beans are an ideal summer food and can pacify increased pitta due to their sweet and cooling nature. Mung beans are considered an alkaline food, since they are rich in minerals such as calcium, magnesium and potassium. They also have a low glycaemic index (GI), which means they provide a slow release of energy to the bloodstream from their breakdown in digestion.

I could easily have it as part of my diet several times a week. When mung beans have been skinned and split, it is referred to as mung dahl, and this process makes them easier and quicker to cook. I often use split yellow mung in my kitchari, for dahl, a soup or as a sautéed side with vegetables and spices. It is the most digestible form of mung and suitable as part of any detox process or fasting diet. Split green and yellow dahl are quicker to prepare, as they don't need soaking, and rinsing in tepid water suffices.

When whole mung beans are used, I recommend that they are steeped in room-temperature water first for several hours or overnight before cooking. The same applies to all legumes.

Sprouting mung beans and friends

Sprouting is a great way to optimise the nutritional value of grains, seeds and legumes as the sprouts contain the energy, enzymes and vitamins needed to transform seeds into strong healthy plants. If we go on the premise that we are what we eat, imagine the nutritional value. By the simple method of sprouting, mung beans, aduki beans, chickpeas, fenugreek, red clover, sunflower seeds, rye berries, alfalfa and some grains would be considered superfoods. These foods can be eaten as a tasty addition to a cooked salad and stir-fries, and can also be lightly sautéed with ghee and spices as a snack. This is my favourite!

Sprouted beans are alkalising and are a 'live' food, with high concentrations of vitamins, minerals, proteins, antioxidants and phytochemicals. Packed with all this goodness, sprouted foods help fight against toxins and boost the body's immune system.

Grow your own sprouts

Growing your own sprouts is easy. Simply take 2 cups of mung beans, wash them in cold water until the water runs clear and place them in a sprouter or glass bowl in room-temperature water (two or three parts water to one part seeds). Leave them to soak overnight (8–12 hours) – soaking neutralises the enzyme inhibitors. Rinse them thoroughly and drain them off the next day. Place them in muslin, a damp cheesecloth, sieve or colander and rest in a covered bowl. Leave them at room temperature, out of direct sunlight. The seeds need to be kept damp and aired, but not wet, otherwise they could spoil. Leave for two to three days, rinsing them gently every 12 hours. For larger sprouts, leave them for four to five days. Most sprouts are edible as soon as you see a tail (the root) emerging from the seed.

Maximum mung effect

Mung beans and dahl are super-versatile. Here are a few ideas for how you can use them in different dishes. Lightly sauté some cumin in ghee in a large, heavy-based pan. Add some turmeric and ginger and then the mung sprouts and sauté for 10–12 minutes. Season with lime or lemon, salt and paprika.

Halwa is a sweet dessert that can be made with yellow mung dahl. It is a delicious, gluten-free pudding that can be spiced and garnished with nuts of your choice – almonds and walnuts work well with saffron, cardamom and nutmeg.

Yellow mung can also be roasted, like peanuts, and salted or spiced and eaten as a bar snack. They can also be used in Bombay mix. Mung bean flour makes a great alternative for gluten-free breads too. The recipe options are endless.

7. Rice

Rice comes in so many different varieties – short, long, white, brown, red, wild, arborio, shali, Japanese, black, basmati, and so on – and is a staple food around the globe. In fact, there are over 40,000 known rice varieties. Symbolising prosperity and fertility, many cultures throw rice at newlywed couples or in ceremonial offerings. Rice can also come in different forms – whole, flaked, puffed, milled (flour). Brown rice and red rice are considered to have the most nutritional value. They are unpolished (unprocessed) and so retain the vitamin content that polished rice loses. Brown rice and red rice have a medium GI, so energy is released at a steady pace.

Rice is considered the king of grains in Ayurveda, as it is nutritious, strengthening, revitalising, regulating for blood pressure and sattvic. However, all rice is not the same. The older the grain, the easier it is to digest. Rice that is more than one year mature after harvest is better than newly harvested rice. In the case of rice, fresher does not mean better. Think of it like wine – it needs some time to mature.

It is an ideal food in cases of weakened or poor digestion, making it the grain of choice if you are recovering from an illness. On the whole, rice has a sweet quality and can be balancing for all three doshas. It is soothing to the nervous system, relieves thirst and helps the body to push out toxins. Rice water, known as *kanji*, is the first ingredient that is taken after an Ayurvedic purgation therapy to help bind the stools again.

In the West, we go to the supermarket and buy a pack of rice (often new grain) or even buy precooked rice; this is quick and convenient but how the food has been prepared and processed affects its quality and health benefits. These options lack the life-promoting benefits, the prana, of freshly prepared old grains.

Thoroughly washing and soaking the rice for an hour before cooking helps to lighten the grain for digestion and also to remove the naturally occurring traces of arsenic found in rice. In most Indian households, rice is usually cooked with more water than needed (five parts water to one part rice) and then strained, making it even lighter and easier to digest.

Rice is the most versatile of grains and can be used in a variety of dishes. The most nourishing and balancing would be rice pudding (see p. 169). Savoury rice can be made to suit any cuisine – paella, risotto, rice and beans, biryani, pilau, stir-fried rice, rice noodles, stuffing for sushi. Rice can be used in pastry for dim sum, and puffed rice, flaked rice and rice cakes can be used for snacking. You can also sweeten rice with jaggery and spices – the list could go on and on.

8. Takra (buttermilk)

Ayurvedic buttermilk is an elixir for restoring beneficial intestinal bacteria. Its unique formula is excellent for helping your gut to assimilate food while providing essential digestive microbes. It is different to the commonly served lassi or mango lassi in Indian restaurants, as it is lighter and easier to digest, and can even be consumed in moderation by kapha types.

Nearly all of my family still make their own fresh yoghurt at home, which makes it easy to make buttermilk, or *chaas*, as we call it in my native language, Gujarati. Chaas is a popular drink with my family, and something that we almost always have over the summer months. Below is the recipe for a home-made buttermilk (chaas) that my family has been using for as long as I can remember. This is very different from shop-bought buttermilk.

....

Chaas

Serves 1
Ingredients:
¼ cup natural set yoghurt (make your own fresh, if possible)
¾ cup purified cold water
¼ tsp ground cumin
Pinch or two rock salt (pink Himalayan rock salt is best)
Fresh coriander leaves, finely chopped (optional)

Method:
Simply blend or churn the yoghurt and water with a hand whisk or blender for 1–2 minutes.

Remove the froth that foams at the top – this is the fatty part.

Whisk again if the foam is not fully extracted – it should look like opaque, cloudy water.

Add the cumin and salt.

Add the finely chopped coriander leaves if desired, stir and serve at room temperature.

....

9. Chyawanprash

One of the best-known rasayanas in Ayurveda is chyawanprash. I like to think of it as the perfect herbal food supplement for vitality. One of the key ingredients in this nutritive jam is amalaki, the Indian gooseberry, a fruit with one of the highest natural sources of vitamin C, giving it a powerful antioxidant quality. Chyawanprash contains several *yogavahis* (catalytic agents), such as honey, ghee and sesame oil, which help the action of the herbs in the jam to deeply penetrate into the body tissues.

This classical formula is a rejuvenative and supports all the tissues in the body, particularly the heart, blood, muscles, lungs and reproductive organs. It helps kindle the digestive fire and gently encourages elimination of toxins while supporting a healthy immune response, by building ojas.

Chyawanprash is now available in many health food stores throughout the UK and Europe; if you can't find it in the shops, there is no shortage of reputable online suppliers. Since taste plays an important role in digestion, chyawanprash is designed as a 'lickable' medicine, as it can trigger the body's natural mechanisms of healing. As such, children and adults alike can dip a spoon into the jar and eat the delicious-tasting paste directly, kind of like that Nutella in your cupboard. Not all of my clients enjoy it this way; if that's the case, I suggest diluting it in warm water and taking it as a juice, or spreading it on toast like a jam.

Ayurveda and vegetarianism

I am often asked by clients in consultations if they need to become vegetarian in order to follow an Ayurvedic lifestyle. The short answer is no, but it is a little more complex than that; some consideration should be given to the rationale behind meat consumption and a plant-based diet from an Ayurvedic perspective. The more awareness you have, the better choices you can make for yourself so that your decisions feel right for you.

A vegetarian-based diet is most definitely encouraged in Ayurveda. A diet rich in fresh vegetables, fruits, whole grains, legumes, nuts and seeds and moderate amounts of dairy foods is easy to digest, nourishes the tissues and brings clarity to the mind. These foods are vibrant, full of prana and sattvic in nature.

Meats are heavy in nature and difficult to digest; they are considered rajasic and mentally stimulating in nature, and over time they can lead to an accumulation of ama. We take on the energy of that which we choose to eat, and so the hormones released in the animal at the point of slaughter remain in the flesh that is eaten.

In Ayurveda, opting for meats that are aligned to your body type is recommended and I am, of course, referring here to meat that is either naturally and ethically farmed or that is wild meat. Some meats, such as salmon and oily fish, are suitable for vata types. Beef is also good as a tissue-builder for vata types. Pitta and kapha types can digest white meats such as chicken, turkey and freshwater fish, but red meats should be limited or avoided.

So, if you do eat meat, I suggest that you limit consumption to only a few times a week and, where possible, eat meat at lunchtime, as you are likely to break it down and digest it better than in your evening meal. It is also a great idea to have one or two meat-free days a week so that your digestive system gets a break to cleanse and rebalance itself.

You can improve the digestibility of meats by adding appropriate seasoning. Pungent and digestive spices such as cumin, black pepper, fennel, cayenne, garlic and ginger can help you digest the meat. You should also eat meats cooked and hot.

It is definitely not a bad idea to question modern farming methods and to know where and how the meat you consume was produced. The quality of your meat (and all foods) should always be questioned, as this has an impact on your health. Levels of toxicity can build in your body as a result of factory-farmed meats. There is a high correlation between health issues such as heart disease and obesity and long-term diets high in saturated animal fats.

Ayurvedic classical texts do, however, recommend meat in cases of debilitation and emaciation, where the body tissues need essential repair and rebuilding. In this instance, meats are considered to be medicinal. Start with easy-to-digest meat broths and soups (*mamsarasa*), and then move on to flesh as digestion improves. For those individuals who have grown up on and are habituated to eating meat, switching to a vegetarian diet may be difficult. Based on the principles of your Ayurvedic mind/body type and the gunas (the qualities) of ingredients, choosing the most suitable meat is essential, as is moderation, just like with any other food.

If you are keen to move to a vegetarian-based diet, I recommend a gradual shift, first cutting out red meats for a month, as this is the heaviest of meats, then cutting out white meats for a few weeks, and then fish after that. As you transition, introduce more plant-based proteins, such as lentils, beans, tofu, nuts and seeds. Take time to observe how well you digest meat and if you should consider making changes to the basis of your diet. It is ultimately a personal decision, but being aligned to your body type will ensure long-term balance and support for preventative health.

Go SLO (Seasonal, Local and Organic)

Today in the West, and especially in cities, we have become so far removed from our natural food sources. We have all types of seemingly fresh foods available all year round, so we have no clue what foods are naturally in season. This is the result of produce being flown in from countries afar, where the local climate supports their production, or crops that are produced more locally in an artificially created environment. Neither of these options is really aligned to eating in the way that nature intended. What's more, the energy required to fuel the planes so that we can have fresh berries in winter and mangoes in the summer is phenomenal, not to mention the nutritional quality that gets lost in transit.

Ayurveda encourages a diet consisting of plant-based foods that are available from the land that you reside in. This means 'local'! Local produce will always be fresher and harvested when it is ripe and ready for consumption. These foods are vibrant and full of prana, as they retain the phytochemicals that have antioxidants, vitamins and minerals that we want to get from our foods, as well as being environmentally friendly. These foods are translated into the right kind of nutrients in your digestion – a bit like putting the right type of fuel in your car to ensure it runs smoothly. In the UK, for example, the peak of the strawberry season is June and July. You will find this fruit in abundance over the summer months, and at this time they are likely to be sweet and juicy in nature. Nothing beats the fresh British strawberries while you watch Wimbledon.

There is much confusion over 'organic' food labelling, and it can be difficult to know what organic means these days. Is it 100 per cent organic, or made with all or some organic ingredients? When it comes to fresh fruit and vegetables, opting for local, organic produce means that it will be free from pesticides, herbicides, fungicides and artificial fertilisers which are foreign to your body and damaging to the environment. There is now an increase in organic foods produced on a mass scale, which we find in major supermarkets. The question is, can we be sure that this is truly organic and ethically produced? To my mind, making the healthiest choices available in your circumstances is already a step in the right direction. The more people choose truly fresh, organic, locally produced and seasonal food, the more the balance of supply and demand will shift over time; communities will be supporting the local farmers, reducing their carbon footprint and reducing the environmental pollutants that surround us.

Not all Indian food is Ayurvedic

It would be a fallacy to think that because Ayurveda is a science born on the Indian subcontinent, all Indian food is naturally Ayurvedic. This is not the case at all, and it can sometimes confuse my clients. Likewise, you don't have to eat Indian food to follow an Ayurvedic diet, but rather adapt the concepts to your everyday meals. I definitely advise my clients to reach out for those spices that will aid their digestion, which are of course commonly used in Indian food preparation. Spices are carefully selected based on your dosha type and imbalance. Ayurvedic dishes are always simple, clean, fresh, light and always eaten warm, giving you vital energy and a nourishing feel-good factor. Many Indian dishes can be heavy to digest, especially those foods immersed in heavy sauces, rich desserts and those tasty deep-fried street foods. Despite the fact that all Indian foods carry beneficial spices, they are not all 'Ayurvedic'.

The raw food myth

The trend to go raw has become increasingly popular in recent times. Sure, raw foods potentially contain maximum levels of untampered nutrition within them; however, they are often the nuance that can quickly irritate your gut. The process of cooking helps to increase their digestibility. Some foods you have to cook, such as legumes, grains and most meats, but we often opt for raw vegetables, fish, meats and fruit. Have you ever noticed feeling uneasy or bloated after eating raw broccoli, carrots, beetroot, cabbage, cauliflower and other raw vegetables? Lightly cooked vegetables are easier to digest, and using some digestive spices such as ginger, cumin, fennel and black pepper can enhance their absorbability without creating adverse side effects in the gut. Ensure you do not overcook or burn foods, as this can also create toxins and digestive disturbance.

Of course, fresh salad items such as lettuce, cucumber and most fruits can be enjoyed raw over the summer, especially if they are local, seasonal, fresh, ripe and ready to eat. These foods are better in the lunch meal, when digestion is strongest. Stewed apples make a great light and easy-to-digest breakfast, a great option for those who find fruits acidic on digestion. Spice them up with cinnamon and garnish with mixed seeds. Have you ever felt heaviness or discomfort with cold milk in cereal? This form of milk can also be difficult to digest; boiling the milk removes the heavy milk proteins, making it more digestible. Add spices like cardamom or cinnamon to increase its digestibility.

Raw foods and cold foods such as cold pasta or other grain

salads, sandwiches and sushi are particularly difficult to digest if you are predominantly vata type or are experiencing vata imbalance. If your digestive fire is low, even fresh, healthy, raw foods can be toxic to the body.

The importance of fats and oils in Ayurveda

If you have ever experienced anything Ayurvedic or have had time to have Ayurvedic treatments in India, you will know that you can often spend a lot of time immersed in oils. This is because oils play an important role in our health and are central to Ayurvedic cleansing processes. Oils are central to Ayurvedic purification treatments, both internally and externally, as deep-seated lipid-based toxins can only be removed using a lipid carrier, such as ghee, sesame oil, coconut oil etc.

Oils can balance vata, provide energy, add flavour and texture to food, help the absorption of vitamins A, D, E and K, insulate and protect the body, help the body digest slowly and act as muscle fuel.

Healthy fats from natural sources are best – vegetable oils, nuts, seeds, milk, eggs, olives, sesame and other seeds and most of all ghee.

Pitta types should exercise moderation with this food group. Kapha types need to be a little more cautious, as they are most susceptible to increased body weight.

Modern food concerns

Food intolerances

One of the biggest health concerns that I see on the rise in clinic is that of food intolerances. They have become such a norm that clients often forget to mention them as presenting complaints. Over time, due to improper diet and lifestyle choices, the digestion can become weakened and the gut can fail to break down certain foods into digestible components. Simply eliminating the food is just a short-term solution and never the best long-term option in Ayurveda.

Ayurveda focuses on rebooting the digestive system so that it can once again digest optimally (see chapter 10). Many of my clients who made adjustments to their diets and focused on digestive strengthening have been able to tolerate foods that they had developed an intolerance to (including lactose and gluten).

Some early signs of food intolerances can include tiredness, nausea, bloating and abdominal distension after meals. You might also experience heart palpitations and altered blood pressure or heartbeat. As we have discovered, every person is unique, and understanding the root of the intolerances and how you are personally affected will dictate the path of your treatment through Ayurveda. If you suffer from life-threatening allergies, please consult a health professional.

Cravings and addictions

A food only becomes 'bad' for you when you are overindulging, abusing or misusing it for some form of gratification. This lack of discretion is what quickly leads to an imbalance of the doshas. It is a vicious cycle, and when your doshas start to spiral out of balance, you can become susceptible to abnormal cravings.

Anything can become an addiction when a substance is taken in excess for prolonged periods, including foods and drinks (sugars, fats, chocolate, caffeine, salt, alcohol), drugs, cigarettes, sex, work, thought patterns and, believe it or not, even exercise. Realising that a pattern exists is the first step to resolving addictive behaviours. Have you stopped to think about your possible addictive eating patterns? Where is this craving stemming from? Are you trying to escape from any stresses? Breaking habits is not always easy, but it is definitely possible, either through self-commitment to transforming a habit or by seeking professional guidance.

Once you find the groove of your prakruti, you will quickly become familiar with the nuances that can unbalance you and the foods and habits that can bring back balance. Ayurvedic treatments and **yogic** practices such as pancha karma, breathing exercises and meditation are geared towards restoring the energetic balance of prakruti by addressing the underlying stresses that cause unhealthy habit patterns. When your body and mind are suitably nourished, your unhealthy craving can start to fade away. One of my clients was consuming in excess of four to five coffees daily, and believed that she would not be able to stop. She recognised this as an addiction, but she was determined to make a change and she did. She now has just the occasional Americano and has replaced her coffee habit with ginger and honey or lemon and honey tea, and she loves it. As a result (after pushing past the initial resistance), she feels much more vibrant and clear in the mind, with reduced headaches and skin reactions.

Did you know that just a few centuries ago, sugar was seen as a luxury commodity? Today, refined white sugar has become a highly addictive substance, and is considered to be nothing more than 'empty calories', giving the body energy without any nutritional value. With the abundance of processed and packaged foods available in the supermarket, most of the time we have very little awareness of how much sugar the foods we eat even contain.

This refined white sugar gets absorbed directly into the bloodstream, bringing instant energy to the body, which can be helpful in emergency cases, where immediate energy is needed. If continuous consumption of sugar persists, however, it puts pressure on the digestive organs to constantly regulate blood glucose; the body starts to lose its functionality and ama quickly starts to form. Natural sugars (simple carbohydrates) found in fruits and sweet vegetables do provide nutrients on the other hand, as well as essential digestible fibre. Complex carbohydrates, found in grains, nuts, seeds, legumes and vegetables, are always favoured, as they release a steady flow of energy as well as providing the body with essential nutrients – proteins, vitamins, minerals, fats and phytonutrients. If your prakruti is vata- or pitta-dominant, complex and some simple carbohydrates can be balancing. Kapha types will need to moderate complex carbohydrates and limit simple sugars, as they could quickly lead to weight gain. An excessive intake of sugar has been linked to diabetes, anxiety, depression, adrenal dysfunction, hyperactivity and more.

My top tips to prevent cravings
- Manage underlying stress (this will stabilise underlying cortisol, adrenalin and insulin release)
- Eat regular meals. Skipping meals can make blood sugars dip, making you likely to reach for a sugar quick fix
- Do not eat on the run – your body and brain are trying to communicate, do not disturb this process
- If blood sugar levels are difficult to manage, have smaller portions and increase your meal frequency from three meals to four or five. Allow 2–3 hours between each meal
- Moderate your portion size to no more than a half-filled stomach
- Drink a warm water or herbal drink as a substitute for cravings
- Opt for fresh, home-made, nutritiously balanced meals that contain all six tastes. When all tastes are satisfied, cravings will subside

---

Coffee can sometimes be a real point of contention with my clients. Coffee taken in the right way can be beneficial. The issues arise when coffee is being used as a stimulant to wake up, to work when tired, to stimulate a bowel movement or generally to help get you through the day – that is not a healthful use of coffee. Coffee can be unbalancing and inhibit mineral absorption, and can lead to hyperacidity, ulcers and IBS (especially on an empty stomach), fatigue, increased blood pressure, anxiety and adrenal dysfunction if abused.

Coffee has bitter and astringent tastes and so is not suitable for vata types, as it is drying for the body as well as overstimulating for the mind. It can be tolerated by pitta types in limited amounts, and it is fine for kapha types to consume as part of a balanced diet.

Coffee before a meal can inhibit digestive enzymes from doing their job. After breakfast is the best time. Between 6 a.m. and 10 a.m., which is the heavy, cool, sluggish kapha time, a hot, dry and stimulating coffee can be beneficial for the digestion and mind. What is not advised is constant cups of coffee throughout the day, which can become a habit in a sedentary day job. Opt for organic coffee, which contains fewer pesticides, and preferably freshly ground, which is less prone to oxidation.

Avoid coffee if you have hyperacidity, hypertension, skin rashes, dehydration, disturbed sleep, dry hair or skin, feel agitated or feel restless, as your vata or pitta may already be out of balance.

If you can't resist the coffee, this is how you should take it, so it is suitable to your dosha type:

- Vata: have a maximum of 1 cup a day and make it milky and sweet, using natural sugars
- Pitta: have a maximum of 1 cup a day and make it black and sweet, using natural sugars
- Kapha: have a maximum of 1 cup of unsweetened black coffee a day

CHAPTER 14

Spice Up Your Life

'The secret to health and happiness is through the artful
use of herbs and spices'

Geeta Vara

Spices have been such an integral part of my life since childhood.
The more I immerse myself in the sea of spice, the more I fall in
love with food, flavours, cooking, and all the magic that happens
in between.

Your intuitive desire for different foods and tastes at different
times will be led by what your body needs, so that it can be
sufficiently nourished and balanced. Since we don't always apply
mindful practices to our eating habits, we can often miss these signs.

In this chapter, I'd like to bring you up to speed with some basic
everyday spices and ingredients that are versatile, flavourful and
packed with medicinal properties. In the same way that every
food has an energetic profile based on taste, quality, potency and
post-digestive action, every ingredient, herb and spice has a
specific energetic profile too, which can balance and heal you. For
me, this is where the magic of Ayurveda comes to life – you can
become your own alchemist!

Your kitchen store cupboard may be just the ticket to put you
back on the mend without having to visit the pharmacy. Lurking
away in your store cupboard is a myriad of herbs and spices which
are full of medicinal properties, and you don't even know it.

Based on the tenet that like increases like and opposites create balance, we can use all herbs and spices as medicines once we have become familiar with their inherent tastes and attributes. Once you have an insight into your mind/body type and where your imbalances lie, you can start to fine-tune your dietary and medicinal herbs to sustain your mind/body equilibrium beyond your basic diet. Eventually you will be guided by your intuition (not to be confused with cravings) when it comes to the taste and flavour of your food to bring your health back into balance.

Everything in your kitchen has some healing properties – cloves, cinnamon, honey, coriander, black pepper, cumin seeds, fennel, ginger, garlic, onion, asafoetida, basil leaves, mint, turmeric, sandalwood, camphor, this list could go on and on. Let's focus on a few of my favourite common kitchen ingredients that will become your digestive friends for life.

Turmeric

Botanical name: *Curcuma longa*
Quality: dry, light
Taste: pungent, bitter, astringent
Potency: heating

Once upon a time, this deep and brightly yellow-coloured spice was called the poor man's saffron, but today it has made the headlines as the star spice of the popular 'golden milk'. This herb is considered a symbol of happiness and prosperity and, with its bitter taste, this kitchen staple has many health benefits. Turmeric has strong antioxidant properties and is therefore immune-boosting and protects against damage caused by free radicals. Turmeric is a powerful anti-inflammatory, reducing histamine levels in conditions such as eczema, psoriasis, asthma, arthritis, osteoarthritis, colitis and cold sores. This multi-use spice is also helpful in detoxifying and maintaining liver and gallbladder functions.

Curcumin is the active agent that gives turmeric its medicinal reputation. Numerous studies have found curcumin to be a potent chemical compound and useful in some of life's biggest threats, including cancer, type 2 diabetes, Alzheimer's, high cholesterol, asthma and more. You can buy the fresh rhizomes in many specialist food markets and I love eating this as an accompaniment to any meal. Just peel, slice and steep in salted water to preserve.

Decongestant

Turmeric is great for clearing obstructions in the chest and lungs. At home, we often add turmeric in small amounts to milk and give this to my nieces and nephews when they are wheezy. For your children, boil ⅛–¼ tsp turmeric in a mug of milk. Bottle and add honey – yes, this is 'golden milk'!

Cuts and grazes

With powerful antiseptic and antibacterial properties, turmeric is perfect for application to external cuts, grazes and wounds, particularly when mixed with honey. This is my go-to antiseptic in my home; it also miraculously stops the bleeding. Mix a little turmeric with honey and apply directly to the cut.

Skin irritations

On the outside, it is great for any skin irritations when mixed with aloe vera. It helps maintain healthy skin via blood purification if taken internally and is also a useful ingredient in beauty creams and lotions, giving a glowing complexion. Mix a paste of turmeric with fresh aloe vera gel and apply directly to the skin. You can also drink ¼ tsp turmeric with 30ml aloe vera juice to clear skin from within.

Colds and flu

Turmeric is very useful for colds and flu. You can add it to a decoction of ginger and lemon with a drizzle of honey. Make a tea with a mug of water and 1 tsp each turmeric and freshly grated

ginger, a little black pepper, lemon juice, add honey at the end and
drink warm.

Ginger

Botanical name: *Zingiber officinale*
Quality: light, oily
Taste: pungent, sweet
Potency: heating

Another truly wonderful herb with numerous healing properties is
ginger, a thick tuber root herb that has been used both in its fresh
and dried form for over 2,500 years. It is effectively used to balance all
three doshas in Ayurveda. Gingerol is an active chemical compound
present in ginger, giving it antioxidant, anti-inflammatory, antiviral
and antibacterial properties. Ginger is therefore useful for multiple
health ailments, such as cancer, asthma, high cholesterol, migraine,
stroke, indigestion, nausea, colds, flu and more.

Digestion
Ginger acts as a digestive tonic and calms stomach upsets, cramps
and flatulence when taken with lime juice; it stimulates digestion
when taken with rock salt and keeps intestinal muscles toned and
increases bile flow. Have a shot of ginger juice (5–10ml) before
your meal as a digestive stimulant. Add ginger to your sweet treats
to help the digestion.

Inflammation
Ginger has anti-inflammatory properties and therefore can be
used for external pain, swelling and arthritis if applied as a local
paste or ginger-infused oils. Make a ginger (1 tsp) and turmeric (½
tsp) infused tea and drink warm 2–3 times daily. Make and take a
paste of fresh ginger and jaggery (1 tsp each) and eat at the end of
your meal.

Nausea no more

Motion sickness or morning sickness – no matter the cause of your queasiness, ginger is a prime choice for its anti-nausea and anti-emetic action. Fresh ginger, dried ginger and ginger in a variety of products, such as teas, jams and crystals, are widely available, making it very versatile and my go-to for anytime I go to sea! Just throw some crystallised ginger into your travel bag.

Cinnamon

Botanical name: *Cinnamomum zeylanicum*
Quality: dry, light, sharp
Taste: pungent, sweet, astringent
Potency: heating

A heating spice with a sweet, pungent and bitter taste, cinnamon is a very versatile ingredient for home remedies. As one of the oldest known spices, Ceylon cinnamon has positive healing effects on digestion, respiratory conditions such as asthma and coughs, insect bites and urinary infections, and helps to pacify vata and kapha doshas. It is also believed to help digestion of fruits and dairy products. Cinnamon is most commonly combined with raw honey and is useful to lower LDL cholesterol. It is a powerful blood sugar-balancing spice and therefore useful in type 2 diabetes; it is also helpful in preventing spikes in blood sugar after meals.

Insect bites

Mix one part honey to two parts water and 1 tsp cinnamon, and apply to itching skin. Or simply apply cinnamon oil.

Diarrhoea

Mix ½ tsp ground cinnamon and a pinch of nutmeg with 1 tbsp yoghurt. Take this mix 3 times a day.

Weight management
Mix ½ tsp cinnamon with 1 tsp honey as a paste and have on an empty stomach in the morning with a little warm water.

Urinary tract infections
A great ingredient to prevent urinary tract infections. Taking ½–¾ tsp cinnamon and 1 tsp honey with a glass of lukewarm water can destroy bacteria in the bladder.

Garlic

Botanical name: *Allium sativum*
Quality: oily, heavy, penetrating, mobile
Taste: Sweet, pungent, bitter, astringent
Potency: heating

Once known as the 'stinking rose', this pungent, heating and characterful aromatic is commonly used all over the world and has many wonderful benefits. Medicinally, it lends itself to preventing infections such as colds and coughs due to its antifungal and antiviral properties, and reduces intestinal complaints.

Heart health
Garlic has the ability to lower blood cholesterol and gently thin blood, similar to the way in which aspirin is used. Garlic is great for keeping all the arteries supple and free-flowing as it reduces arterial plaque. Chew 1–2 cloves fresh garlic on an empty stomach in the morning (if you can stomach it!). Raw garlic acts as a natural aphrodisiac, supports brain functions and strengthens bones.

Earache
Squeeze a drop of fresh garlic juice or garlic oil in each ear for earaches or ear irritation.

Cumin

Botanical name: *Cuminum cyminum*
Quality: dry, light
Taste: bitter, pungent
Potency: cooling

Love, love, love! If I was stuck on a desert island with only one choice of seeded spice, this would be it. It is by far my most favourite seeded spice and one that I use in abundance. Not only does it lift every dish with its gorgeous aroma and flavour, it is famed for its ability to enhance appetite and digestion. It clears toxins from the digestive system and reduces bloating and upward wind which cause nausea and indigestion. It acts as a carminative, diuretic, antispasmodic and decongestant.

It is used in postpartum care as it reduces pain and inflammation, and enhances lactation.

Basically, put it on everything either in whole seed form or ground.

Bloating and gas

For bloating and gas simply chew 1 tsp of cumin seeds really well and wash down with warm water. Alternatively, combine with fennel and cardamom and have it as a tea infusion.

Black pepper

Botanical name: *Piper nigrum*
Quality: light, penetrating
Taste: pungent
Potency: heating

At one time, black pepper was worth more than gold; now it is a common condiment in the West and rightly so – black pepper is a versatile and powerful jump-start for the digestive system, right from the point of the taste buds. It helps burn away toxins and cleanse the digestive tract. It is great to have black pepper on raw foods and salads to help balance the coldness of the food. It is useful for chronic indigestion, sinus congestion and colds. Add black pepper to increase the absorption of turmeric.

It tones and lines the intestines, and its heating properties help stimulate digestion and enhance the metabolism of food and medicines.

Aloe vera

Botanical name: *Aloe barbadensis*
Quality: oily, heavy, sticky
Taste: bitter, sweet, astringent
Potency: cooling

The gel from inside the leaves of an aloe plant is a powerful anti-inflammatory, bringing a cooling and soothing action to the body. Due to its bitter taste, it is detoxifying for the liver, spleen and blood; it also enhances the regulation of sugar and fat metabolism. Its clear cooling effects make it a perfect option for pacifying pitta dosha. It can be used as a form of laxative and can balance the stomach acids and inflammations in the digestive tract, such as colitis. If you have ever tasted the juice of aloe you will know its strong, bitter taste; so dilute it with a little water or apple juice or add honey to make it palatable. Add a pinch of turmeric to give a cleansing boost to the blood and skin.

PMS
Useful in premenstrual syndrome, heavy cycles, hot flushes and the menopause. You can safely consume 2–3 tbsp aloe juice a day; add a pinch of black pepper and take preferably before food.

Skin conditions and sunburn

The fresh soothing gel is commonly used externally on the skin on cuts, burns, sunburn, rashes, sores, herpes, and so on. Always keep some gel or better still nurture a plant in your home.

Liquorice

Botanical name: *Glycyrrhiza glabra*
Quality: heavy, moist
Taste: sweet, bitter
Potency: cooling

When you think of liquorice, do you have visions of sticky black sweets? After processing, this is what it becomes, but in its natural state, liquorice is a rough-looking root. This is a multitalented and restorative herb and a great expectorant, helping to liquefy mucus and soothe dry coughs, sore throats and inflammation in the chest.

It is sattvic in nature, meaning that it is calming to the mind, nourishes the brain and supports cerebrospinal fluid. If you enjoy singing, this is a great supportive herb, as it improves the voice as well as vision, complexion and hair.

Dry cough and voice enhancement

The easiest way to have liquorice is to boil the crushed root or powder with water and drink as a tea.

Children's constipation

Sweet and safe for children with constipation as it is a mild laxative. Give as a warm tea or natural liquorice sweets.

Nutmeg

Botanical name: *Myristica fragrans*
Quality: light, sharp, unctuous
Taste: pungent, bitter, astringent
Potency: heating

What I love about this spice is how it makes you sleep like a baby with its sedative action, not to mention the gorgeous aroma when it is freshly grated. It's one of the best spices for calming the mind, anxiety, depression and vata, and helping to moderate the nervous system. It increases the absorption in the small intestines, relieves indigestion, wind, bloating and muscle spasms. It can be taken with buttermilk to stop diarrhoea. It is also a great reproductive tonic for low libido, irregular or painful menstruation and impotence.

Nutmeg is used in dishes all around the world, from jerked curries, to German potatoes and French béchamel to an array of Indian desserts, and not forgetting the festive eggnog.

Insomnia/disturbed sleep
Just mix ¼ tsp ground nutmeg and ¼ tsp ground cardamom with boiled milk before bed for some sedative action.

Cardamom

Botanical name: *Elettaria cardamomum*
Quality: light, dry
Taste: pungent, sweet
Potency: heating

With its delicate aroma and flavour, cardamom is a perfect flavour partner with nutmeg for a bedtime milky drink. The little seeds that come out from the cardamom pod are a safe digestive stimulant for agni and for removing excess mucus from the digestion and relieving stomach aches. It is sattvic in nature and opens the flow of energy throughout the body, bringing clarity to the mind and joy to your heart. One of its magic properties is its ability to neutralise the adverse effects of caffeine. It improves loss of taste and hoarseness of voice.

Cardamom is calming for both the gut and respiratory system, as well as helping in conditions of high blood pressure and heart disease.

Mouth freshener
You will find many people simply chew on a cardamom pod as a mouth freshener. Just pop 1–2 whole pods in your mouth after meals.

Fennel seeds

Botanical name: *Foeniculum vulgare*
Quality: dry, light
Taste: pungent, sweet
Potency: cooling

Ever wonder what those little sugar-coated seeds that you get at the end of your Indian curry night out are? Well, they are roasted fennel seeds and are often eaten at the end of a meal to freshen the breath but also to aid digestion. This wonderful aromatic is in fact one of the best digestives, strengthening agni without unbalancing pitta, removing bloating, nausea, vomiting and flatulence and reducing the risk of digestive cramping and piles.

Fennel seeds are a gentle and safe seed to help stimulate digestion in children. They nourish the mind and create alertness. Combined with coriander, they are a great decoction to take for urinary problems. These seeds are a sound anti-inflammatory that can be taken in many chronic conditions, such as inflammatory bowel disease, Alzheimer's, dementia, arthritis and cancer.

Digestive aid

Chewing on a teaspoon of fennel seeds is great for all digestive upsets. Great as a post-meal digestive.

Nursing mothers

A decoction with other seeded spices can be given to nursing mothers to help increase lactation and to calm colic in babies. They can also help to relieve menstrual cramps.

Holy Basil (Tulsi)

Botanical name: *Ocimum sanctum*
Quality: light, dry, penetrating
Taste: pungent, bitter
Potency: heating

There are around thirty different varieties of basil and although holy basil is different from the regular basil we are used to eating, it can contain similar properties. One of the best herbs for treating colds, coughs and flu, as well as for reducing inflammation and headaches. Considered a youth-promoting plant, holy basil has brilliant anti-stress and clarifying properties, and is a sattvic herb, bringing purity to the mind and opening the heart. With strong volatile oils such as eugenol (also in parsley), tulsi has antibacterial and antifungal properties.

Colds and flu

Tulsi helps reduce excess mucus in the lungs. Make a tea with tulsi leaves, a few whole cloves and a little salt when you have a cold or flu. You can use this as a throat gargle too.

Skin irritations

Tulsi leaves can be used externally as a paste for itching and urticaria (hives) and the juice can be used as eardrops for earaches.

Garden mint

Botanical name: *Mentha spicata*
Quality: light, dry, penetrating
Taste: pungent, sweet
Potency: cooling

Mint is a universal herb hit, and used far and wide, from Moroccan mint tea, mojito cocktails and mint sweets, to mint raita, mint sauce to accompany your lamb and mint chocolate ice cream. Also known as spearmint, this lush, fresh, green, aromatic herb is soothing, cooling and clarifying in action. It is useful to the nervous system and digestion and can be helpful in irritable bowel syndrome and indigestion. The aroma of mint helps awaken the mind, relieve stress, stimulate saliva and activate the digestive system. Mint can gently clear any stagnation in the stomach and digestive tract.

Urinary tract infection
It is useful in cases of urinary inflammation or cystitis. Just steep a small bunch of fresh leaves in hot water and drink the fresh tea.

Nausea
Mint can be useful to relieve feelings of nausea generally and even during pregnancy. You can make a mint tea or chew on fresh leaves.

Parsley

Botanical name: *Petroselinum crispum*
Quality: light, dry
Taste: pungent, bitter, sweet
Potency: heating

Flat leaf and curly parsley are more commonly used in the Western diet. More than just a decorative garnish, parsley is a good dietary choice as it is packed with minerals, vitamins A and C, and iron. Parsley is a great antioxidant and an antioxidant enhancer (since it contains flavonoids, apigenin and lutein). It is mildly stimulating to the digestion and mildly cleansing to the blood. Its chemical compound makes it useful for fighting cancer, heart disease, diabetes and ulcers. It can be useful as a mild diuretic and can promote menstruation, relieve premenstrual cramping, water retention and headaches. It can also help to dispel stones from the kidneys and gall bladder but must be used with caution in cases of inflammation in the kidneys. You can get parsley into your diet by cooking it in your soup or adding to your smoothies.

Pomegranate

Botanical name: *Punica granatum*
Quality: light, unctuous
Taste: astringent, bitter (rind); sweet, sour (fruit)
Potency: cooling

Sure, so pomegranate is neither a spice nor a herb, but it is definitely worthy of a mention, as it contains powerful healing properties and is now a trendy health food. This fruit of ruby-coloured kernels is one that reminds me of early autumn in the UK, and what is so great is that every part can be used for medicinal purposes, from the fruit seeds, to the skin, pulp and root. The juice of this fruit makes a strong tonic for blood cleansing, balancing increased pitta and promoting digestion. The rind of the fruit is the part that is most astringent and acts as an anti-inflammatory. This juicy and tasty fruit is actually useful in the removal of worms, soothing a sore throat, bronchitis, colitis, ulcers, diarrhoea and dysentery.

Section 3:

The Art of
Preventative Healthcare

CHAPTER 15

Anchors for Health – Sleep, Exercise and Sex

Sleep – a core pillar of life

'Sleep is the best meditation'

Dalai Lama

Do you have trouble getting to sleep or suffer from disturbed sleep? In my practice, I see dozens of cases of disturbed sleep and for some it can be really debilitating. These disturbances stem largely from life stresses – work stress, financial and health worries, relationship issues – inconsistent sleep patterns, excessive stimulation before bed and frequent travel. When we have worries, it can keep us lying awake at night for hours on end, tossing and turning.

During a major stressful period of my life, where I was shaken to my core, my nervous system was completely derailed, my anxiety levels were through the roof and I was a prisoner to overthinking; my vata dosha was severely imbalanced and inevitably I suffered from deep sleep disturbances, which got me caught up in a catch-22 situation. My immune system was breaking down. It was then I decided that my only resolve would be to put into practice everything I had learnt from Ayurveda and I have never been so grateful to this wisdom.

Sleep is a critical component to our health and wellbeing; in fact, Ayurveda considers sleep to be one of the three pillars for sustaining life. We spend on average a third of our lives sleeping. It is the one activity, or rather inactivity, that allows our body to repair damaged cells, rejuvenate and replenish at a cellular level. This is a time when the body is focused on eliminating toxins. So, staying awake late at night or eating before bed can interfere with the process and result in an increase in toxins. In this instance, the body starts to focus on digesting when it should be focused on cellular cleansing and repair. In order to enjoy a life full of vibrancy, it is in our interest to respect the cycle of rest and activity.

Sleep stemming from mental fatigue, increased kapha, physical exhaustion, mental inertia or acute illness is not natural or healthy. Healthy sleep results from the disengagement of the mind with the senses. The quality of your sleep will affect the health of your digestion, your mental alertness and your ability to process information and make decisions.

Vata types tend to have light, irregular sleep patterns. If imbalanced, vata types can find it hard to fall asleep and can awake at night and find it hard to get back to sleep. They may grind their teeth, sleepwalk or sleep-talk.

Pitta types generally sleep well throughout the night. If they are disturbed, their minds may get overactive between 10 p.m. and 2 a.m., thinking of work and projects or thinking critically about themselves, people and situations.

Kapha types are usually heavy sleepers and could literally sleep anywhere. Kapha types actually need less sleep than vata and pitta types. If kapha gets out of balance, they will feel lethargic and overindulge in sleep.

Get your milk on!

When I was a child, in our family home, we would often have guests visit us in the evenings after dinner, and the beverage of choice was boiled and spiced milk. I always wondered why adults would choose such a childlike drink. Now that I am older, I have come to appreciate that this drink has numerous benefits and is perfect as a pre-bedtime drink, as milk is sattvic, a substance that is pure and balancing in nature.

In order for milk to be digested properly, it should be brought to the boil for 2–3 minutes. The process of boiling changes the molecular structure of the milk, breaking down the milk proteins into digestible amino acids, ensuring that it is easier and lighter to digest. Taken with spices such as cardamom and nutmeg, freshly ground almonds and pistachios, and a little saffron or turmeric, this drink has grounding properties (due to the milk and nuts), while the spices are mildly sedative. This is an excellent way to induce the heaviness (tamas) necessary for a good-quality sleep.

Sleep well with shirodhara

I never leave India without having a shirodhara. In this unique treatment, found in no other system of health, warm oil is poured continuously across the forehead for 30–60 minutes. This treatment is used therapeutically for patients with insomnia, high stress and anxiety, and to induce deep relaxation. This profound treatment is considered to have a deep and positive effect on the physiological body. The pineal gland (corresponding to the crown chakra) and the pituitary gland (corresponding to the third-eye chakra) are the twin centres of the endocrine system. The pituitary gland is a small, pea-sized gland resting deep at the base of the brain that regulates metabolism, tissue growth and development, blood pressure and pain-relieving endorphins. The pineal gland is seated deep in the brain and secretes two vital hormones to balance our emotional and mental health. Serotonin, the 'happy hormone', is secreted in the pineal gland, as is melatonin, the hormone that is responsible for regulating our natural sleep. Hence, the deep relaxation induced by the pouring of warm oil, subtly stimulating these glands deep in the brain, is considered to be the natural antidote to anxiety and insomnia and can help rebalance the endocrine and nervous systems. After this treatment, my clients always feel a complete sense of Zen; they have reported improved sleep and a feeling of deep relaxation that they have never experienced before. In fact, many of my clients actually fall asleep during the treatment itself.

Our bodies function on circadian rhythms, and we stay in synchronicity with our natural rhythms when we have regulated sleep patterns. It may seem impossible, but I recommend going to bed as near to 10 p.m. as possible and waking close to 6 a.m. or earlier, so that you are more alert for your day. If sleep is the single most medicinal activity, why would we want to deprive ourselves of the luxury? Post 10 p.m., we enter the pitta period of the night, when our minds start to get active again, making it difficult to fall into a deep sleep. Sleeping from midnight to 8 a.m. is not as restful as sleeping from 10 p.m. to 6 a.m.

It's called a 'bed' room for a reason

This is your tranquil space, designed for rest and love-making. Design and decorate your bedroom in an inviting, cosy, and peaceful way. Ensure there is fresh air circulating and the room is at a comfortable temperature for you. You can have natural, sleep-inducing incense, oils or candles with scents like lavender, camomile or bergamot, or even fresh flowers. You can use soft, calming music to enhance the relaxed space. If my clients don't wake up naturally with the sunlight, I encourage them to use a traditional alarm clock and leave the electromagnetic radiation-emitting mobile phone charging in another room.

Sedative foods

If you are suffering from insomnia or sleep disturbances, opt for foods that are moist, oily and sweet in quality. For example, sweet fruits, avocado, banana, milk, root vegetables, nuts, fish and black gram. Foods that are spicy, bitter, dry, raw and light can be aggravating. Alcohol, coffee and sugar are all sleep vampires; instead, opt for a soothing camomile tea or spiced milk.

Night-time rituals for better sleep

- Ensure you have finished your evening meal at least 2–3 hours before you intend to sleep
- Minimise industrial lighting where possible; opt for dim lighting or candles
- At least an hour before bed, prepare the mind and body for sleep. Turn off the TV (yes, that means *Game of Thrones* too!), mobile phones and tablets, put down that gripping novel you're reading, avoid any disturbing music, news or stressful conversations, and refrain from exercise. Instead, take a gentle walk or engage in pleasant conversations with friends and family, or read inspirational or spiritual material, or write in your journal
- Take a warm bath with soothing oils to relax the body and mind
- Give yourself a warm sesame oil foot and scalp massage – this has been known to promote sleep and reduce stress
- Have a warm, spiced milk drink 20–25 minutes before bed
- Do some breathing (ujjaya and **bhramari**) and meditation to balance your brain chemistry, nervous system and hormones
- Reflect on the day with gratitude – end on a positive note
- Sleep at or around 10 p.m. – try to get 7–8 hours of restful sleep
- Exercise in the morning to balance energy
- Get exposure to morning light to reset rhythms

I urge you not to underestimate the power of these simple rituals. Apart from in a few specific instances – such as pregnancy, illness, travel and grief – or in the case of young children and the elderly, day sleep is best avoided.

If you feel that excessive sleep is more of an issue, I recommend that you follow a regime that is focused on reducing kapha.

- Avoid heavy meals and dull, lifeless foods, such as fried, canned and packaged foods
- Opt for vegetarian-based evening meals – kitchari is ideal
- If you eat meat, limit it to the lunch meal
- Exercise portion control so you don't feel heavy in the stomach
- Increase physical exercise
- Avoid sleeping in the day
- Engage your mind in creative arts to reduce inertia

Exercise – life in motion

'A mind free from all disturbances is Yoga'

Patanjali

Do you love pounding on the treadmill, or are you more accustomed to rolling out that yoga mat? Body movement of any kind is exercise, in my book. My only rule for exercise is that it must be enjoyable, otherwise you won't be motivated. If you are anything like me, you will find more enjoyment in exercise that is fun, such as dancing, walking, yoga and team sports. Physical exercise should bring alertness to the mind and energy to the body, not complete exhaustion. Just observe the way children play – they are so joyful. Wouldn't it be great if we could take a more childlike approach to exercise and just have fun? My nieces and nephews just love active play, and getting acquainted with the trampoline recently with them was invigorating and just so much fun.

Our bodies are designed for movement, and movement is a crucial element to our vitality. Each and every one of us is different in the shape and structure of our body, so exercise that works for one person won't always be the most suitable for the next. Again, the key is to listen to your body and honour how you feel. Regardless of your choice of movement, regular exercise can increase your strength, stamina and resistance to disease. Your suitability to certain exercises can be determined by your constitution. Exercise helps the body to stay light and agile, as well as maintaining a balanced body weight.

Since our body follows a seasonal pattern, so too does our strength and desire for exercise. Winter and spring are the seasons when we definitely want to focus on exercise, as these are the kapha-influenced months. Exercise should be customised according to the person's age, condition and capacity. It should be light and carried out until you break a sweat on your forehead, your breath deepens and your heart rate increases. This is sufficient for most people on a daily basis. The more you get attuned with your body, the more you will know when you have reached your exercise threshold.

Move yourself healthy

Exercise brings many health benefits:
- It increases mental and physical stamina and strength
- It improves resistance to disease
- It relieves tension
- It improves circulation of the blood
- It aids lymphatic flow and the elimination of waste via sweat
- It improves the lustre of your skin
- It improves your digestive power
- It combats inertia, depression, anxiety and laziness

The Ayurvedic approach to physical fitness is focused less on the size of the muscles or being 'body beautiful', and more on the body's capacity to handle aspects such as cold, heat, hunger and thirst, as well as the capacity to bend and flex and have firmness without rigidity. The aim is to improve the efficiency of the body's natural functions.

Exercise for a vata person

Since vata can become easily imbalanced, vata types do best when they focus on light, gentle, grounding exercise such as walking, cycling, swimming, golf, dance, tai chi and hatha yoga. I recommend movement that encourages agility, coordination, balance and stretching.

Exercise for a pitta person

The most suitable type of exercise to balance a pitta-dominant person is exercise of moderate intensity and of a non-competitive nature. Let's face it, if you are pitta-dominant, you are likely to have a competitive streak, and this is sometimes counterproductive for you. Since you like a challenge, activities such as jogging, cycling, swimming, yoga, brisk walking, skiing, snowboarding and mountain climbing are all great options.

Exercise for a kapha person

Vigorous exercises that improve strength and endurance will help kapha types to stay in balance. Since kapha types have a naturally strong stamina, high-intensity exercises are suitable. You can opt for activities such as running, cycling, aerobics, dancing, swimming, weight training, racquet sports, hiking and rock climbing.

Enough is enough

The more you move, the more energy you will generate. How much exercise is enough exercise? If you are not able to hold a conversation while you are exercising, you need to reduce the intensity. Safety in exercise should always be observed and this means including in your routine a warm-up of flexing and stretching, an active phase and a cool-down phase.

Excessive exercise can also lead to some health complications, including vomiting, fever, anaemia, excessive thirst, exhaustion, distaste for food and delirium. So, please exercise with caution and listen to your body before you start to feel any of these signs. I advise you to refrain from exercise if you have indigestion, if you have just eaten, feel exhausted, hungry or thirsty, are overworked, in menstrual flow, have had a lack of sleep, have been travelling, are feeling unwell (physically or emotionally) and also directly after sex.

Yoga

When your mind, body and spirit are truly in union, you are practising yoga. Yoga stretches far beyond the physical realms that we have come to experience in the West, where yoga predominately refers to the practices of holding or flowing through postures knows as yoga **asanas**. Nowadays, the mysticism of yoga has been removed and the stigma that was attached to it as some cult-like practice has disappeared. Yoga is as scientific, accessible and practical as Ayurveda. Nowadays, every third person walking down the street has a yoga mat, and there are yoga studios popping up in cities everywhere. It's a phenomenon!

If you are a seasoned yogi (male) or yogini (female), you may have come to know that the practice of yoga extends far beyond the practice of asanas. In the *Yoga Sutras*, Patanjali focuses on ashtanga yoga – literally meaning 'eight limbs' – to reach enlightenment. Starting with ethical living and self-discipline (*yama* and *niyama*), then performing asanas to connect with yourself, creating freedom through breath (*pranayama*), freedom from sensory engagement (*pratyahara*), practice of focused concentration on one point (*dharana*), uninterrupted contemplative meditation (*dhyana*) and finally a pure blissful state (**samadhi**).

Yoga is the sister science of Ayurveda and both are firmly rooted in Samkhya, one of the six schools of Vedic philosophy. My discussion on yoga here is focused on the physical asana practice.

A practice that is gentle, respectful and kind to your body. The purpose of your practice should be to move with mindfulness and bring focus to your breath in each pose; this is the essence of yoga. Yoga not only directs and channels prana, your life force energy, as you engage your physical body, but also encourages the flow in the channels of your subtle body.

Once you start to identify yourself with your dosha type, you can begin to customise your yoga practice with postures to create balance and harmony. Yoga postures are designed to help stretch, massage and tone the body muscles and organs. With regular practice, you can build strength, stamina, flexibility and heightened awareness. Yoga is now widely recognised for its health benefits, such as bringing down high blood pressure and high blood sugar, reducing the risk of heart disease, alleviating depression and anxiety. So, maybe it's time to get in on the action!

My simple yoga practice really enables me to connect with my body and keeps me grounded and stable so that I can face challenges that come my way. A qualified yoga instructor will guide you to modify your practice so that you can first move away from your vikruti, your imbalanced state, and then continue a practice that is aligned to your prakruti, your balanced state. They can also help you adapt your practice to suit the season and time of day. Here are just a few examples of postures to balance your dosha.

Vata yoga
- *Tadasana* (mountain pose)
- *Vrksasana* (tree pose)
- *Malasana* (garland pose)
- *Dandasana* (staff pose)
- *Uttanasana* (standing forward bend pose)
- *Virabhadrasana* I and II (warrior I and II pose)
- *Marjaryasana/Bitilasana* (cat/cow pose)
- *Balasana* (child pose)
- *Savasana* (corpse pose)

If you have identified yourself with a dominance of vata, a practice that is warming, grounding and stabilising is most suitable. A practice that is at a slow and steady pace will be balancing. Vata types should avoid postures that are overstimulating to the nervous system, such as repetitive sun salutations or vinyasa flow, and be careful not to put pressure on weak areas of the body. The right yoga postures can really help relieve stress and anxiety, and get the bowels moving.

Pitta yoga
- *Bhujangasana* (cobra pose)
- *Dhanurasana* (bow pose)
- *Setu Bandha Sarvangasana* (bridge pose)
- *Parivrtta Utkatasana* (revolved chair pose)
- *Balasana* (child pose)
- *Vrksasana* (tree pose)
- *Ustrasana* (camel pose)

If pitta is your dominant dosha or a current imbalance, encourage fun in your practice. Postures that are heart-opening, calming and which evoke compassion and are in a slightly cool environment can help balance the intense pitta. A moderate pace will be pacifying. Hot yoga is most definitely not for the pitta person, nor is intense yoga in the pitta season – it is way too heating and stimulating. Using balancing pitta postures, you can alleviate conditions such as hyperacidity, acne and ulcers, as well reduce anger, irritability and resentment. Headstands are not for pitta types!

Kapha yoga
- *Viparita Virabhadrasana* (reverse warrior pose)
- *Bhujangasana* (cobra pose)
- *Dhanurasana* (bow pose)
- *Utkatasana* (chair pose)
- *Ustrasana* (camel pose)

- *Tadasana* (mountain pose)
- *Surya Namaskar* (saluting the sun)

If you identified yourself with a kapha dominance or a kapha imbalance, your practice will be supported by a fast or flowing pace with plenty of standing postures. Your practice should focus on creating space, warmth, stimulation and precision. Postures that focus on opening and creating movement in the chest area are great to prevent kapha types suffering from congestive conditions of the chest and lungs.

Surya Namaskar (saluting the sun)

The 12 Surya Namaskar Postures

This ingenious twelve-posture yoga sequence known as *Surya Namaskar* can be tailored to suit your constitution by adapting the pace to suit your body type. It is a fluid warm-up sequence that is performed at the beginning of the day. Unlike aerobic exercise, this sequence is done slowly, purposefully and gently with a focus on your breath.

This sequence helps stimulate blood circulation, regulate the nervous system, clear the brain and bring lustre to the eyes. You will simply glow!

As with Ayurveda, there is no one-size-fits-all approach to yoga, so be guided by what feels right both in classes and in your own practice at home.

The science of healthy sex

'Good memory, intelligence, long life, health, nourishment, sharpness of senses, reputation, strength and slow ageing are gained from disciplined indulgence in sex'

Ashtanga Hridayam

As part of a complete approach to wellness, the ancient sages of Ayurveda gave thorough guidelines on the art of healthy love-making by following the rhythms of nature. The philosophy of tantra that is nowadays commonly interwoven with *Kama Sutra* enables us to explore a mind, body and spiritual connection within intimate interaction that can help you to experience transformational sex and powerful orgasms. In this book, however, I want to bring your awareness to the guidelines on sex given to help you sustain your health and vitality.

Nourishing the tissues

Our reproductive tissues are the last of seven bodily tissues to form and get nourished. The body works really hard to produce both shukra dhatu and artava dhatu, the male and female sexual fluids – after all, these are the very tissues that have the capacity to form a new life. Over time, what we eat gets converted into these body tissues, and the quality and health of all tissue formation is dependent on the ability to first properly digest food. This is the very reason that as a practitioner I focus so heavily on digestive health, as it plays a central role in our entire health ecosystem.

Ojas is the vital energy that is present in every cell of the body, the *je ne sais quoi* that sparks our creativity and talents. It is the end result of the food we eat, which has been metabolically transformed. Sex can deplete our ojas. By having a rasayana-based diet and following seasonal and daily routines, the reproductive tissues and ojas can be protected and enhanced.

Celebrate sexuality

Sexuality is something that has always been celebrated in the Indian culture and Vedic traditions, encouraging a connection to our inner divine feminine and masculine energies. Exploring our sexuality not only brings sensual enjoyment on a physical level but also encourages emotional intimacy. Ayurvedic scriptures encourage slow and relaxed intimacy to bring deeper contentment, self-respect and ultimately freedom. As with most guidance given in Ayurveda, nothing is prescriptive and everything has a rational explanation and a middle path. Neither indulgence nor abstinence is encouraged. Healthy sexual engagement can help promote physical and mental strength, intelligence, sharpness of sensory organs, improved lustre, renewed youthfulness and inner joy.

The physical union between two partners in a mutually loving, respectful, affectionate relationship is a natural occurrence. The ancient texts considered sex to be divine and the basis for creation and preservation. It is our prerogative to maintain a healthy sexual relationship without depleting our bodies.

The health benefits of sex

Research conducted at the University of Toronto Mississauga Canada indicates that sex once a week can be optimal and can maximise happiness and have many health benefits.[1] Excessive sexual interaction did not seem to increase the health benefits. Love-making once a week can help reduce the risk of depression and heart disease, and can strengthen the pelvic floor. Engaging in sexual activity can also enhance the release of oxytocin, stimulating a greater connection with your partner. Research also suggests links between sex and a slimmer waistline, a stronger heart and a better mood.

Season for sex

Your sexual energy and strength mirrors the seasons (rtu), as well as your age and your stage of life. You will naturally feel inclined to be active and dormant in certain seasons. The question is, how many people are actually tuned in to their natural body rhythms? Nowadays we eat, sleep and have sex at unnatural times.

Of course, I realise that our human nature can be rather impulsive when it comes to sex. But understanding your body's natural pattern when it comes to sex can help you to maintain balanced reproductive tissues and support your vital energy (ojas). When our vital energy is depleted, we see symptoms such as reduced creativity and zest for life, mild depression, decreased sex drive and fatigue. Over time this depletion can contribute to longer-term issues such as impotency, premature erectile dysfunction, reduced fertility and difficult menopause, at which point herbs, diet and interventions have limited effects.

The season that supports sexual activities is the winter, the kapha season. Your natural body strength is higher in the cooler months, so your body has the natural capacity for even daily sexual activity provided there is good body strength. Over the transitional seasons of spring and autumn, your body has moderate strength and energy, so sexual activity can be moderated to approximately twice weekly. As we transition into the summer, the heat of the sun depletes your energy and your body strength is weakened. So it is best to be mindful of preserving your vital energy when you are engaging in sex in the summer months.

The 24-hour sex cycle

Like the seasonal rhythm, the diurnal clock supports sexual activity in the kapha times of the day, when your natural strength is higher. The best times for sex are between 6 p.m. and 10 p.m. and 6 a.m. and 10 a.m. All other times are not recommended as they can deplete energy. Of course, based on your own body, the recommended times may flex a little each way.

Prepare for the occasion

- Ensure that you have eaten and have allowed enough time for digestion to take place
- Use natural fragrances, flowers and candles to awaken your senses during sex
- Take a warm bath/shower after, wear fresh clothes and have a sweet milk drink to replenish your body tissues

Prevent ojas depletion

Here are some tips on how to prevent your vital energy from becoming depleted:
- Avoid excessive pungent, salty, astringent and bitter foods – these increase vata and pitta
- Avoid too much dry food; opt for healthy oils such as ghee, which support shukra/artava and ojas
- Avoid excessive fasting and irregular meal patterns as this disturbs vata

- Avoid indulgence in alcohol (although a little regulated wine is fine!), coffee, carbonated drinks, smoking and recreational drugs
- Avoid frequent late nights – sleep is crucial for tissue replenishment
- Avoid excessive exercise
- Avoid processed foods

Client story

'I decided it would be helpful to meet with Geeta again, focusing this time on preparation for getting my body healthy and in balance for conception, pregnancy and birth. As I have been influenced by the work and research surrounding conception and birth by Dr David Simon, and by Dr Deepak Chopra's work around the benefits of Ayurveda, yoga and meditation, Geeta's input was invaluable in outlining a diet and routine plan for each stage. As I followed the guidance of Geeta's plan, I visibly noticed the change in my skin, eyes and energy levels, and others noticed the difference too, commenting on how much better my appearance had become. I also felt that while I prepared psychologically for the transition into motherhood, it was vital also to prepare physically. This preparation was naturally aligned to the holistic approach to life I had already been transitioning to.

By the time we conceived, I felt more confident my body was as prepared to manage the levels of change biochemically as it was psychologically. Geeta was able to offer perspectives on all the different aspects of healthcare, and gave me a detailed written plan for the duration of my pregnancy and suggestions for the post-partum stage.'

Sreety

Enhance your vital energy

Foods that rejuvenate your body tissues are key to supporting your vital energy (ojas). Opt for foods that are fresh, organic, local and seasonal and for foods that have a sweet taste and contain fat (ideally ghee).

Type of food	Example foods
Grains	Kitchari, millet, oats, rice (basmati, red and brown), wheat
Vegetables	Asparagus, beetroot, cooked onion, potato, pumpkin, spinach, sweet potato, winter melon
Fruits	Sweet and heavy fruits – avocado, banana, coconut, dates, figs, grapes, mango, peaches, pears, plums, pomegranate, raisins
Meat and fish	Buffalo, chicken, crab, deer, duck, goat, partridge, pork, quail, rabbit, turkey
Legumes	Black gram, mung beans/dahl
Herbs and spices	Ajwain, cardamom, cinnamon, clove, cooked garlic, cumin, ginger, saffron, turmeric
Nuts and seeds	Almonds, pine nuts, sesame seeds, sunflower seeds, walnuts and nut butters
Sweeteners	All natural sugars especially jaggery
Dairy and eggs	Butter, buttermilk, chicken eggs, cream, duck eggs, fresh cheeses (paneer), ghee, goose eggs, milk, ostrich eggs, pheasant eggs, sweetened yoghurt

CHAPTER 16

Daily Health Rituals

'Yesterday I was clever, so I wanted to change the world.
Today I am wise, so I am changing myself'

Rumi

I am no stranger to the concept of rituals, as I grew up surrounded by such practices and ceremonies. However, despite the religious connotations of the word, 'rituals' to me have become more about commitment to practices that you follow on a day-to-day basis for the benefit of self-development of both the mind and body. I don't see rituals as a set of strict 'must-dos' but more as guidelines to help you live a happier and healthier life and to help you remember that simple changes will bring balance to your doshas.

I welcome you to explore Ayurvedic rituals that will not only bring about many preventative health benefits but also practices that you will really enjoy. Once you get into a routine, you will wonder how you ever started your day without them. These daily regimens, known in Sanskrit as **dinacharya**, are easy day-to-day Ayurvedic and yogic lifestyle regimes that enhance the quality of your life, keeping your mind and body cleansed.

When we are making plans with friends, we often say, 'Oh I don't mind, I'm happy to go with the flow'; if only we had that conversation more often with our inner self. With our busy day-to-day work life, we are often at the mercy of timings dictated to us by a modern society. We are now working longer hours than ever before. Technology has enabled us to stretch time in all sorts of ways; we can go to the gym at 2 a.m. if we want, we can get blackout blinds to sleep in the day and we can work all night with unlimited industrial lighting.

On top of this, some people manage two jobs, some study and work at the same time, to change the direction of their life, and many juggle work with raising and caring for children. With so much going on, it is no surprise that we have lost all sense of our body clock. So, if you stop to think about it, are you really in the 'flow' of your day? We so often get caught up with a false sense of the time that we forget to listen to our inner signals.

The daily clock

Our bodies are designed to follow natural circadian rhythms so that we stay in a healthy flow. After all, timing is everything! We can roughly split our 24-hour clock into six time zones. This daily clock is so important, as it influences our natural energy in relationship to the cosmic forces. Natural structure and routine can really support life (*ayus*).

Dominant dosha	First cycle	Best time for
Kapha	6 a.m. to 10 a.m.	Physical activity/exercise, sexual engagement
Pitta	10 a.m. to 2 p.m.	Eating your main meal of the day (ideally lunch)
Vata	2 p.m. to 6 p.m.	Engaging in creative mental activities This is a great time for meditating

Dominant dosha	Second cycle	Best time for
Kapha	6 p.m. to 10 p.m.	Disengaging from mental stimulation, relaxing and preparing for sleep This is the best time for sexual engagement
Pitta	10 p.m. to 2 a.m.	Deep sleep that enhances physical rejuvenation
Vata	2 a.m. to 6 a.m.	Sleep that enhances mental rejuvenation. Preparing to wake

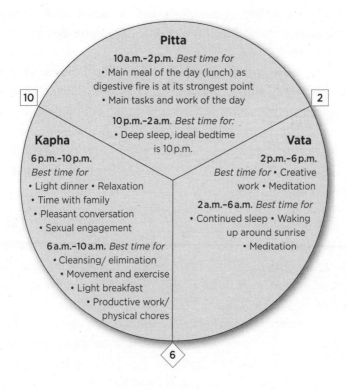

The Circadian Clock

Kapha dominates the morning, when most of us are getting up, and the body feels heavy, slow, relaxed and cool. By choosing to wake earlier and be active, we can prevent sluggishness from setting in and kapha from increasing. Have you ever noticed that you feel more tired the later you wake up? The kapha time, is when we experience a natural heaviness and grogginess in the body. So, it is best to awake at the beginning of the kapha phase or preferably earlier, that is, 6 a.m. or earlier. In the morning we can balance this with activities that have opposing qualities to that of kapha – it's a great time for cleansing, for physical exercise, for working and for doing anything that stimulates the mind and body. As such, it is not recommended to have a huge and heavy breakfast in these hours, as it can make you feel heavy and dull – contrary to popular belief, we don't need to have breakfast like a king! It's more a time for some stimulating ginger and lemon tea.

As we move into the late morning and early afternoon, our minds are active and our metabolic activities are now in full flow. It's a time to continue with work and digest, both physically and mentally. This is when we are most alert. At noon, as the sun reaches its highest point, our appetite should mirror this high and hunger should be present. As mentioned earlier in the book, lunch is considered the main meal of the day in Ayurveda.

In the most part of the latter afternoon, vata dominates the energy, which means variability sets in for digestion, mental activity and mood. This is an optimum time for light mental activity and creative work. I recommend practices that calm the nervous system, such as breathing, meditation, creative arts and creative work.

As we enter the second phase of our diurnal cycle, from 6 p.m. it's a time to slow down, so not the best time for the gym or heavy meals. Have a light early evening meal followed by pleasant conversations and reflections, and preparation for sleep. Aim to go to bed at around 10 p.m., while the heaviness of kapha can aid a deeper sleep. The later we sleep, the more active our minds become. Read chapter 15 for more on sleep.

Have you ever noticed that the later you go to sleep, the more unrested you feel? Or do you get the midnight munchies? As the metabolism powers up again, if we don't listen to what the body needs we will eat foods that do not digest and that disturb the quality of sleep. Ideally, when we transition (in sleep) over pitta stage (between 10 p.m. and 2 a.m.), our body goes into repair mode, and this is the time when our cells and tissues rejuvenate.

We continue to sleep into the early hours, and our body continues to rest, now repairing our mental faculties. Since the time between 2 a.m. and 6 a.m. is dominated by vata, those with worries and stresses will find that sleep can be disturbed and light, and dreams and thoughts can start to take over. As we get towards 5 a.m., in the depths of the vata time, it's a perfect time to awaken the body. Many yogis use this time to rise early, before the sun, and ground themselves when nervous energy can increase, by practising yoga, breathing and meditation. It is a perfect time to be with our 'self', and certainly not a time for engaging in stimulating activities.

Morning rituals

From the moment you open your eyes, you are actively engaged with every action, consciously or unconsciously. When we apply awareness to our morning routine, we can change the biodynamics of our being. Anything that we do regularly becomes a routine, routines become rituals and rituals become a way of life. Ayurveda is a way of life, rather than a dictation of dos and don'ts. I am a firm believer in the experiential approach to health changes, and the proof is in the experience of the way you feel as a result of the changes. If you try any of these guidelines for forty days, you will start to feel some change. I also believe that the more holistic your approach, the more you will feel the benefits. The key words here are 'gradual transition'; if you start to feel stressed with too many changes, it can be counterproductive to your wellness, so slow down and do what feels manageable.

Morning rituals

Your typical Ayurvedic morning rituals can include the following:

- Wake up early with an attitude of gratitude
- Ensure you eliminate your bowels and bladder first thing
- Cleanse orally – brush your teeth, scrape your tongue, oil pulling
- Perform nasal cleansing with a **neti pot**
- Cleanse and awaken the eyes
- Brush your body and massage with oil
- Bathe or shower
- Practise yoga or light exercise
- Practise breathing and meditation (see chapter 17)
- Drink warm lemon water
- Eat a light breakfast if you feel hunger
- Continue with your morning work and activities

An attitude of gratitude

We don't need to wait for a special day to be thankful for all the wonderful gifts in life. When we have gratitude in every moment of our lives, especially in the morning, every cell in our body responds with enthusiasm. I see every day as a blessing and, no matter how many curveballs life throws at me, I know there are always so many small things to be grateful for. This practice can have an immediate impact on your state of mind and mood, washing away the negative emotions such as anger and sadness that affect our health.

Every cell of your body responds to the attitude that you carry with you. Wouldn't it be so much nicer to wake up and appreciate the positive things, rather than observe what is missing and crave for something more? Wouldn't it feel nicer to immerse yourself in nature instead of reaching for your smartphone and filling your mind with negative news or celebrity gossip? We become a product of our beliefs and thoughts. The philosophy coined as the 'law of attraction' can help us manifest positive experiences in our lives by creating uplifting belief and thought patterns. On this basis of 'like attracts like', everything can be considered to be pure energy and we can attract what we think or believe.

Awakening

When we wake up before or around 6 a.m., we have a tendency to feel fresher. Ideally we want to wake up aligned to the sunrise. Of course there are times where we feel sluggish and keep hitting that snooze button, but does the sun say, 'I feel tired, maybe I will rise later today'? Try getting up at the weekends naturally, without an alarm, and monitor how your body responds. After some practice, my body now wakes naturally most days. Eventually your body will wake up naturally at the right times too.

Nature flows in its own rhythm. When we sit and ponder this, it's really incredible. So why don't we try to mirror our lives the way nature intended? Our waking time is the starting point to staying in tune with nature throughout the rest of the day.

Let that sh*t go

Surprisingly, healthy elimination is something many people struggle with, yet we are not open when it comes to talking about our bowel movements! Over my clinical years, I have come to know the intricacies of elimination. This is one of the cornerstones to maintaining a healthy digestive system, and one that I simply can't gloss over in this book or in clinic.

Movement in the body is governed by vata and the early morning is the most natural and ideal time to empty the bowels, without any force. This helps to clear any accumulations and makes us feel light in the body and mind. If we truly want holistic health, we cannot ignore disturbances in any element of our natural body habits.

Due to our busy lives and erratic eating habits, many of us now have varied bowel habits. Abnormal has become normal. Gas, constipation, pain, bleeding, mucus and loose motions are all signs of an unhealthy digestive system, but we are so used to living with bad patterns that we almost don't consider them as an issue. An ideal stool should be soft and formed and it should pass easily. You can refer to the Bristol stool chart online, to check where your bowel habits fit, and share this with your practitioner.

A lot of people don't pay much attention to what comes out the other end, but it's your single most obvious indicator of your gut health. A person with healthy movements will experience several or all of the below:

- An urge to evacuate at least once a day – usually first thing in the morning
- The urge to evacuate at a regular time daily
- Motions that are soft and formed
- Motions that have no profuse odour
- Stools that are a medium brown-yellowish colour
- Stools that float and do not sink
- A feeling of satisfied evacuation
- No discomfort or pain on evacuation except a mild pressure

Characteristics of healthy and unhealthy bowels

Dominant dosha	Healthy bowel movement	Unhealthy bowel movement
Vata	Daily movement in the morning. Easy evacuation. Soft and well-formed stools, slightly dark in colour	Irregular movement, can skip a day or more. Painful or difficult defecation. Dry, hard motions. Dark brown or blackish in colour. Gas and flatulence. Tendency towards constipation
Pitta	One to two daily movements. Easy evacuation. Soft and formed stools, yellowish in colour	More than two movements a day. Loose, unformed stools. Undigested food matter, foul odour, burning sensation, bleeding, sticky stools. Yellow/greenish or red in colour
Kapha	One to two movements a day with easy evacuation. Bulky, soft and formed stools, pale brown in colour	Sluggish movement. Bulky, sticky stools, pale-coloured. Tendency towards constipation or feeling of incomplete evacuation

In my clinic, many clients feel that not having a daily motion is quite normal and unrelated to their diet and lifestyle habits – that it's 'just the way it is'. However, constipation is a growing concern; in 2016 it was reported that constipation cost the NHS £145 million a year. In 2014 and 2015 more than 66,000 patients were admitted to hospital for issues related to constipation. Even more shockingly, a survey revealed that one in five people were too embarrassed to go to the GP about their bowel health. Reports also show that around 6.5 million people in the UK have health issues of the bowel.[2] As I see it, 90 per cent of the time this is a lifestyle-induced health concern and one that can be taken care of through preventative measures, if people just knew how to recognise the signs early on.

What initially starts as a simple discomfort can turn into various complications, not to mention the reabsorption of toxins back into our system due to stagnation. Signs that you have constipation include:

- Infrequent bowel motion
- A reduced urge to pass stools
- Difficulty, strain and pain on passing stools
- Abdominal bloating, distension and pain
- Small, hard, dry and often sticky stools
- A feeling of incomplete evacuation
- Head and body aches
- Bad breath and coating on the tongue
- Loss of appetite
- Nausea

Laxatives are increasingly being used as a solution to constipation, but this is not a long-term answer – even in the case of natural laxatives – as it encourages the body to develop a dependency on them. Over time, the body becomes resistant to laxatives and they stop having the desired effect. When we make small changes to our diet and lifestyle, we can start to address the root of the problem and encourage the body's natural function to reboot. Constipation is predominantly triggered by an increase in the vata dosha.

Here are some tips to encourage a daily morning bowel movement:

- Avoid heavy, late-night meals and irregular mealtimes
- Avoid cold, heavy, dry foods; favour warm foods and drinks
- Take a squat position to encourage bowels (*ashwini mudra*) in the morning

- Drink warm lemon water in the morning and liquorice tea in the day
- Be patient with your body – it is trying to create a new habit
- Use a toilet with good ventilation, space and privacy – be comfortable
- Give yourself a clockwise abdominal massage (you can try castor oil or a vata-balancing oil)
- Focus on the task at hand (no phone, magazines or any other distraction while on the loo)
- Do not suppress urges – if you need to go, then go! That means even if it is at work
- Eat only digestible / soluble fibre (citrus fruits, apples, peas, barley, psyllium and oat bran, for example)
- Avoid incompatible foods (see p. 190)
- Drink a 50ml / 50ml mix of prune juice and warm water with two pinches of rock salt to encourage a motion
- Take two triphala capsules with warm water before bed the evening before
- Undertake ongoing regular exercise
- Maintain a diet according to your body type
- Manage your stress with breathing and meditation

Your sparkling Ayurvedic smile

So much importance in Ayurveda is given to complete oral hygiene. There is no doubt that you brush your teeth in the morning before you leave for work. But what I noticed growing up in the West was that a lot of my friends opted to brush their teeth after their breakfast. It was something that I struggled to get my head around, as to me the thought of eating with a foul mouth just didn't feel right. What I didn't know then was that oral cleansing *before* food is a key component to Ayurvedic morning rituals.

The problem with fluoride

Fluoride is in our water, in medications, in cookware and, in the West, features heavily in our toothpastes. In fact, we have grown up thinking that fluoride is good for us. Contrary to popular belief, there are some suspicions that fluoride is the robber of iodine, which plays an active role in thyroid function, and that it might also inhibit melatonin secretion (responsible for your sleep and circadian rhythms).

Iodine, fluoride, bromide and chloride are halogens, of which only iodine is useful in the body for the function of the thyroid. Exposure to large amounts of fluoride can be toxic and means that the receptors in the thyroid don't get enough iodine. What's more, the liver is not able to process fluoride. In 2007, the WHO recognised that there is a global increase in iodine deficiency. Some of the health concerns raised include calcification of the pineal gland, toxicity to the thyroid and negative effects on fertility and the kidneys.[3]

Your oral cavity is one of the most absorbent parts of your body, and while dental products on the market might give you a brilliant-white smile, they may not always be the healthiest option. Making a small adjustment such as changing to a natural toothpaste can be a conscious shift towards reducing your fluoride exposure and working towards holistic health.

A natural, fluoride-free toothpaste that has bitter or astringent qualities containing natural ingredients such as fennel, neem, liquorice, clove, cinnamon, triphala or tea tree will go a long way as it is also unlikely to contain other harmful chemicals. A liver cleanse can also help flush out harmful toxins, as can increasing iodine levels in the body through the diet and the Indian household favourite, tamarind. Neem also has a great effect of removing toxins, due to its bitter taste.

Traditionally, in the ancient days, teeth were cleaned with the fingers or with a twig, using herbal powders and oil. Now, I am not suggesting you go back to chewing sticks, but there are a few subtle adjustments that can still help you improve your oral health. Not only for removing bad smells, but to prevent diseases of teeth, mouth, ears, eyes, digestive and respiratory systems, and in some cases even of the heart.

Brushing in the morning before food prevents metabolic toxins accumulated overnight in the mouth from being reingested by your system, which cannot be further broken down by the liver.

Tongue scraping

For me, the completeness of oral hygiene starts after brushing my teeth. Ever since I was a young child, growing up closely with my grandparents, I picked up some age-old traditions, one of which was using a tongue scraper. I thought it was perfectly normal to scrape my tongue morning and night, after brushing my teeth, until I realised that none of my Western friends did it! I stopped for a short period of time, out of embarrassment, but my regime felt really incomplete so it quickly returned to my regime. This tradition now continues with my nieces and nephews, who, like me, are growing up with this ritual.

So, what is the purpose of a tongue scraper, and why was I brought up using one? Well, bacteria don't only accumulate on your teeth – what about the rest of your oral cavity? Your gums, tongue and throat, for example, all house bacteria. Cleaning the surface of the tongue is an important part of daily oral hygiene, along with brushing, flossing the teeth and retaining oil in the mouth. Gently scraping the tongue from the back to the front five to ten times, first thing in the morning after brushing the teeth, can reduce the accumulation of toxic and bacterial substances that can lead to bad breath and disturbed digestion.

Using a stainless steel or copper U-shaped scraper, this quick and easy ritual can eliminate the white or sometimes yellowish coating found on the tongue, as well as enhance the function of taste buds, which stimulate the oral enzymes (the key sensory organ in digestion). When the brain and mind accurately perceive 'taste', only then does your food digest properly. Scraping the tongue stimulates this process, the digestive tract and your digestive fire. A healthy tongue should be pink in colour and free from any coating. Your tongue is a map of your digestion, and it can really tell you what is going on in your gut.

So, next time you wake up and go to brush your teeth, check out your tongue too. Is there stickiness or a coating? If so, then it's definitely time to add tongue scraping to your morning routine. Tongue scrapers are inexpensive and now widely available, but a good-quality copper one will last a lifetime – copper is a non-toxic metal and has healing properties of its own, including being pitta-/kapha-pacifying and healing for mouth ulcers.

Oil pulling

This ancient technique of Ayurveda, known as gandusha, is becoming a popular practice in the West and is known as oil pulling. It is a practice that has been a health ritual in India for over 5,000 years.

As the oil is retained in the mouth, it mixes with the saliva, becoming thinner in consistency and white in colour. This process subtly draws toxins from the local area and the blood by the enzymatic stimulation and lipophilic action, collecting all the fat-soluble toxins ready for expulsion from the mouth and the surrounding areas. If the oil is still yellow, it could indicate that the pulling needs to be done for longer. Cured sesame is widely used in Ayurveda for this practice, as well as numerous other treatments, as it has many therapeutic actions on the body. Coconut oil is another sound choice.

I first did this practice fifteen years ago, on a retreat in France while studying Ayurveda. As my colleagues and I walked barefoot outside in the early morning, swooshing a mouthful of warm sesame oil, I felt something nurturing and cleansing happening, and it has since become a regular practice in my morning routine.

The health benefits of using this technique are plentiful. Here are a few to get you enthused:

- It is brilliant for oral healthcare, preventing gum disease and cavities, firmly rooting teeth, healing bleeding gums, preventing tooth sensitivity and toothaches
- It keeps breath fresh by removing local toxins
- It pulls toxins and removes mucus from the mouth, throat and head
- It improves taste perception and digestive metabolism
- It prevents dryness in the mouth and throat
- It brings clarity to the mind and reduces headaches
- It helps keep sinuses clear and healthy
- It strengthens the jaw, facial muscles and voice
- It contributes to improved overall immunity

Try it for yourself! Use this technique in the morning before breakfast and on an empty stomach. After brushing your teeth and using a tongue scraper, take one tablespoon of warm cured sesame oil or coconut oil. Retain it in your mouth, swooshing gently from side to side for 5–10 minutes and then expel the oil. Simple, easy, inexpensive, harmless and effective.

Please note: this oil should not be swallowed as it has become laced with toxins in the process of pulling. Do not practise the technique if you have a sore throat or a cold.

Nasal cleansing

According to recent research, the human nose isn't just able to smell 10,000 scents but has the ability to differentiate between at least a trillion different scents.[4]

There are millions of microglands in your nasal passages that have a direct connection to your nervous system. Living in an urban environment means that we can lose our sensory sharpness. So why would we not nurture and protect our nasal senses?

Although I was a late adopter of this practice, nasal cleansing has now become one of my favourite daily rituals and one that has made such an impact on my health. It really feels like an extension to my daily practice of tongue scraping. Oh, it feels so good! The traditional yogic practice of nasal irrigation using a warm sterile saline water and a neti pot is truly amazing.

- It clears the sinuses and helps clear blockages
- It helps to prevent allergic reactions
- It relieves cold symptoms (and possibly snoring)
- It pulls out toxins from inner mucosa

This practice is best done once a day, in the morning, usually after your oral cleansing practices. Using comfortably warm sterile water, mix with ½ tsp powdered rock salt in your neti pot. Tilt your head forward and tilt to one side and, using the pot, allow half of the water to trickle in one nostril and out the other. Take a break and repeat on the other side. Blow your nose to clear the solution, along with the excess mucus.

Neti pot irrigation can be followed up where appropriate by oil cleansing of the nostrils, known as *pratimarsha nasya*. You can use a medicated oil such as *anu thailam*, but sesame oil or ghee are just as beneficial. To perform nasya at home, you can take a slightly warm liquid ghee, tilt your head backwards and administer 1–2 drops in one nostril, while closing the other. Take a deep inhalation, and repeat on the other side. You will feel the oil in your throat, which you can spit out.

Nasya protects the eyes, nose and throat against diseases. It has also been said to prevent premature greying of the hair and hair loss. It can nourish the facial skin and strengthen the voice, so it is a great practice for vocalists and public speakers. It can also help loosen stiffness in the neck and jaw, relieve headaches and aid better sleep.

For more serious issues of the ear, nose and throat, consult your Ayurvedic practitioner, who will be able to do in-clinic treatments to give therapeutic relief with this wonderful remedy. Like oil pulling, it is best to avoid it if you are actively suffering from a cold or fever.

I spy with my little eye

With the increased use of industrial lighting, computers and mobile devices, there has never been so much strain on our eyes. Protection against excessive light and heat is important for the long-term health of your eyes. Where possible, avoid long periods of exposure to bright sunlight, wear sunglasses and limit exposure to industrial light and heat. It's a perfect excuse to have regular candle-lit nights in.

Keeping your eyes cool by washing your face with cool water and giving them a cooling eye bath is a great start. One of the practices I enjoyed from an Ayurvedic retreat in India some years back was a rose water eye bath. My eyes felt so cool, clear, nourished and invigorated. There are of course other natural solutions for an eye bath, but I find rose water to be simple and effective.

Can you 'ear me

One or two drops of warm sesame oil or ghee can be dropped into the ears periodically to cleanse and nourish the ear canal. It is particularly useful for vata-type issues such as tinnitus, hearing problems, wax accumulation and deep inner-ear itching.

Nurture your body with massage

We can't all have the luxury of weekly body treatments at a spa, but as advocated by Ayurveda, you can treat yourself to regular self-massage, or abhyanga, with warm nourishing and balancing oils. Regular self-abhyanga helps to improve the condition and tone of your skin, improve circulation and loosen any toxins and fat from the skin. It can also help alleviate joint and muscle stiffness. It's a perfect practice for vata types and an antidote for vata imbalances.

The benefits of Ayurvedic massage

There is no doubt that treating yourself to a massage can leave you feeling relaxed and peaceful, and it can certainly help you to switch off from the daily stresses of life for an hour or so. Bodywork allows you to really stop and give yourself time to fully receive, a necessity that not many people give themselves permission to do.

There are many styles of massage born of cultures all over the world, and whichever technique you decide suits you, massage has numerous proven health benefits:

- It relieves stress and anxiety
- It reduces fatigue in the body and mind
- It boosts your mood
- It reduces muscle tension and pain
- It relieves tension headaches and neck pain
- It improves circulation of prana and strength
- It encourages lymphatic drainage
- It improves immunity
- It prevents premature ageing
- It improves lustre of skin
- It relieves joint pain and stiffness
- It increases range of motion
- It helps you to sleep soundly
- It lowers blood pressure
- It gently improves poor digestion

Ayurvedic abhyanga is traditionally used as a preparatory treatment for deep detoxification or pancha karma. It certainly has all the benefits of massage, but its focus is to help the body loosen the toxins so they can be flushed out.

If you have ever had the opportunity to visit India and have experienced the different types on Ayurvedic body massages, you will know just how nurturing this practice is, from invigorating herbal powder massages to nourishing rice poultice massages. There, abhyanga is not considered a luxury or a treat, as we see it here in the West, but more a daily practice and a health-promoting part of life. In most homes in India, there is a practice of self-massage as part of daily physical health and hygiene. Touch is an integral component to holistic healing, especially for pregnant women, babies, brides and bridegrooms, and the elderly.

Abhyanga is a great practice that can be done for 10 minutes before your shower or bath. What I love about it is that it feels so grounding, invigorating and relaxing all at the same time. Better still, my skin always feels so soft, and I don't have to moisturise afterwards. What's not to love? Since I like my showers steaming hot, a self-abhyanga protects my skin from drying out with the heat of the water.

If you identify more with a kapha body type, then regular dry-brush massage can also help with exfoliation and circulation. You can pick up body brushes in most health stores. Taking a steam bath or shower after an abhyanga enables the body to continue removing the impurities blocked in the pores and tissues and further nourishes the skin. Sweating also releases toxins through the skin.

A simple self-abhyanga technique

Opt for a warm dosha-pacifying oil, a plain cured sesame or coconut oil, for self-abhyanga. The choice of oil plays just as much a part of the massage as the technique itself. Only natural oils should be used, such as sesame, coconut, castor and mustard, and medicated oils designed to have a specific healing effect on dosha imbalances. Daily abhyanga uses a subtle but firm touch, rather than being purely focused on the manipulation of muscle tissues. Attention is given also to the temperature of the oil. In the same way that we opt for warm foods, in Ayurveda the treatments will predominantly use warm oils, specially selected for your specific body type and health issue. The focus is on balancing the doshas and nourishing every level of the body. The oils themselves help to improve relaxation, reduce pain, bring lightness to the body and awaken your spiritual awareness.

Abhyanga is all about liberal application of warm nourishing oils to your entire body, both with love and awareness. Self-massage is best if you take a seated position and allow the oils to absorb fully. Always ensure that you do this on an empty stomach. I don't feel there needs to be any hard and fast rules for self-massage, but it's worth noting these guidelines to help you get started:

- Don't forget to massage your head with your fingertips
- Always massage your abdomen in a clockwise direction – this is in sync with the direction of your digestive system
- Work upwards and out on your neck and face
- On your limbs, massage down and out
- Use circular motions around the joints
- Don't miss any part (toes, fingers, buttocks, back – if you are able to reach it, then massage it)

There are a few occasions when I would advise you not to practise self-abhyanga: when you are suffering from a fever or infection, indigestion or loose motions, if you are menstruating or have a cough or cold.

The power of touch

Your skin is the largest organ of your body, and touch is the first sense to develop as a child. It remains core to human nature throughout life. Expression through the language of touch supports the deep desire for real human contact, comfort, compassion and love. Touch, just like the other four senses, positively impacts your overall health when nurtured.

Your skin contains receptors that directly trigger emotional responses to interpersonal touch. Touch can take many forms, from a handshake to a pat on the back, a compassionate hug, skin-to-skin contact between parents and newborns after birth, therapeutic and healing bodywork, and sensual touch with your partner.

Non-sexual touch is becoming increasingly absent in our digitally developing world and in a world where touch can be misinterpreted or misused. In this instance, protection and safety are a necessary consideration. However, genuine interpersonal touch really helps us to thrive and is a fundamental component of human development. Touch is known to release oxytocin in the body, also known as the 'feel-good hormone', and reduces the release of cortisol, therefore reducing stress on the adrenal glands. Appropriate touch can also reduce violence and anger, while increasing personal development, compassion, intimacy, communication, social bonds and more.

I want to encourage appropriate touch as a means of communication to bond with each other, create trust, increase a sense of genuine caring and enhance our social environment at large. Just ask yourself how your mind and body feel after some healing bodywork. Or have you noticed the difference between how you feel when someone gives you a genuine hug and when someone just hugs you in an obligatory way?

> Touch is something you feel, not something you do, so use touch in a more purposeful and mindful way.
>
> TRY THIS: If you are holding a crying or restless baby, just try rubbing the forehead softly by the third eye and watch them slowly start to calm down.

Conscious bathing/showering

A bath or shower is a perfect follow-on after a self-massage. The warmth of the water enables the oils from your massage to penetrate deeply into the body tissues. The oils also protect your skin from being dried out by the water. A nice warm bath or shower brings many benefits:

- It can help purify your senses
- It removes sweat and relieves itching
- It alleviates exhaustion and increases strength and immunity
- It stimulates your digestive fire
- It improves your mental agility and mood
- It increases your sexual power
- It awakens you and helps you face what lies ahead

I, for one, love the sensation of having a shower or bath, it's my happy place. It really breaks up the day and helps me either to unwind from a heavy day or to feel invigorated for the day ahead.

Showering or bathing is not recommended if you are suffering from a fever, acute indigestion or loose motions, nor should you bath immediately after food.

Move your body

Movement is a crucial part of our daily life. Our lives have become more and more sedentary, so planned and purposeful exercise has become a necessity. Life used to be much more active, and incidental exercise was sufficient, as people worked on farms and walked longer distances to work. Chapter 15 gives more insight into the art of movement for health. Engaging in movement daily in the morning will invigorate the mind and body.

Breathing and meditation

My day doesn't get started without a dose of my short but daily practice of pranayama and meditation. On the odd occasions where I am out of sync with my routine, my day feels incomplete and rather disturbed. I think of these elements of my practice in much the same way as brushing my teeth – I wouldn't leave the house without doing them. See p. 280 for guidance on how to get started with a practice.

Morning cleansing tea

Drinking fresh lemon with warm water on an empty stomach after your morning cleansing practices can enhance digestion, reduce any sluggish and bloated feelings and aid daily elimination. I am a firm believer in learning from first-hand experience – so go on, try it!

'Wow,' you are probably thinking, 'I could be here all morning with these daily rituals. How on earth do I create the time to carry out all these extra morning practices when I already have such a busy schedule?' Well, I always advise my clients to just do what feels manageable and start with the simple rituals that resonate first. You are not supposed to be overwhelmed with a whole new list of to-dos. Some practices you can alternate and some, like the body massage, you can do one or two times a week. You don't have to try to be perfect, but add in these daily rituals over the long term and you will reap the amazing preventative health benefits, especially for your sensory organs, which are constantly overstimulated in this modern world.

The health benefits I feel, having incorporated these practices into my morning, more than make up for the time I commit to carrying them out. It truly just feels like second nature now.

Client story

'The daily abhyanga, nasal rinse and oil pulling are some of the routines I have maintained since my consultation. It helps me to maintain a routine, balance and calmness.'

Sreety

CHAPTER 17

Mind Medicine

'Human beings, by changing the inner attitudes of their
minds, can change the outer aspects of their lives'
William James

You take time to cleanse and nourish your physical body, whether
it's having a daily shower, brushing your teeth, eating meals or
sleeping daily. But what about cleansing for your mental and
emotional faculties? After all, as we have discovered, our health
issues can stem from beyond just our physical body. Personally,
cultivating a sense of inner peace has always been my strongest
desire and my hardest challenge, but now that I truly understand
that a healthy mind is just as important as a healthy body, I give
more time and energy to my daily practices.

Is it all in your head?

Similar to the physical doshas, your mind balance is influenced by
the interplay of the three gunas (qualities) – sattva, rajas and
tamas – which we mentioned briefly in chapter 2.

Rajas is the quality that drives your passion, movement and
activity; without it, life would be static, as all activity is influenced
by the quality of rajas. Tamas is the quality that triggers inertia
and lethargy, but without it you would not be able to sleep or rest,
and therefore it is an equally essential quality. However, an excess
of either of these qualities can have a disturbing effect on the
mind and so the aim is to keep them in healthy balance, just like

the physical doshas, and to increase the uplifting and pure qualities of sattva, the pure and balanced state of mind.

A sattvic person will reflect qualities that express an intelligent and calm mind with a sound memory. Sattvic people usually have a positive demeanour, demonstrating happiness, enthusiasm, forgiveness, politeness, helpfulness, honesty and humbleness. Quite the perfect person, don't you think? We all have these inherent qualities within us, but they get masked by our various experiences and emotions and the interplay of rajasic and tamasic energies.

When rajas becomes excessive, it brings hyperactivity and restlessness to the mind, increasing agitation, fear and anxiety. Individuals with an imbalanced rajasic mind will tend to become strong influencers, rather fanatical, easily jealous, competitive, selfish, manipulative, cynical, rude and often aggressive.

If there is an excess of tamas, you may become dull in the mind, lazy, depressed and can be indulgent and self-destructive.

Don't take my breath away

When we are born, our life starts with it and when we die, our life ends with it – prana (our life force energy). What an incredibly powerful function is the breath! Nothing is as powerful as the medicine of breath, and for me it supersedes any dietary change when it comes to influencing your mental faculties and physiological health.

You see, your body can exist without food for several weeks and without water for several days, but without breath for even a few minutes, you would not survive. If our breath is able to sustain our very existence, why would we choose not to nurture it?

Prana is the subtle energy form of vata that governs all functions of your body and mind, taking responsibility for the coordination of breathing, the senses and the mind.

In today's sedentary and stressful lifestyle, most of us live on a shallow and quick breath, using only a fraction of our total lung capacity and living on just enough energy supply for the body to function. This way of breathing limits our vitality and our resistance to diseases, and potentially starves our brain of essential oxygen, creating tiredness, irritability, disturbed sleep cycles, and so on.

Let it breathe

'The breath is the link between the body and the mind'

Sri Sri Ravi Shankar

Pranayama is not only a deep and profound set of breathing exercises, but one of the eight branches of Patanjali's discipline of yoga.

This profound knowledge of careful direction and circulation of prana aims to manipulate the respiration rate, deepen and elongate the breath, and therefore sustain life.

It costs us nothing to sit and use this wisdom of breath to enhance our wellbeing, so we have nothing to lose and everything to gain. You don't need to believe me. Just try it for yourself – you will feel the calm, peace and physical benefits, even after just a few minutes. Although I outline guidelines here, if you are uncertain, consult a practitioner, who can safely guide you through various practices suitable for your mind/body type.

Deep inhalation and exhalation of breath increases the level of oxygen being supplied to the blood and as a result it improves the quality of your bodily tissues. Many studies highlight the positive effects of breathwork on medical conditions such as type 2 diabetes, heart disease, migraines, obesity, asthma and high blood pressure, as well as many stress-related conditions, such as depression, anxiety and insomnia.

Just as we can tailor our diet and lifestyle to suit our mind/ body type, we can also select breathing exercises that are suitable for our needs.

Set the scene

Setting up the right environment will enhance the clarity and focus of your mind during the practice of pranayama and meditation. Set up your space so that it is clean, clutter-free, noise-free (no TVs, phones or music on), with plenty of ventilation so that fresh air is able to enter the room. Keep some comfort provisions, such as cushions and blankets, nearby in case you need extra support, padding and warmth. When you practise pranayama, you should sit in a comfortable position, ideally seated on the floor or on a chair, with the spine erect, chest open and the focus on your breath.

For all breathing exercises outlined here, begin by sitting comfortably on the floor with legs crossed (*siddhasana / padmasana*) or sitting on your knees (*vajrasana*), or on a chair with your back straight and feet firmly flat on the floor.

Take care!

Pranayama is integral to holistic lifestyle changes, and if you are new to focused breathwork, please take care. Gradual and slow progress is recommended to prevent imbalances from occurring – 5–6 minutes in the morning and evening is a sufficient starting point.

Avoid any straining or uncomfortable holding of the breath. If you start to feel light-headed, short of breath or dizzy, you must stop and let your breath resume normality, while relaxing the body and keeping the eyes closed. If your nose feels blocked, allow the body to clear it naturally. Use neti pot cleansing to help clear long-term blockages.

Please note: breathing exercises should be done on an empty stomach.

Vata-balancing pranayama

Bhramari Pranayama (bumblebee breath)

Benefits: A technique that helps promote restful sleep and helps overcome insomnia. It is great at silencing the mind. The vibration of this breath does not allow any thoughts to enter the mind. This is truly blissful.

Method: Take a normal breath in, then let go and relax. Then cover your ears with your thumbs and your eyes with your fingers as shown below, to block out external disturbances and enable you to go inward. Take a deep inhalation to your natural full lung capacity, then, as you slowly exhale, make a low humming sound in your throat until your breath is complete. Repeat at your own pace for 2–3 minutes. This is a great exercise pre-bedtime. This practice is suitable for pitta and kapha types too.

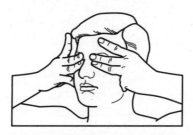

Position for Bhramari Pranayama

Nadi Shodhana Pranayama (alternate nostril breath)

Benefits: This breath is designed to cleanse the channels of the physical and subtle body. Alternate nostril breathing will help you to balance the left and right side of the brain, the sympathetic and parasympathetic activity, helping you to bring your awareness to the breath and stimulating a grounding sensation. This practice is also suitable for pitta and kapha types.

Method: Using your right hand (reverse, if you prefer left), place your right thumb beside your right nostril and your ring and little finger beside the left nostril. Gently close the right nostril with your thumb and exhale out of your left nostril. Inhale with the left nostril to your natural capacity (usually a count to four as a guide). Then close the left nostril and breathe out through the right. Inhale with the right nostril, close the right nostril and exhale from the left. This completes one full cycle, but you can continue in this rhythm for 4–5 minutes at a time, ideally in the morning.

Ensure that you take a moment to pause between each inhalation and exhalation – this will help you to keep your breath slow, steady and just slightly deeper than normal. The depth should be to your natural lung capacity only.

Position for Nadi Shodhana Pranayama

Ujjaya Pranayama (victorious breath)

Benefits: This breath helps remove the heat from the head, as it cools the back of the throat. It is a great way to draw oxygen into the lungs, helping you to expand, deepen and lengthen your breath. It helps remove phlegm in the throat, and relieves the symptoms of asthma and other pulmonary diseases. Ujjaya increases resistance to diseases of the nerves, dysentery, dyspepsia, enlarged spleen, coughs and fever. This practice is also suitable for kapha and pitta types.

Method: Sitting comfortably, inhale a slow breath through the nose that travels down the back of the throat and into the lungs, to a full but comfortable lung capacity (sounds like a Darth Vader-like breathing noise). Hold it for as long as is comfortable (or four counts), then slowly release it in the same manner as inhalation.

Pitta-cooling pranayama

Shitali Pranayama (cooling breath)
Benefits: This breath is a cooling breath, so if you are feeling agitated, angry or overheated, this one is for you. It helps quench thirst and appeases hunger. Shitali pranayama cools the physical body, especially the back of the mouth and throat. It reduces inflammation of chronic diseases, fever and indigestion.

Method: Protrude your tongue and make it like a tube/straw as illustrated below. Draw air in through your tongue to your natural lung capacity with a hissing sound, and exhale slowly through both nostrils – 2–3 minutes is sufficient for this exercise. If you struggle to make a tube you can try *Sheetkari Pranayama* below.

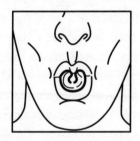

Position for Shitali Pranayama

Sheetkari Pranayama (hissing breath)

Sheetkari pranayama has similar benefits to shitali pranayama. It is known as the hissing breath.

Method: touch the tongue to the roof of the palate and gently clench your teeth. Open your lips widely so the teeth are exposed and breathe in through the mouth to your natural full lung capacity from the abdomen through to the chest, and then slowly release through the nose. Repeat for 2–3 minutes.

Kapha-stimulating pranayama

Kapala Bhati Pranayama (skull shining breath)

Benefits: This vigorous, energising breath helps to stimulate stagnation of kapha in the body. It stimulates and strengthens your abdominal muscles and diaphragm. It also massages and improves the function of your digestive organs, purifies the channels of the body and clears the lungs, bringing clarity to the mind and warmth to the body.

Method: Since this is an energising breath, it is best to do this in the morning only. You can do this when you are cold or when you are feeling sluggish. Start by exhaling your breath and then, in quick motions, take a passive breath in through the lower abdomen, then forcefully exhale the breath while pulling the navel towards the spine. The emphasis is on the exhalation while you contract your abdomen. Take a cycle of 15 breaths and repeat 3–4 times, with a short gap to rest between each cycle.

Do not do this exercise if you are pregnant, menstruating, have heart conditions, hypertension or any digestive issues, or after meals or if you start to feel too light-headed.

Bhastrika Pranayama (bellow breath)

Benefits: Another energising breath that will increase your prana and purify the subtle channels. This exercise will help stimulate your digestive power, giving you improved appetite and metabolism. The bellow breath brings clarity to the mind and warmth to the body. The stimulating nature of this breath helps to combat phlegm and reduce diseases of the nose and chest, including asthma.

Method: Sitting comfortably with your eyes closed and body relaxed, inhale deeply and exhale deeply using the belly. This is similar to kapala bhati but with an emphasis on both inhalation and exhalation from the abdomen. Go at a steady pace. You can do 3 rounds of 20 breaths, with a short break in between.

As with kapala bhati, do not do this exercise after meals, during pregnancy or menstruation, if you have hypertension and heart conditions, glaucoma or any issues surrounding anxiety, vertigo or panic.

After your practice

Take some time to rest after each breathing exercise to observe the sensations that you are feeling in your mind and body. You are not trying to orchestrate any experience, you are simply allowing your body to be free in the moment. Use this time to let your awareness be present in the body. You might like to direct your attention to different parts of the body, such as the forehead, the chest and the hands. Just observe what you experience in that part of the body for a short while. It is really special, as you will start to notice subtle movements, sensations and changes in the physical body as your awareness expands. This is a perfect opportunity to lead into your meditation practice.

Engaging in pranayama practices can bring numerous benefits:
- It increases the capacity of your lungs to energise the body with a fresh supply of oxygen
- It reduces your breathing rate, which can reduce hypertension
- It expels toxic waste from the respiratory system

- It improves the health of your heart
- It strengthens the respiratory and nervous systems
- It helps increase metabolic activity and digestion
- It reduces stress, and calms the mind and nervous activity
- It increases awareness and concentration
- It increases energy and vitality by providing stimulation for the internal organs
- It reduces negative emotions, such as anger, irritability, depression, greed, arrogance and jealousy

Meditation: medicine of the mind

So many of my clients feel alienated at the thought of meditation. 'I don't know how', 'I don't have time', 'It's not for me', 'I can't focus', 'I can't clear my head', 'I am already too busy', 'I don't know what is right for me', 'I am not sure I am doing it right'; these are just some of the reservations my clients have that make them shy away from meditative practices.

It's true, we live in a busy world that continues to get more frantic, more technology-focused and more distant from our true human nature. We are no longer able to understand what it means to be in the present moment. And for this reason alone, I believe meditation is more important than ever before.

Meditation can feel unfamiliar, not to mention mystical, too New Age or overly complicated. It did for me, too, when meditation became a part of my self-development and spiritual growth. With so many different techniques and disciplines, it is hard to know what is right for you. But what is important is that anyone can do it, no matter your age, background or culture.

What is meditation?

Let's demystify this a little. In meditation, we are actually not trying to achieve or 'do' anything. Meditation is simply a state of 'restful alertness'. Yes, there are many forms of meditation, but don't be overwhelmed. You can start with simple techniques and, as you become accustomed to a regular practice, you can then expand with techniques of meditation that resonate with you. There is no right or wrong. This is about self-awareness and connectivity to your deeper consciousness. You can use meditation to bring yourself into a state of deep physical relaxation and inner awareness.

Meditation has become increasingly popular and even trendy in recent years, with more and more people turning to meditation for peace of mind. Any stigma that once was attached to this discipline is slowly fading. Ironically, technology has made meditation much more accessible and, while it is not ideal to use devices to achieve the benefits of meditation, they can still serve as a fantastic introduction to and way of experiencing some of the numerous benefits.

Like everything else in Ayurveda, there is no blanket approach. Meditation comes in all different shapes and sizes. There are hundreds of different types of meditation, including popular practices such as: mantra-based meditation, mindfulness meditation, guided meditation, sound meditation, kundalini meditation, Zen meditation, Transcendental Meditation (which became popular with the Beatles), Vipasanna Meditation, loving-kindness meditation, yoga meditation, and so on. So there will be a practice that will work perfectly for you.

In any given day we have on average 60,000–80,000 thoughts. If you go on the premise that through meditation you will be able to stop all thoughts altogether, meditation will seem like an impossible task. So much of the noise in our minds is generated by our own internal dialogue, impressions of past memories and anxieties about the future. The aim is not to force the mind to be quiet, but to connect to the stillness that already resides within. This is our happy place, the place of higher awareness. The home of love, compassion, empathy and joy.

Why meditate?

The more you believe that your mind cannot be calm and that meditation is a waste of time, the more I say you probably need it. People have been meditating for thousands of years to expand awareness and stay in the present moment. The reasons and paths to meditation are plenty, but one thing is for sure: our minds have become more frenzied than ever before, and we can sometimes lose control of our emotions. Meditation helps us to regain this control over our emotions and nerves by quietening the mind. Through the process of meditation, you can start to reduce the number of thoughts that take over your day. Over time, you will be able to reduce negative emotions, such as fear, grief, anger, greed and jealousy, which trigger the release of stress hormones that can affect your physical health. Connecting to your consciousness and increasing and deepening your intuition are very supportive when trying to make healthful dietary and lifestyle choices.

The health benefits of meditation

Your state of mind is at a different frequency during meditation than it is in your sleep. There are numerous studies that emphasise the physical, mental and emotional benefits of engaging the mind in meditation. Physiologically, meditation can help to:
- Lower blood pressure and regulate heart rate
- Lower levels of cholesterol
- Induce restful sleep
- Increase immunity
- Reduce stress and anxiety

A simple way to meditate

In the same way you made your surroundings comfortable for your breathing practices, so should you do in your meditation practice. In fact, if you have just done some breathing exercises, you will already be in the zone and ready for meditation.

Sit in a quiet, comfortable place with your body relaxed and spine erect. Place your hands on your legs or knees, palms facing up. Close your eyes and start to deepen your breath. Bring your awareness to your breath and keep your focus on the rise and fall of your chest area as you gently breathe in and out. Just be gentle and breathe naturally. If you notice your mind wandering into thought mode, just bring your focus back to the chest area and continue to breathe. Continue for as long as you can – up to 20 minutes, ideally. This is the simplest way to get started with meditation. If you want to use other tools such as mantras, **mudras** (see below) and visualisations as focal points, then that is fine too. Just be aware not to fall asleep.

Life in your hands

In India, classical dancers move with a lot of soul and use their entire body as a form of expression, from the tiniest of eye, eyebrow and mouth movements to rhythmic pattering on the bare ground. They also use focused and deliberate movements of the hands, and each of these hand gestures has a meaning in the dance. These hand signs are known as mudras.

In the context of health, mudras are specific postures of the hands and fingers that can have an influence on our mind, body and mood. They are used particularly in worship and rituals in the Hindu, Buddhist, Christian and other faiths and are also used in many cultures to greet people.

I always wondered why in the UK we greet people by shaking hands, in Europe you do an air kiss on each cheek and in India you place both hands together in prayer (*anjali mudra*), bow the head slightly and say 'Namaste'. I then learnt that this anjali mudra with the word 'namaste' translates as 'The divinity in me bows to the divinity in you', as a way of being welcoming and respectful to all, including family, friends, teachers and even natural sacred sites. While preserving your personal energy, prayer hands help you to connect both the right and left hemispheres of the brain at the same time, representing unification. Now, don't you think that is just beautiful?

In yoga, this gesture serves as an 'offering' of yourself as you commit to your practice. Prayer hands engage your awareness to the spiritual heart centre in your chest.

Mudras can be used as a focal point in the practice of meditation, pranayama or yoga. These hand gestures have been used in the East for thousands of years, not only as a way of connecting to your higher self and channelling energy in meditation but also as a way to heal physical ailments, improve clarity and concentration, and encourage love and compassion. Mudras are quick and easy to learn, so you can start to reap the benefits straight away.

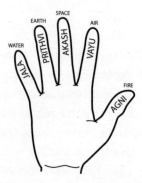

The Five Elements Associated with Each Finger

As mentioned earlier in this book, we are composed of five elements and each finger represents one of these elements. The thumb represents fire (agni), the index finger represents air (vayu), the middle finger represents ether (akash), the ring finger represents earth (prithvi) and the little finger represents water (jala). Since all diseases are ultimately due to an imbalance in the body caused by lack or excess of any one of these elements, when balance is maintained in line with your Ayurvedic constitution, the body can naturally heal itself. As a healing modality, our fingers can be understood to contain electrical circuits, channelling the flow of prana that is present at these release points. As we focus our attention deeper into the body, balance can be achieved within.

A very familiar and commonly used mudra, the *gyan mudra*, or mudra of knowledge, is thought to help sharpen the memory, and enhance concentration and the capacity to learn. By touching the tips of the forefinger and thumb together to form an 'O', a union of the fire and air elements is created. When used in a lotus pose, this mudra closes the circuit of energy in the body, preserving prana. Similarly, other hand gestures stimulate different parts of the body.

Mudra	Gesture	Action on the body
Gyan		Stimulates the root chakra and is grounding. Calms and improves concentration.
Vayu		Prevents wind in the body, which can lead to conditions of gas, sciatica, gout and rheumatism.
Akash		Increases the space within the body and mind. Increases intuitive power and alertness. Beneficial for bone diseases, ear pain and toothache.

Prana		Gives energy, reduces fatigue and nervousness. Calms, brings inner stability, improves vision.
Prithvi		Increases energy and inner stability. Can stimulate body temperature, the liver and the stomach.
Agni		Increases heat, energy and strength in the body; decreases kapha, fat and phlegm.
Jala		Increases and restores water balance in the body; reduces dryness in the skin, congestion in the lungs.

Practising mudras with yoga and meditation, together with a healthy diet, appropriate routines, adequate exercise and rest will naturally lead to optimal health. Mudras can be practised daily, for anything between 10 minutes and up to a few hours at a time. But a short practice will suffice, as this will be new to many. You should sit comfortably, with your back straight and hands relaxed on your thighs, your shoulders relaxed and your chin pulled back slightly. Keeping the breath even and slow, with hands in your selected mudra position, you are ready to begin a journey of contemplation. This really is an extension of meditation.

Magic in your mouth

Feelings such as love, joy, emotional pain and sorrow are just some of the human emotions we can't quantifiably measure, but that does not mean that we don't 'feel' them. Faith-based healing is a subject that many authors and spiritual leaders have written about, but we remain fixated on the need to qualify everything through the modern scientific paradigm.

In our hour of need, when all else fails, many of us turn to prayer as a request for help and assistance from a higher source. Most religious and spiritual beings have used prayer in circumstances where science can no longer provide answers. Prayer helps to restore a sense of hope and comfort and helps us 'feel' better.

Now, it doesn't matter your faith, religion or belief structure. What is important is that we understand that our words carry power, both internally and externally, and what we believe becomes our reality; it is the placebo effect. Prayer is communication with your consciousness.

What is your mantra?

Mantras are energetic sound vibrations, and they can enhance the more non-tangible 'feel-good' health benefits when used in meditation. 'Mantra' seems to be a real New Age buzzword, but what does it really mean? *Man* is the root of *manas*, meaning 'the mind' or 'to think', and *tra* is a suffix that means 'tool' or 'instrument', so mantra quite literally means the tool for the mind.

Mantras are sounds that produce vibrations within your body as you chant. This chanting bridges you to your 'higher self', the universe, consciousness, divine, or however you wish to identify with this energy.

Mantras are considered the main tool for influencing and calming the mind in yoga and Ayurveda; in fact, most ancient Vedic scriptures are written in mantras or **sloka**(s) and it is a language in itself. Mantras enable the spread of knowledge, bringing positive changes to the conscious and subconscious mind. This powerful technique of sound channelling can also influence deep-seated emotional patterns, exercise, increase the strength of the mental faculties, open our intuition and increase our awareness.

The Gayatri Mantra is a powerful classical mantra chanted in many instances for awakening, liberation, health and healing:

'Om Bhur Buvaha Svaha,
Tat Savithur Varenyam,
Bhargo Devasya Dheemahi,
Dhiyo Yonaha Prachodayath'

Gayatri Mantra

Swami Vivekananda translated this simply as:

'We meditate on the glory of that being who has produced this universe; may he enlighten our minds'

Mantra	Meaning and influence
Lam	Related to the earth, root chakra and adrenals. Bringing groundedness, contentment and stability.
Vam	Related to water, sacral chakra and reproductive glands. Encourages willpower.
Ram	Related to fire, the solar plexus and the pancreas. Gives power of movement and direction.
Yam	Related to air, the heart centre and thymus. Gives space and force.
Ham	Related to ether, the throat chakra and the thyroid.
Ksham	Related to the third eye chakra and the pituitary gland.
Om	Related to the crown chakra, the centre of consciousness and pineal gland.

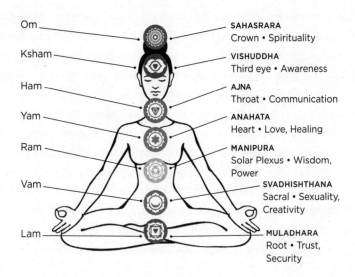

Om — SAHASRARA
Crown • Spirituality

Ksham — VISHUDDHA
Third eye • Awareness

Ham — AJNA
Throat • Communication

Yam — ANAHATA
Heart • Love, Healing

Ram — MANIPURA
Solar Plexus • Wisdom,
Power

Vam — SVADHISHTHANA
Sacral • Sexuality,
Creativity

Lam — MULADHARA
Root • Trust,
Security

Positions of the Seven Chakras and their Related Mantras

Mantras are a great technique to incorporate with the practice of yoga, pranayama and meditation, as the vibration generated can help balance the chakras and the five elements.

It is the *beej* or seed mantras that are commonly used as part of daily meditation and yoga practices. These mantras stimulate positive energy and healing for their associated organs, chakras and elements and associated planets.

Laughter really is the best medicine

'In the sweetness of friendship let there be laughter, and sharing of pleasures. For in the dew of little things, the heart finds its morning and is refreshed'

Kahlil Gibran

Have you ever noticed how time flies when you spend an hour or two with good friends, chatting away and ending with belly-aching laughter? You feel free and elated, and are totally in the present moment. Laughter, by its very joyous nature, is infectious and you should have laughter every day. In the moment where there is laughter, there can be no space for sadness, anger or stress. In fact, it should be a prescriptive medicine because of its amazing health benefits.

Laughter triggers the release of endorphins in your body, which help your mind and body to feel more relaxed. Every cell of your body responds to laughter. Pain-relieving chemicals and hormones such as dopamine and neuropeptides are released, improving your mood and your response to stress and disease.

Laughter is universal, breaking all boundaries between cultures and ages. What's more, laughter connects you with other people, while burning a few calories too, as you have yourself a little abdominal workout.

As crazy as it sounds, in many countries there has been a surge in laughter meditation groups, gatherings where a few people instigate group laughter for no reason, followed by a period of silence. I highly recommend trying it. No matter how ridiculous it feels and no matter how much you try to resist the laughter, it is just not possible to contain yourself – laughter is just contagious. When I tried this a few times, it made me feel so expansive and free. Do it with friends, it's even funnier!

A prescription for laughter

- First, grant yourself permission to be happy and to laugh
- Prioritise moments for laughter every day
- Reflect on your day, even if it was stressful, and find a laughable moment – share your moment
- Ensure you spend time with friends who lift your spirits and make you laugh
- Find a laughter meditation group near you or start one
- Lighten up – take time to laugh at yourself
- Watch comedy programmes or read a funny book or article

CHAPTER 18

Ayurveda Beyond Today

'The part can never be well unless the whole is well'

Plato

Beyond the day-to-day

In these chapters, we have looked at the many facets of Ayurvedic preventative healthcare, but Ayurveda extends far beyond the scope of this book. Ayurveda is a complete system of medicine, and if you are suffering from complex or chronic health issues there are many treatments, herbs, deep-cleansing processes and retreats that can give you relief and potential disease reversal without harmful side effects. Find a practitioner near you by looking at the Ayurvedic Professionals Association website: apa.uk.com.

A good diagnosis is central to Ayurveda, so that you can adopt the most suitable preventative measures at home. A practitioner will be able to work with you on curative measures so that treatments, herbs, diet and lifestyle specifics can be tailored to your needs.

When you visit a practitioner, you won't necessarily walk away with a label to your ails, but with knowledge of your mind/body type that will be central to your ongoing health and healing. Many patients come with pre-diagnosed conditions, and your practitioner can certainly work with this, but the same doshic approach and principles will apply. Each practitioner may work in a slightly different way, but they will use both traditional and modern methods of diagnosis.

Aside from taking a detailed patient case history, a practitioner will assess your physical strength, digestive power, energy levels, age, constitution, dosha imbalance, lifestyle habits, diet, immunity, psychological state, body functionality, tissue structure and family history. They will examine or ask you about your urine and faeces, and observe your eyes, voice, skin and nails as indicators of health. Two of the most significant diagnostic tools used in Ayurveda are the pulse and tongue. A practitioner is looking at the size, shape, colour, coating and characteristics of the tongue, which will give deep insights into your digestion and more. The highly skilled technique of the pulse diagnosis provides insight into your prakruti, vikruti, strength, state of body tissues and more. All these measures of inference and observation help the practitioner to spot the early signs and presenting symptoms of a potential disease and identify the possible root cause.

Ayurveda offers a vast array of therapeutic body treatments tailored to your body type and condition, as well as purification therapies to correct deeper imbalances. What's more, herbal medicines are tailored to your needs, to be taken at appropriate times in a conducive form (powder, tablet, herbal wine, paste, decoction, smoke or tincture) and with a suitable carrier. As I have said before, there is no one-size-fits-all when it comes to Ayurveda.

There has been a surge in the number of Ayurvedic residential retreats in India and around the globe recently, offering one-, two-, three- and four-week programmes to support your wellbeing. You just have to find the place that suits your needs, time and budget.

A Final Word from Me

'Be the change you want to see in the world'
Mahatma Gandhi

When I came to the realisation that all change starts with a thought, a light bulb went off in my head. Of course! We just need to have a shift in our thoughts when it comes to health and wellbeing. Ayurveda is not magic but a method, a very profound and empowering one. It is always a great moment when we decide to take back the power and responsibility for our health and life.

What struck me and many of my clients is that you don't have to believe my praises or passion about Ayurveda. Just trust in yourself and follow the guidance of Ayurveda; your experience will give you all the belief that you need. Healthcare is easy if you take the time to listen to your inner wisdom.

Ayurveda takes us on a journey to understand how to create health and wellbeing, rather than treating a disease, by accepting our body, mind and spirit as a complete biological ecosystem. Everything is energy and inherently connected. However, in our technologically advanced world, we have become far removed from the natural way of life that nurtures wellbeing. Important aspects of our lives, such as cooking, family, exercise, rest and playtime, have become secondary priorities.

When Steve Jobs gave his speech at the Stanford University graduation ceremony of 2005, he spoke about 'connecting the dots' and how looking backwards coupled with faith will somehow connect in the future. Let's take a deeper look at our lives the way nature intended and take our lead from there.

What is your story? What path do you want to pave for your future journey, both in health and life?

Each and every one of us deserves a life of vitality; after all, health and happiness are our birthright. I truly believe that if you have reached this point in the book, your Ayurvedic journey awaits you in whatever capacity you choose. Are you ready to awaken to optimal health?

'And you? When will you begin that long journey into yourself?'

                                                          Rumi

Glossary

Abhyanga	Warm oil body massage
Agni	The element of fire
Ahamkara	The ego or the 'I am'
Ahara	Diet or food
Ahararasa	The end product of digested food
Akash	The element of ether/space
Ama	Undigested food waste and toxins in the digestive system
Amla	Sour taste
Anjali	An Ayurvedic measure for food. One anjali equals palms cupped together
Anupana	A substance that serves as a medium to carry herbs to the body tissues. For example, ghee, milk, water
Artava	Female reproductive tissue
Asana	Yoga posture or pose
Ashtanga Hridayam	An authoritative and influential text of Ayurveda written by sage, Vagbhata
Asthi	Bone tissue
Ayurveda	The ancient system of healing and natural medicine known as the science of life
Bhastrika	Yogic breathing technique (bellow breath)
Bhramari	Yogic breathing technique (bumblebee breath)
Bhutagni	The digestive fire that breaks down ahararasa to each of the five elements (space, air, fire, water and earth)

Brmhana	A substance, process or treatment that tonifies, builds and nourishes the body. Anabolic in nature
Buddhi	The universal intellect
Chakra	A Sanskrit word for 'wheel' or 'vortex'. There are seven primary energetic vortices (or nerve plexus centres) that form part of the energetic body found near the spinal cord, where a number of subtle energy channels known as nadis intersect
Charaka	A sage of the Ayurvedic system of medicine and lifestyle. He is famous for writing the medical treatise called the *Charaka Samhita*
Chikitsa	Any type of Ayurvedic treatment or therapy intended to correct or manage an imbalance or a specific disease
Chyawanprash	A traditional rejuvenating herbal jam
Deepana	Natural substances that kindle the digestive fire and strengthen appetite
Dhatus	The seven tissues that give basic structure to the body
Dhatvagni	The digestive fire located in the body tissue
Dinacharya	Ayurvedic daily health regimen
Dosha	A natural energy force in the body, of which there are three: vata, pitta and kapha. Doshas are responsible for all functions in the body and each has distinct characteristics, making up your unique constitution
Gandusha	Ancient oral hygiene technique known as oil pulling (retention of oil in the mouth)
Ghee	Clarified butter
Guna	1. The quality or attribute of a food, spice or herb 2. Referring to the quality of the mind

Jala	The element of water
Jatharagni	Fire responsible for digestion and absorption of food
Kapala bhati	Yogic breathing technique (skull shining breath)
Kapha	Kapha is the dosha that governs structure and cohesiveness. Kapha is predominated by the earth and water elements. It is heavy, slow, cool, oily, smooth, dense, soft, stable and cloudy
Karma	The action of a substance on the body
Kashaya	Astringent taste
Katu	Pungent taste
Kitchari	A dish made of rice and mung dahl
Langhana	Reduction and lightening therapies usually referring to fasting and detoxification. Catabolic in nature
Lavana	Salty taste
Madhura	Sweet taste
Majja	Nerve and bone marrow tissue
Malas	The waste products that are excreted out of the body, primarily through urine, faeces and sweat
Mamsa	Muscle tissue
Manas	The mind
Manda agni	Slow or weakened state of the digestive fire. Can be considered hypometabolism
Mantra	Sacred words or phrases that are recited aloud or in silence. They hold a vibration in the body
Marma	Energy points on the surface of the body that correlate to subtle channels of the body. They relate to specific organs, channels and energies. Used in healing treatments
Meda	Fat tissue

Mudra	A hand sign or position commonly practised in yoga
Nadi	A tubular channel of the physical or subtle body, for example, a vein or artery
Nadi shodhana	Yogic breathing technique (alternate nostril breath)
Nasya	The therapeutic administration of medicated oil in the nasal passages to clear imbalanced doshas in the ear, nose and throat area. One of the five purification treatments
Neti pot	A small watering can-style pot used for nasal cleansing
Ojas	The subtle energy of kapha. The end product when tissue formation is complete and the foundation of our immune system
Pachana	A substance that neutralises toxins and ama in the body
Pancha karma	Five purification treatments that fall under shodhana therapies
Pancha mahabhutas	The five great elements of akash (ether), vayu (air), tejas (fire), jala (water), prithvi (earth)
Pitta	Pitta is the dosha that governs all digestion and transformation in the body. Pitta is predominated by the fire and water elements. It is light, penetrating, hot, oily, liquid, and spreading
Prabhava	The special effect of a food, herb or spice that is present beyond the logic of samprapti
Prakruti	1. Your mind/body constitution derived from a unique composition of vata, pitta and kapha 2. The force responsible for creation
Prana	The subtle energy of vata. Considered the life force energy associated with incoming energy from breath, and also water and food
Pranayama	A series of yogic breathing techniques

Prithvi	The element of earth
Purusha	The consciousness or the soul
Rajas	The quality of action, energy and stimulation that generates sensual reaction, pleasure, pain
Rakta	Blood tissue
Rasa	1. The taste of a food (sweet, sour, salty, bitter, pungent, astringent)
	2. The name of the plasma tissue (rasa dhatu)
Rasayana	A substance that nourishes, heals and rejuvenates, acting as a tonic for the entire body (cells, tissues and organs)
Rishi	An ancient Vedic sage
Rtu-charya	Seasonal regimen according to the natural cycle of the seasons
Sama agni	Balanced and resilient state of digestion
Samadhi	Highly evolved state of consciousness attained through meditation
Samkhya	A Hindu philosophy founded by Kapila that gives a systematic explanation for cosmic evolution according to twenty-five categories
Samprapti	The pathogenesis of disease
Sanskrit	One of the oldest ancient languages from which Hindi derives
Sattva	The quality of purity that gives rise to lightness, luminosity and harmony in the mind and body
Shamana	Palliative therapies
Sheeta	Cold quality
Shirodhara	Therapeutic treatment of a stream of warm oil poured over the forehead
Shitali	Yogic breathing technique (cooling breath)
Shodhana	Ayurvedic cleansing therapies aimed at removing excess dosha, ama and other toxins from the body

Shukra	Male reproductive tissue
Sloka	A verse of an ancient Vedic scripture
Srota	The channels of the body
Sushruta	A sage of the Ayurvedic system of medicine and surgery. He is known as the father of surgery, writing the medical treatise, the *Sushruta Samhita*
Swasthavritta	The theory and practice of preventative health using daily and seasonal regimens
Tamas	The mental quality of dullness, darkness and inertia
Tejas	The subtle form of agni or pitta in the body that governs intelligence, discernment and enthusiasm
Tikshna agni	Acute, strong and intense state of digestive fire. Can be considered as hypermetabolism
Tikta	Bitter taste
Tri-dosha	A combination of the three doshas, vata, pitta and kapha
Tri-doshic	Pacifying substance for all three doshas
Triphala	A traditional Ayurvedic compound of three fruits – amalaki, haritaki and bibhitaki. Its properties help to gently cleanse and detoxify the digestive tract, support regularity and nourish the tissues
Ujjaya	Yogic breathing technique (victorious breath)
Ushna	Hot, fiery or heating quality
Vastu (shastra)	Vedic system of architecture based on sacred and spatial geometry
Vata	The dosha primarily responsible for all movement and communication in the body. Vata is predominated by the ether and air elements. It is light, cold, dry, rough, mobile, subtle and clear

Vayu	The element of air
Vedas	The earliest collection of ancient Indian scriptures. They consist of four bodies of wisdom including, *Rig Veda*, *Sama Veda*, *Yajur Veda* and *Atharva Veda*
Vedic	Belonging to the traditions of the Vedas
Vikruti	The imbalanced or current state of your health
Vipaka	The post-digestive effect of a food substance experienced in the latter stages of digestion
Virya	The heating or cooling potency of an ingredient in the process of digestion before vipaka
Vishama agni	Irregular or unstable digestive fire
Yoga	Yoga is a collection of physical, mental and spiritual practices intended to transform and liberate the mind and body
Yogic	Belonging to the yoga/Vedic tradition

Notes

1 Muise, A., Schimmack, U. and Impett, E.A., 'Sexual Frequency Predicts Greater Well-Being, But More is Not Always Better', *Social Psychological and Personality Science*, vol. 7, issue 4, 295–302, 2016.

2 Coloplast, 'The Cost of Constipation report'. Retrieved from www.coloplast.co.uk/Global/UK/Continence/Cost_of_ Constipation_Report_FINAL.pdf.

3 De Benoist, B., McLean, E., Andersson, M. and Rogers, L., 'Iodine deficiency in 2007: Global progress since 2003', *Food and Nutrition Bulletin*, vol. 29, no. 3, 195–202, 2008.

4 Bushdid, C., Magnasco, M.O., Vosshall, L.B. and Keller, A., 'Humans Can Discriminate More than 1 Trillion Olfactory Stimuli', *Science*, vol. 343, issue 6177 1370–1372, 2014.

Bibliography

Bhishagratna, Kaviraj Kunjalal, editor-translator. **Sushruta Samhita**. 4th ed., 2 vols. Varanasi: Chowkhamba Sanskrit Series Office, 1991.

Frawley, David. **Ayurvedic Healing: A comprehensive guide**. Delhi: Motilal Banarsidass Publishers, 1992.

Hirschi, Gertrud. **Mudras: Yoga in your hands**. New Delhi: Sri Satguru Publications, 2002.

Lad, Vasant. **Ayurveda, the Science of Self-healing: A practical guide.** Santa Fe: Lotus Press, 1984.

Lad, Vasant. **The Complete Book of Ayurvedic Home Remedies.** New York: Harmony Books, 1998.

Lad, Vasant & Frawley, David. **The Yoga of Herbs: An Ayurvedic guide to herbal medicine.** Santa Fe: Lotus Press, 1986.

Rieker, H.U. **Hatha Yoga Pradipika: Yoga Swami Svatmarama.** London: The Aquarian Press, 1992.

Saraswati, Niranjanananda. **Gheranda Samhita: Commentary on the yoga teachings of Maharshi Gheranda.** Munger: Yoga Publications Trust, 2012.

Saraswati, Vishnudevananda. **The Complete Illustrated Book of Yoga.** New York: Three Rivers Press, 1988.

Sharma, Ram Karan & Dash, Vaidya Bhagwan, editors-translators. **Charaka Samhita.** 3rd ed., 3 vols. Varanasi: Chowkhamba Sanskrit Series Office, 1992.

Srikantha Murthy, K.R., editor-translator. **Ashtanga Hridayam by Vagbhata.** 2 vols. Varanasi: Krishnadas Academy, 1991–1992.

Srikantha Murthy, K.R., translator. **Bhavaprakasha by Bhavamishran.** 2 vols. Varanasi: Krishnadas Academy, 1998.

Srikantha Murthy, K.R., translator. **Madhava Nidanam by Madhava Acharyan.** Varanasi: Chaukhambha Orientalia, 1993.

Srikantha Murthy, K.R., translator. **Sharngadhara Samhita: A treatise on Ayurveda.** Varanasi: Chaukhambha Orientalia, 1984.

Acknowledgements

I must begin by first counting the blessings of many spiritual guides through my Ayurvedic journey. This has been the true source that has kept me grounded and clear about my life purpose.

I am grateful for the family values and traditions instilled by my grandparents, my mum, Bhagwati and my dad Bhagwanji, in my early years. Despite my parents' early concerns about whether Ayurveda was 'real work', they have always been my strongest support pillars.

My quest to bring Ayurveda to you would not be possible without the encouraging and tenacious support of my sisters, Leena and Preeya. You have been the glue in my life. I am eternally grateful.

Gratitude goes to my wonderful clients, Aline, Dugald, Eve, Ioana, Joey, Nicky and Sreety for sharing their Ayurvedic stories in this book. I thank all my clients for being my biggest teachers and allowing me to facilitate their journey of wellness. It is an absolute pleasure working with you.

My dearest soul family and friends Vivienne, Ranjana, Andrew, Amita, Angie, Ragini, Mahnaza, Anjla, Lepat, Elizabeth, Niall and Esha. I am indebted to your endless support and enthusiasm not just for this project but through all of life's challenges.

My inspiring mentors, Dr Mauroof Athique and Dr Palitha Serasinghe who were among the earliest and most devoted pioneers of Ayurveda in the UK. Thank you for your expertise and limitless dedication.

I am forever grateful for the unwavering support and encouragement of my literary agent, Laetitia Rutherford who magically appeared when this book was ready to emerge. Your invaluable insights have kept me on track.

This process would not have come together without Olivia Morris and the publishing team at Orion Spring who worked humbly behind the scenes to deliver Ayurveda.

My personal and professional growth is a result of all the wonderful souls that have touched my life. You are sincerely cherished.

About the Author

Inspired by her Indian roots, British-born practitioner Geeta Vara brings the timeless wisdom of Ayurveda to her clinic and workshops in London and online as well as international retreats.

Using a holistic approach in her health consultations, Geeta helps resolve a host of complaints and health conditions by addressing the root cause through herbs, diet, nutrition, lifestyle coaching, therapeutic treatments, yoga, breathing and meditation. With a background in conventional diet and nutrition as well as a BSc/PGDip in Ayurvedic Medicine, Geeta makes Ayurveda accessible to the modern mind.

Her mission is to inspire conscious living and empower individuals to be the healthiest version of themselves.

www.geetavara.co.uk
Instagram: geetavara
Twitter: geetavara
Facebook: GeetaVaraAyurveda